POWER
of the Weak

STUDIES ON MEDIEVAL WOMEN

Edited by
Jennifer Carpenter
and
Sally-Beth MacLean

University of Illinois Press   *Urbana & Chicago*

Publication of this work has been supported in part by a grant from the Centre for Medieval Studies, University of Toronto.

This book is printed on acid-free paper.

Library of Congress Cataloging-in-Publication Data

Power of the weak : studies on medieval women / edited by Jennifer
Carpenter and Sally-Beth MacLean.
        p.   cm.
    A selection of papers presented at the annual conference of the
Centre for Medieval Studies, University of Toronto, Feb. 1990.
    Includes bibliographical references and index.
    ISBN 0-252-02169-X (cloth : acid-free paper). — ISBN 0-252-06504-2
(paper : acid-free paper).
    1. Women—History—Middle Ages, 500–1500. I. Carpenter,
Jennifer, 1962–   . II. MacLean, Sally-Beth.
HQ1143.P69   1995
305.4'09'02—dc20   94-45063
                                                            CIP

Power of the Weak

Contents

Acknowledgments

It is a pleasure to have the opportunity to acknowledge the generosity and scholarship of many who have contributed to this volume of essays. Our collaboration originated in the planning of the annual conference for the Centre for Medieval Studies at the University of Toronto in February, 1990. Both the initial response to the conference topic of "Power of the Weak?" and the stimulating exchange of ideas amongst participants and audience during those wintry days several years ago encouraged us to pursue the publication of a collection of essays selected from the papers delivered at the conference.

Our first thanks must therefore go to the Centre for Medieval Studies, which fostered our interest in this topic, hosted the conference with warmth and efficiency, and through the unwavering personal kindness of the director, Jill Webster, supported our lengthy editorial endeavors. This support has been made tangible through a publication subvention by the Centre for Medieval Studies to the University of Illinois Press. We are grateful, too, for the continued commitment of the newly appointed director, Roberta Frank, to our project.

We also want to pay special tribute to Susan Mosher Stuard, the scholar who delivered the keynote address at the 1990 conference and inspired everyone with her learning and personal grace. We have continued to benefit from her generous encouragement and perceptive advice since that time, and are fortunate to have made her acquaintance.

Our long-suffering contributors have endured a process of assessment slower than we could ever have imagined at the outset of this venture and brought on in part by our own editorial zeal. The most bizarre phase of assessment returned the entire collection dripping wet to Sally-Beth's desk, after what was described as an "airport incident" at Long Island! The cooperation and loyalty of our contributors have more than matched the determination of the editors—we thank them all for their dedicated work. In particular we would like to single out John Parsons, who coordinated the conference session featuring early versions of the three queenship essays; we have taken advantage of John's own editorial experience and presence in Toronto to consult him in detail about these essays as well as other aspects of the collection, including the introduction.

Although we cannot record the names of all those who agreed to read and comment anonymously on the essays, either individually or as a whole, we do want to convey our gratitude to a selfless company of scholars. The comments received were outstandingly constructive and stimulating—we are sure that all our contributors would agree that their work has been enriched by the reports from these silent partners in our collaboration.

There are others whose names we can list with thanks for sharing their expertise. Particular care was taken to check all translations, and we would like to thank K. Janet Ritch, a friend at the Centre for Medieval Studies, for generously sharing her expertise in Anglo-Norman and French, and John Corbett, also of the Centre for Medieval Studies, for reviewing the Hebrew translations. We owe the warmest possible thanks to Jennifer's husband, Andrew Connolly, who has been a behind-the-scenes partner in this endeavor from the beginning. It is no exaggeration to say that there is hardly a passage in the book, except for this one, which he has not read and commented on. In particular, we owe him thanks for his painstaking review of all the translations from Latin in this volume, a considerable task which he undertook with unfailing good cheer.

We have also benefited from the assistance of Joseph Goering, again of the Centre for Medieval Studies, an astute critic whose comments have helped us greatly in our editorial task. We are especially grateful to Joe for the serene patience he cultivated as Jennifer's thesis supervisor when this project lured her away from her doctoral thesis.

The later stages of producing this book have been facilitated with friendly efficiency and attention to detail by our editor, Karen Hewitt, and our copy editor, Patricia Hollahan. We have appreciated the care they have taken on our behalf. On a more domestic front, Sally-Beth would like to thank her husband Paul for encouraging her to pursue her interests in a field centuries away from his own and enduring the ensuing distractions, not to mention piles of proofs, on the home scene.

Our final tribute must be a sad one. Our editorial team initially included a third member, Prudence Tracy, a valued associate of the Centre for Medieval Studies and senior editor at the University of Toronto Press. We have happy memories of sharing ideas and experiences over lunch with Prue at the Fare Exchange where the future of this collection was debated. When she died prematurely in 1993, we mourned her loss as a wise colleague and friend. We are pleased to dedicate this volume to her memory.

Introduction

Jennifer Carpenter and Sally-Beth MacLean

HIS BOOK WILL APPEAR IN PRINT nineteen years after the publication of *Women in Medieval Society*, edited by Susan Mosher Stuard.[1] Stuard's pioneer collection helped to establish the collaborative, interdisciplinary path which much future scholarship in the field would follow. Nineteen years on, the essays collected in this volume bear witness to the continuing vitality and diversity of scholarship on medieval women, and to the continuing importance of the essay collection as a forum for that work. These two points are perhaps not unrelated: in recent years, a number of new and fascinating questions, approaches, and sources have enlivened the study of women in the Middle Ages. Detailed, close analyses have been needed to unravel the many-layered cultural narratives which shaped their thought and behavior. Nuanced case studies have illuminated the strategies individual women used to negotiate the accepted concepts and practices of society at large, and have helped us understand the slipperiness and ambiguity of that concept we call "power." We are only too aware of the complexity of the picture which has emerged, a complexity which has tended to make general narrative histories of medieval women difficult to write, and unsatisfying to read. In these circumstances, it is no surprise that collections of smaller studies on medieval women which allow the reader to build layers of insights from a number of different research perspectives should remain attractive. We are pleased to offer this collection as a contribution to a healthy tradition.

One direction in recent scholarship on women has focused on uncovering and describing the discourses which governed people's thinking about the categories of "male" and "female." In the present volume,

Jacqueline Murray's essay follows this course, and seeks to lay bare the underlying understanding of the relationship between men and women implicit in the pastoral manuals used by medieval clergy to help them with their duties of preaching and hearing confession. Murray concludes that the two pastoral manual authors she investigates provide contrasting approaches to the differences between men and women, both of which, however, are more favorable in their assessment of women than the more learned discourses of theology and canon law. Her analysis of these little-examined sources leads her to call for a more sensitive understanding of the varied conceptions of gender which operated within medieval society.

Jocelyn Wogan-Browne's contribution to the collection approaches the vexed question of the relationship between historical women and the literary narratives which represent them, by exploring the nexus between the female writer who translated the *vita* of St. Etheldreda into Anglo-Norman and the known female audience of the work. Wogan-Browne points out the ways in which the translator of the Anglo-Norman life gives greater emphasis in her work to the agency of "Audrée"— French for Etheldreda—and how she illuminates her saint's point of view in ways distinct from the Latin *vita* from which her work derived. The essay then moves into a discussion of how Audrée's life as a wife, widow, virgin, manager of estates, and patron-founder might have found resonance with the experience and interests of Anglo-Norman aristocratic nuns who lived in communities such as Campsey Priory and listened to *La vie seinte Audrée* at mealtimes. Wogan-Browne thus offers fresh insights into not only the ways in which women chose to create female models in writing but also the ways in which women readers may have appropriated such models.

Jennifer Carpenter's essay approaches the question of the relationship between individual agency and the constraints of culture by attempting to reconstruct the subjective experience of mothering in the life of the recluse Juette of Huy (d. 1228), in the context of established cultural narratives of sainthood and motherhood. This essay first explores the history of Christian attitudes toward the compatibility of motherhood and sanctity, and then proceeds to investigate Juette's own experience of mothering and being mothered, as it can be retraced in the *vita* written about her not long after her death. Carpenter discusses the ways in which "motherhood," understood both as an ideal and as a practical social role, provided established patterns which could work to restrict women's activities or to provide a structure on which to graft innovative behavior.

Libby Garshowitz's essay is a significant contribution to the study of Jewish women, a group too seldom represented in standard collections of medieval and early modern European women's history. Garshowitz presents her subject, Gracia Mendes, as a striking example of a woman who successfully negotiated several communities with varying legal, social, and religious expectations, as she lived as a *conversa* (converted Jew), a secret Jew, and finally, an openly professing Jew. Gracia's shrewd intelligence, and her courage, together with her privileged status as a wealthy widow, enabled her to preserve and expand the financial empire she had inherited, while at the same time resisting attempts to redirect her fortune and to prevent her from achieving her ultimate goal, which was to move her household to Turkey where she would be welcome to practice Judaism without hindrance. Garshowitz's essay is especially welcome for the material it provides for the comparative study of medieval Jewish and Christian women.

A particular feature of the collection is the three essays offered on medieval and early modern queenship. The complementary studies of Lois Huneycutt, John Parsons, and Elizabeth McCartney draw upon social, legal, and political history as well as anthropological analysis of ritual and authority to form a valuable contribution to our understanding of these important women and their office. The essays of both Huneycutt and Parsons present some of the models of queenly behavior available to medieval people and explore in some detail how these models were actively interpreted by the queen and those who wished to influence her. In a wider perspective, both essays expand our understanding of the dialectic relationship between cultural ideals of female roles and the ways in which medieval women and men manipulated those roles.

In her study, Huneycutt focuses on the use of the Old Testament queen, Esther, as a model for the perfect queen, and especially as a model for a queen who successfully intercedes with her husband for her people. Huneycutt explores her theme by offering a case study of how the twelfth-century English queen Mathilda understood her role in society. Parsons's essay also considers the nature and implications of the intercessory role of medieval queens, concentrating on the model of the Virgin Mary as perfect queen and merciful intercessor. Instead of focusing on the importance of the Virgin for the queen herself, Parsons makes imaginative use of disparate sources to suggest how the Marian model for queenly intercession may have become known to the queen's more ordinary subjects and how Marian imagery was then manipulated by those making petitions for the queen's intercession.

Elizabeth McCartney's work analyzes the theoretical underpinnings of the legal status and authority of late medieval and early modern French queens which are to be found both implicitly demonstrated in their coronation ceremonies and explicitly asserted in the works of French legal scholars. McCartney demonstrates how the ceremonies which marked the queen's coronation publicly acknowledged that she held a unique status in the kingdom, and was, as the king's wife, associated with the "dignitas" of the crown and accorded the honors, privileges, and prerogatives assumed with royal office. McCartney's study of the pivotal coronation of Anne of Brittany in 1504 traces the evolution of the French queen's rights and privileges as second only to the king's and endorsed by early modern constitutional writers. Their affirmation of the royal widow's independent right to enjoy her husband's privileges and honors was later to empower the queens regent of late sixteenth- and seventeenth-century France.

Scholarship on medieval women and, to a lesser extent, on early modern women in history and literature has always had to be aware of the elusiveness of its subjects, as well as their agency, their absence as well as their presence.[2] It is difficult for us to trace the women who spoke to their priests in confession, and how they negotiated their experience of confession, not to mention their penance; we are frustrated that the audience of the life of Audrée has to be reconstructed from such meager evidence; we will never know exactly what Juette of Huy thought about her own life, or to what Gracia Mendes attributed her success, much less her inner strategies for financial, social, and political survival.

We are also constantly made aware of the constructed nature of the "reality" which we find in our texts, and of the "reality" our own scholarly texts create. And yet, despite these difficulties, our contributors have tackled their elusive subject perceptively from a variety of angles and with a wide range of interdisciplinary sources at their command. Murray's essay covers the widest time span and leads the collection from the theoretical misogynist texts of classical and medieval philosophers and theologians to the late twelfth-century pastoral manuals which bring us closer to the actual experience of that most elusive class, ordinary medieval women.[3]

Hagiography continues to be a fruitful area for reexamination by historians and literary scholars in search of medieval women's experiences: Carpenter and Huneycutt both make fresh use of their twelfth- and thirteenth-century *vitae*, while Wogan-Browne discovers an authentic woman's voice in the neglected Anglo-Norman text derived from the twelfth-century male-authored *Liber Eliensis*. The difficult and specialized *responsa* literature used by Libby Garshowitz extends the range of the collection beyond traditional cultural boundaries and across the artificial barrier frequently erected between medieval and early modern studies. Her sixteenth-century focus is echoed by McCartney's analysis of legal treatises, iconography, and coronation *ordines* from this later period. The other two contributors on queenship, Huneycutt and Parsons, draw upon a remarkable range of historical documents, including letters, petitions, and other exchequer records, as well as the sophisticated iconography with which women were represented in the high Middle Ages. The writers have explored a wide range of Latin works, making innovative use of new and familiar sources. In addition, several writers have used texts and documents in vernacular languages— Anglo-Norman, medieval and early modern French, and Hebrew— which usually present a less clerical, more popular point of view.

We have given this collection the title *Power of the Weak* because it suggests something of the contradictory nature of medieval women's independence of action, influence, and self-expression. It is not intended to suggest an overarching theory or create an artificial unity, although the essays do, finally, reflect on some demonstrable points of access to influence available to women in the period covered. In pursuing their independent studies of medieval women in various social, religious, and political roles, the authors have been sensitive to the possibilities of medieval women's formal and informal power, and the possibilities for influence that may have paradoxically been available to women despite, and sometimes precisely because of, their subordinate position in society.[4]

For example, that most traditional, and very often most restricting, role, motherhood, could provide a model for religious leadership and active charitable service, as we see in Carpenter's study of Juette of Huy. The role of the daughter, likewise traditionally a lowly one, could also be emphasized in order to create and reinforce significant ties. As Huneycutt has shown, Mathilda placed great importance on her symbolic inheritance from her famous saintly mother both privately and publicly. Mathilda also chose to closely associate herself with Archbishop Anselm by styling herself as his "daughter."

Our collection illustrates the special prominence of three kinds of medieval women, namely, widows, holy women, and queens, a prominence which reflects the opportunities available for such women. And yet in each case, the foundation of the very real influence these women exercised was precarious and fragile, and was often dependent on their family and financial circumstances.

Widowhood, like motherhood, was an ambiguous state.[5] Poor widows were traditionally seen as the most vulnerable and pitiable members of medieval society. And yet the opportunities for independent activity available to widows as heads of their own households, often with independent control over economic resources, are evident in the essays by Wogan-Browne, Carpenter, Garshowitz, and McCartney. Garshowitz presents the case of a wealthy non-Christian woman who exercised considerable economic influence in her struggle to find personal freedom while developing a role as social benefactor and patron. Wogan-Browne's study reflects upon a widow who chose a religious context in which to gain authority, her personal and socioeconomic autonomy assured through her rerouting of her dower lands to the monastic community of Ely. In another context, McCartney has demonstrated that the legal rights and status of the widow were so well established as to provide a model for political theorists who wished to define queenly power as flowing from a change in status which the queen irrevocably underwent at the time of her marriage to the king.

Medieval holy women, who were not infrequently also queens and widows, were an especially conspicuous group whose lives and writings are well represented in our sources. Murray has used the writings of Hildegard of Bingen in her analysis of medieval concepts of gender, while Wogan-Browne and Carpenter have based their research on hagiographical texts which commemorate in some detail the lives of two holy women.

The religious life could bring women control over their bodies and a legitimate career alternative to marriage. For Audrée it brought administrative power in Anglo-Saxon England; both for Audrée and for Juette in thirteenth-century Huy the holy life brought reputation and sanctity with lasting influence beyond the grave through the dissemination of hagiographic texts representing them as positive role models. Women, as Wogan-Browne's essay points out, could also function as authors and literary or monastic patrons, using their influence to extend recognition of their favored subjects.

At the highest level of society we can see in the queenship essays some aspects of influence observed by Murray in the pastoral manuals representing the experience of women in the lower classes. Queens were similarly able to exert influence through the affectionate bonds of marriage to intercede for worthy causes or through pious activity such as almsgiving or other lay religious practices. The opportunities for lay religious activity such as this increased through the period, even as another option, the power enjoyed by an Audrée or a Hildegard as abbess, receded. Not only were queens among the most powerful of medieval women, they were also ritual figures, with prominent public roles. The ambiguity of the queen's position of power, resting as it did on informal familial ties, is one of the most interesting aspects of medieval queenship, as can be seen in the essays of Huneycutt and Parsons. McCartney's study of conflicting theoretical understandings of the nature of the queen's power in Renaissance France demonstrates that the ambiguity continued to be an issue in the sixteenth century.

The cumulative political influence of queens is clearly delineated by Huneycutt, Parsons, and McCartney over a period of five centuries. Beyond the considerable status afforded the queen, through her ceremonial role and her privileged opportunities for intercession, are recorded acts of public authority such as witnessing legal documents, presiding over councils, and regency during military campaigns and the minority of her son. The sixteenth-century legal research which upheld the independent juridical rights of queenship for McCartney's Anne of Brittany was the culmination of centuries of women claiming their rights of action within a precarious position of dependent authority. This kind of struggle on the part of women is surely indicative of the very real fragility of the "power of the weak"; and full recognition of the courage and ingenuity of medieval women in considering their options does not disguise the effort involved in reacting against restrictive circumstances or the narrowness of the avenues within which influence and independence might be achieved.

Notes

1. *Women in Medieval Society,* ed. Susan Mosher Stuard (Philadelphia, 1976).

2. For a discussion of these issues in feminist literary criticism, see Sheila Fisher and Janet E. Halley, "The Lady Vanishes: The Problem of Women's Absence in Late Medieval and Renaissance Texts," in *Seeking the Woman in Late Medieval and Renaissance Writings: Essays in Feminist Contextual Criticism*, ed. Sheila Fisher and Janet E. Halley (Knoxville, Tenn., 1989), 1–17; see also Christiane Klapisch-Zuber, "Including Women," in *Silences of the Middle Ages*, ed. Christiane Klapisch-Zuber (Cambridge, Mass., 1992), vol. 2 of *A History of Women in the West*, gen. eds. Georges Duby and Michelle Perrot. See esp. 6–9.

3. Medieval peasant and working women are not, however, as elusive as they may seem from the contents of this collection, and we would direct the reader to these valuable studies: Judith Bennett, *Women in the Medieval English Countryside: Gender and Household in Brigstock before the Plague* (New York, 1987); Martha C. Howell, *Women, Production, and Patriarchy in Late Medieval Cities* (Chicago, 1986); Peter Biller, "The Common Woman in the Western Church in the Thirteenth and Early Fourteenth Centuries," in *Women in the Church*, ed. W. J. Sheils and Diana Wood, Studies in Church History 27 (Oxford, 1990), 127–57; and the articles in *Woman Is a Worthy Wight: Women in English Society c. 1200–1500*, ed. P. J. P. Goldberg (Stroud, Gloucestershire, 1992).

4. A number of writers have discussed the deep appreciation of narratives of inversion which characterized Christian culture. The centrality of inversion in the Gospel story, in which Christ, poor and humble as a human, though in reality great in majesty as God, had his triumphant moment at the hour of his defeat in death, was a cogent model for considering the qualities of powerlessness. St. Paul himself was the first writer to explore the theme of Christ's strength through weakness, using the analogy to find power in his own weakness (2 Cor. 12:8–10, 13:3–4).

The paradoxical nature of the recurrent Christian theme of the "power of the weak" has been explored by Victor Turner and Edith Turner in *Image and Pilgrimage in Christian Culture: Anthropological Perspectives* (New York, 1978), see esp. 154. Exploration of these themes, and their complex relationship to the lives of medieval women, has been a particular interest of Caroline Walker Bynum in *Jesus as Mother: Studies in the Spirituality of the High Middle Ages* (Berkeley, 1982), 110–65; "Women's Stories, Women's Symbols: A Critique of Victor Turner's Theory of Liminality," in *Anthropology and the Study of Religion*, ed. Robert L. Moore and Frank E. Reynolds (Chicago, 1984), 105–25; and "'. . . And Woman His Humanity': Female Imagery in the Religious Writing of the Later Middle Ages," in *Gender and Religion: On the Complexity of Symbols*, ed. Caroline Walker Bynum, Stevan Harrell, and Paula Richman (Boston, 1986), 257–88.

5. There is a growing literature on medieval widows and the options

available to them in secular and religious life. See Margaret Wade Labarge's case study, "Three Medieval Widows and a Second Career," in *Aging and the Aged in Medieval Europe,* ed. Michael M. Sheehan, Papers in Mediaeval Studies 11 (Toronto, 1990), 159–72; M.-T. Lorcin, "Retraite des veuves et filles au couvent: Quelques aspects de la condition féminine à la fin du Moyen Age," *Annales de démographie historique* 38 (1975), 187–204; and now Sue Sheridan Walker, ed., *Wife and Widow in Medieval England* (Ann Arbor, 1993), esp. the articles by Joel T. Rosenthal ("Fifteenth-Century Widows and Widowhood: Bereavement, Reintegration, and Life Choices" [33–58]) and Barbara Hanawalt ("Remarriage as an Option for Urban and Rural Widows in Late Medieval England" [141–64]). For widows in literature, see Louise Mirrer, ed., *Upon My Husband's Death: Widows in the Literature and Histories of Medieval Europe* (Ann Arbor, 1992).

ONE

Thinking about Gender:
The Diversity of Medieval
Perspectives

Jacqueline Murray

ONCEPTS OF GENDER, like any other set of ideas, are influenced by their historical context. The recognition that gender is socially constructed and historically rooted is now commonplace.[1] As part of the efforts to explain human nature and the similarities or differences between women and men, the concepts of sex and gender have occupied humanity, and especially philosophers, since at least the pre-Socratics.[2] The study of gender in history is a complex dialogue of past and present. As with any other area of historical enquiry, we moderns never really leave ourselves behind. Present agendas and personal experiences necessarily inform our interpretations of the past. In a society as complex and diverse as that of the Middle Ages, it is possible for the scholar to find whatever she wants, whatever will best serve her hypothesis. In this way the interpretation of the past is frequently used either to validate the present or to promote a vision of the future. This is especially true for women's history, for which the contradictory myths of progress and of a Golden Age hold particular appeal.[3]

The paucity of sources that troubles every area of medieval scholarship presents serious difficulties for the study of gender. Most medieval literature was, of course, written by men for men and not just any men but an elite caste of celibate males who occupied a privileged place in the social order: the clergy. There are few sources written by women and fewer still that were self-consciously written to present a woman's perspective.[4] Consequently, there is a tendency, even among medievalists, to view the Middle Ages as somehow having had a single interpretive stance, one shaped by a single ecclesiastical discourse of misogyny. For example, R. Howard Bloch has gone so far as to suggest that such sources are completely irrelevant to women's experience and concludes that "the discourse of misogyny is a discourse by men, for men and of men."[5] Rather than abandon the quest, however, the medievalist who searches for women has instead begun to employ new and innovative techniques, to interpret from silence, and to reread old sources in new ways.[6] As Jo Ann McNamara has asked: "Can we write a history for which there were no historians, from records that resist the project?" Her answer is a resounding yes, although she warns that "This is the history we were all trained not to write: a history in confrontation with our sources rather than in conformity with them."[7]

In addition to writing the history of medieval women in spite of the sources, it is also important to question the hegemony of this ecclesiastical discourse of misogyny. Medieval clerical writers frequently expressed their ideas about the nature of men and women in terms of binary oppositions, a conceptual framework that has been particularly influential and enduring.[8] Caroline Bynum has summarized this misogynist understanding of gender saying: "*Male* and *female* were contrasted and asymmetrically valued as intellect/body, active/passive, rational/irrational, reason/emotion, self-control/lust, judgment/mercy, and order/disorder."[9] This dualism was perpetuated in discussions of good woman/bad woman, for example, in the familiar dichotomies of Mary and Eve or the Lady and the Whore. Women were considered inferior and their virtue was interpreted according to the degree to which they accepted their theoretical and social inferiority. Submission and obedience were virtues. Pride, ambition, and autonomy were perceived ultimately as rebellious, and as crimes against both the natural and the moral order. The best thing inferior woman could do was to know her place.[10] Or so we might conclude from an analysis of those texts which comprise the ecclesiastical discourse of misogyny. However, it is important to remember, as Bynum has observed, that "[there is] no such thing as '*the* medieval attitude toward women.'"[11] Our historical vantage point frequently blinds us to alternative interpretations and dissent from the ideology which prevailed in a society. Joan Scott warns us that: "normative statements depend on the refusal or repression of alternative possibilities, and, sometimes, overt contests about them take place. . . . The position that emerges as dominant, however, is stated as the only possible one. Subsequent history is written as if these normative positions were the product of social consensus rather than of conflict."[12] And, in fact, rather than a monolithic "medieval view," a monovocalic discourse of misogyny, there was a diversity of opinion, even within what might broadly be termed "the Church."

ᏒᏅ

Recent scholarship suggests that medieval ideas about gender were in fact far more varied and complex than a reading of the standard misogynist texts would suggest. For example, from her study of the writings of female saints from the twelfth to fifteenth centuries, Bynum challenges the idea that medieval women internalized the negative image of woman developed in the theoretical literature of the clergy.[13] In a comparative examination of the writings by women and men Bynum found that the image of woman was used differently, according to the author's gender. Women tended to place themselves in the category humanity and did not assume that somehow religious progress meant becoming masculine, as some male writers asserted. Rather, female writers more often use "woman" to mean "human being." Male writers, however, perceived gender in terms of binary oppositions and juxtaposed male power, judgment, discipline, and reason, compared with female weakness, mercy, lust, and unreason.[14] Bynum concludes that "Women say less about gender, [and] make less use of dichotomous gender images . . . it is men who develop conceptions of gender, whereas women develop conceptions of humanity."[15] In writing by women, "Personal and social characteristics were more often shared by the two genders. . . . The female was a less marked category; it was more often simply a symbol of an almost genderless self."[16]

While popular perceptions might be varied and diffuse, in academic circles more standardized understandings of gender prevailed. These were based on the two main philosophical explanations of gender inherited from antiquity, explanations which were subsequently informed and modified in light of Jewish and Christian scripture and theology.[17] The philosophy of gender polarity, articulated by Aristotle, is the source of the male/female binary opposition so familiar to medieval thinkers. According to Aristotle male/female could be juxtaposed with active/passive, form/matter, and perfection/imperfection.[18] Furthermore, these oppositions are not perceived as equal and opposite but rather are in a hierarchical relationship. The female is understood to be the result of defective generation and is, as it were, a deformed male. Since she is imperfect, it is natural that man should rule over woman.[19]

The philosophy of gender unity attributed to Plato is somewhat more complex because it was not presented in a sustained and systematic discussion, and because his evaluation of gender tended to vary from work to work.[20] In general, Plato believed that male and female are essentially the same and only accidentally different. The physical bodies of man and woman differ but they possess the same eternal souls. For Plato, bodily existence has the appearance of reality but it is in fact imperfect and transitory. Ultimately the body will pass away, leaving only the individual's true nature, the soul, which is neither male nor female. Consequently, Plato's body-soul dualism established that woman and man were of the same nature and that woman was just as capable as man of moral and intellectual perfection. Yet, this dualism also relegated the physical to a secondary status. Woman's body was believed weaker and she was more closely linked with the physical world through the process of giving birth.[21] This, then, provided an explanation for woman's evident social inferiority. However, social and physical inferiority notwithstanding, according to Plato women and men were of essentially the same nature and equally capable of the highest wisdom, virtue, and moral perfection.

The values of early Christianity and its understanding that both women and men could achieve individual merit were a departure from those of the surrounding pagan world, especially from the theories developed by the ancient philosophers. The example and teaching of Jesus provided a reevaluation of largely devalued female qualities such as compassion, gentleness, and humility. Women, too, were included in his inner circle and their status was thus elevated by proximity to their great teacher.[22] For the next and subsequent generations of Christians, however, gender relations were a source of friction and concern.

The tensions between a theology of equality within the order of salvation and a hierarchically conceived social order that enforced the subordination of women are evident in the letters of the Apostle Paul. The Pauline epistles themselves record how in early Christian communities women exercised positions of authority and leadership that were in direct contradiction to the ideology of subordination that prevailed in both Roman and Jewish society. In the course of the first few centuries of Christianity women gradually came to be excluded from ministries, exhorted to humility, obedience, and ultimately silence.[23]

The notion of woman's spiritual equality and her social subordination was emphasized in the Pauline epistles. The standard articulation of the spiritual equality of all believers is found in Galatians 3:28: "There is neither Jew nor Greek, slave nor free, male nor female; for you are all one in Christ Jesus."[24] Elsewhere Paul provides equally clear statements of the hierarchical nature of gender relations: "But I want you to know that the head of every man is Christ: the head of woman, man: just as the head of Christ is God" (1 Cor. 11:3). "Wives, be subject to your husbands as to the Lord; for the man is the head of the woman, just as Christ is the head of the church" (Eph. 5:22–23). Thus Paul established an unambiguous hierarchy stretching down from God to Christ to man and finally to woman. Yet he also appeared to believe that social subordination and spiritual equality could coexist. As George H. Tavard has summarized the problem, "Paul's ideas regarding womanhood prove to be ambiguous. They may be, and have been, interpreted in either a misogynist or a pro-feminine direction."[25]

Despite the flexibility or ambiguity of the Pauline epistles, the early Church Fathers, as learned in ancient philosophy as in the Christian scriptures, tended to adopt a rigorist, hierarchical view of gender relations. Woman was not only subordinate, she was dangerous to the salvation of men. While some of the Fathers reiterated Paul's understanding of the spiritual equality of men and women, it was of limited practical influence. Jo Ann McNamara has summarized the situation, saying: "But in essence the equality of which the Christian fathers wrote was a celestial condition, not a temporal one. . . . In general they viewed social inequities, violence, and oppression as evils that grew out of man's original fall from grace."[26] And although the opinion of Tertullian, who characterized woman as "the devil's gateway," may have been extreme, nevertheless, in the course of the Middle Ages, the theoretical spiritual equality of man and woman came to be overshadowed by negative images of woman as frail, seductive, and an impediment to man's salvation.[27]

By the late thirteenth century, as a result of Thomas Aquinas's reconciliation of Aristotelian philosophy and Christian theology, women's inferiority and subordination became grounded firmly on both the theoretical and practical levels. The Pauline assertion of spiritual equality was overshadowed by Thomas's adoption of Aristotelian biology and the consequent negative evaluation has exercised influence down to our own century.[28] In the years preceding Thomas's ultimate intellectual hegemony, however, there was a plurality of belief. For example, in the twelfth century, Hildegard of Bingen developed an understanding of gender which departed from both the gender polarity and gender unity theories. Her theory, which sought to reconcile biological difference and spiritual equality, was completely obscured by Thomas's predominance.

Hildegard, abbess, mystic, philosopher, and theologian, was an extraordinary person. The extent to which she departed from conventional evaluations of gender must be understood in the context both of her specifically female perspective and her personal departure from the traditional behavior prescribed for women.[29] Hildegard divided the soul into masculine and feminine aspects, as Aristotle had done, but she tempered their traditional relationship "by stressing sexual complementarity both in God and in humanity even as she reasserted the principle of sexual hierarchy."[30] Thus she assigned to women and men different characteristics and urged each to work at developing the characteristics of the other gender. She also insisted on the resurrection of the sexual body and the notion that sexual identification was a significant factor in human existence. In doing so Hildegard avoided the Platonic idea of a genderless soul and the consequent devaluation of the physical body, while at the same time she avoided the Aristotelian devaluation of female nature.

Hildegard believed that men and women were complementary in virtue. To account for their unequal social relationships she explained that women obey men by choice, as a means of exercising virtue. This notion of obedience may be better understood when viewed in the context of the Benedictine monastic tradition. Obedience was perceived as neither natural nor inherent but rather was one of the means by which the individual could cultivate virtue. Ultimately, for Hildegard, it was irrelevant whether one obeyed a man or a woman, since she believed that in many circumstances women could and did rule and men obey.[31] This is perhaps a natural conclusion in light of Hildegard's early life in a double monastery in which both monks and nuns obeyed the abbot and of her own experience as an abbess, accustomed to exercising authority and advising both temporal and spiritual leaders.

Prudence Allen, who has placed Hildegard's thought within the framework of western philosophical tradition, concludes that she developed "a realistic and complex theory of sex identity. . . . she used a philosophical method of observation of the senses and analysis of reason to develop the framework for a theory of sex complementarity."[32] She suggests that Hildegard developed her ideas quite consciously based on her personal understanding of theology, her medical knowledge, especially of anatomy and generation, and her own life experience. In other words, Hildegard's philosophical understanding of gender was based on her own experience as a woman. This would seem to parallel Bynum's point that women did not see themselves in the same way as men saw them, though in Hildegard's case she did not blur sex and gender distinctions as did the women whom Bynum studied.[33] Hildegard accepted neither a philosophy of natural inferiority that denigrated her gender nor one of antimaterial dualism that denigrated her humanity.[34] Rather she sought a middle ground that accounted for her own experience as a woman and her understanding of her place in the order of creation.

Hildegard's theory serves to highlight the diversity of the understanding of human nature in the Middle Ages, at least prior to the institutionalization of Aristotelian philosophy after the mid-thirteenth century. Indeed, the notion that there were a number of different evaluations of gender which coexisted in this earlier period is clearly demonstrated in the voluminous literature surrounding pastoral care which in part anticipated and in part was inspired by the religious revival and reforms of the Fourth Lateran Council (1215).[35]

These pastoral manuals began to appear at the end of the twelfth century. Designed to help the simple priest with the *cura animarum,* these books were of a more practical than speculative nature—they addressed the real problems that the individual could encounter in daily life. They touched upon areas where Christian morality and social reality could come into conflict. For example, they might examine such questions as usury, just-price, and prostitution: phenomena which simple condemnation could neither rectify nor obviate. The problems that average people might encounter were considered and solutions suggested.

These manuals were also one of the means by which the doctrines developed by canonists and theologians were disseminated to the lowest ranks of Christian society. As a conscious attempt to inform the parish priest who, in turn, would teach the laity, these manuals bring us near to the average person by telling us the advice her pastor received and was expected to transmit to his parishioners.[36] Consequently, pastoral literature has a number of distinctive characteristics. Because it was intended for minimally educated members of the clergy, the information is presented in a straightforward and simple fashion, freed from the rigid formulae of scholastic discourse. Second, the information is of a practical nature; what a priest needed to know to hear confession, preach, and otherwise care for his flock. Third, because the information was intended to be applicable to daily life, it was timely and took into account the experience of the laity and the problems of living in a complex and imperfect world. Thus pastoral literature tended to be more concrete in nature than the canon law, theology, or philosophy from which it was derived. There was no room for lauding the unrealistic ideal and ignoring the uncomfortable or ambiguous situations that could arise in daily life.[37] In addressing the experience of the laity these manuals mitigated theory to take practice into account. And the further removed from the courtroom or the classroom, the more summarized, condensed, and simplified the manual, the more likely it was to have actually been consulted by the parish clergy and thus to have touched the lives of the laity.

Rather than consulting the small and accessible handbooks, historians have traditionally relied on scholarly and expensive tomes for information about pastoral care and the values taught at the parish level.[38] Works of monumental proportions, for example, the *Corrector et medicus* of Burchard of Worms or Raymond of Peñafort's *Summa de casibus,* frequently are examined for information about pastoral care in the Middle Ages. But by their very nature, these books were more likely found in a reference library than in the hands of a parish priest. In short, such mammoth works were too learned and too expensive to have been consulted by the simple priest. These sources, so closely tied to the schools, have perpetuated the view that the learned discourse of clerical misogyny, so apparent in the schools and the courts, was the only understanding of gender found within the medieval church.

If indeed preachers and confessors had perpetuated the prejudices of the ecclesiastical establishment, not only with regard to the nature of woman but also about the evils of trade, of military activity, of marriage, and so on, why then would anyone have listened? It is possible to legislate obligatory annual confession or weekly preaching, but that does not mean the laity will listen to advice that is irrelevant, insulting, or at odds with their own experience and values. What is more, ecclesiastical writers, released from the conventions imposed by scholasticism, may have been able to interpret the Church's teaching in light of their personal experience, as men who knew women, not only as penitents and sinners but also perhaps as mothers and sisters, housekeepers, and friends. Pastoral writers, freed from the *expectation* of writing from a stance of clerical misogyny, could bring to their manuals on pastoral care a more compassionate and realistic understanding of the workings of daily life.[39] It has become commonplace to analyze confession as a means of social control and to view the Church as co-ercing women and men to conform to an irrelevant and oppressive moral code. But this rigid understanding of medieval social dynamics unnecessarily limits our ability to appreciate the complexity of medi-eval cultural and religious values.[40] Pastoral manuals, in fact, present a diversity of opinion and their evaluations of gender reflect a practical understanding of the interaction of women and men that belies the idea of a monovocalic medieval discourse of misogyny. The works of two authors, Thomas of Chobham and Robert Grosseteste, will serve to illustrate this point.

Thomas of Chobham and Robert Grosseteste were both interested in the *cura animarum* and how to prepare priests to exercise better their pastoral functions. Both men lived and worked in England in the first half of the thirteenth century, and were influenced by the interest in pastoral theology that emanated from the Paris theology faculty, un-der the leadership and inspiration of Peter the Chanter.[41] Both wrote pastoral manuals that were immensely popular. Despite these similar-ities in their education, outlook, and cultural context, they arrived at quite different understandings of gender.

Thomas of Chobham, subdean of Salisbury and rector of the village of Chobham, wrote a *Summa confessorum* that was finished and circu-lating by 1216.[42] He had an academic interest in the *cura animarum*. As a Master of Theology, Chobham may have been involved in the education of the clergy; his manual makes it clear that he also had a practical understanding of the issues pertaining to pastoral care. In his *Summa confessorum* Chobham reflects on human nature and the prob-lems that individuals could encounter in life, and his work allows for some concrete conclusions to be drawn about his perceptions of gen-der in both the public and private spheres.

Most of the information pertaining to women is found in passages that discuss the sacrament of marriage, the interaction of spouses, and the problems peculiar to the marital relationship. Chobham says that marriage ought properly be called *coniugium* "because it pertains equally to the man and the woman."[43] While establishing that the union en-gages both spouses equally, he also clearly believes that the relationship is a hierarchical one in which the husband holds the dominant posi-tion. For example, he warns confessors to exercise care when assigning penance to a married woman. The penance must be such that it will not disclose the woman's sin to her husband and must also be one that her husband will allow her to perform. Thus, if fasting is enjoined as penance but the husband orders the woman to eat, she must obey her husband rather than her confessor.[44] In this vein Chobham clearly reinforced the hierarchical nature of Christian marriage articulated by St. Paul in his letter to the Ephesians.[45]

Chobham would have argued that woman and man complement each other within marriage. He discusses at length the relationship between spouses whom he sees as exercising a mutually beneficial influence on each other. He advises that the confessor "should persuade the husband to manage his wife with decent demands, and to exhibit the respect owed as to a part of his own body. And if she is foolish, he should rebuke her moderately and decently, and if there is need, he should chastise her. For he should employ greater diligence in guarding his wife than in guarding any earthly possession because nothing should be more dear to him than his wife."[46] Women, on the other hand, are enjoined to persuade their husbands to upright behavior:

> Women should always be urged in confession to be preachers to their husbands. For no priest can soften a man's heart as a wife can. Hence the sin of a man can often be imputed to his wife if, through her neglect, the husband does not mend his ways. When they are in their bedroom and in each other's arms, she ought to speak to her husband soothingly, and if he is hard and merciless and an oppressor of the poor she ought to incite him to mercy, if he is a plunderer to detest his plundering; if he is a grasping man, let her inspire generosity in him and let her secretly give alms from their common property and let her make good the alms which he fails to give. For it is licit for a wife to give out much of her husband's property without his knowledge for purposes advantageous to him and for pious causes.[47]

Thus, women and men are not only considered equal in the moral forum but each complements the other's behavior. A woman has the responsibility to correct or compensate for her husband's moral failures.[48] This moral responsibility, however, should not be confused with de facto equality. The wife is enjoined to use her charm and her feminine wiles, as well as her ability to cajole and persuade. If necessary, she is to manipulate her husband into altering his behavior. He, on the other hand, has the authority to correct or punish her. Thus this recognition of woman's influence over her husband could be interpreted as reinforcing her subordinate position. While both spouses may be responsible moral agents, in daily life it is the man who exercises authority over the woman and the woman who obeys.

It is possible that ideas similar to Hildegard's philosophy of gender complementarity underlie Chobham's manual. Certainly, he appears to see women and men as complementary: a husband's harshness can be balanced by his wife's mercy, a quality Hildegard identifies as feminine. In her analysis of Chobham's advice to wives, Sharon Farmer has concluded that: "In choosing to advocate the persuasive role of wives rather than husbands, Thomas remained consistent with the gender dichotomy that had already associated women with embodiment and the realm of the concrete. Unlike many male clerical authors, however, Thomas fully endorsed this realm and saw an advantage in women's association with it."[49] In addition to providing an alternate understanding of gender roles, Chobham's advice has also been interpreted as having a rehabilitating effect on the contemporary perception of women.

While Thomas of Chobham questioned neither the social structures that restricted women to this realm nor the gender stereotypes that ensued, his discussion of persuasive wives implicitly challenged the symbolic hierarchies that have frequently devalued and degraded sensual, concrete, and domestic life while valuing immaterial, abstract, and public existence.[50] While this evaluation may not have influenced the social reality of a married woman, it may have served to accord her dignity and respect within the home and in the eyes of her husband. Indeed, the home and the intimate relations of husband and wife are the context for Thomas of Chobham's second challenge to the traditional misogynist evaluation of women.

One of the most frequent negative comments made about female nature in clerical discourse followed in the tradition of Tertullian and asserted that women were more sexual creatures than men. Women were perceived as irrational, more prone to lust than men, and at every turn waiting to seduce men. There is no hint of this sort of rhetorical, conventionalized denunciation of the "daughters of Eve" in Chobham's manual.[51] If anything women are presented as more continent or sexually controlled. While warning men to beware of keeping company with lascivious women and prostitutes, Chobham also suggests that men are more likely to have trouble controlling their sexual urges. He warns that a husband who constantly seeks sexual relations with his wife

because he is consumed by lust, either because of her beauty or because
he has been solicited by prostitutes, in fact commits a sin. He describes
such men as being consumed by lust and harassing their wives day and
night, as if they were in bed, and he accuses them of sinning through
lascivious kisses and filthy embraces. Such men should do serious penance because "they abuse as objects of lust those wives whom they may
have for necessity" and "they ought not to lead their wives to lust but
rather to sanctity."[52]

This characterization of human sexuality is very different from the
misogynist characterization of women as the source of lust. Rather,
Chobham paints a picture of a continent wife who is harassed daily by
the excessive sexual demands of her husband. Chobham would say that
by trying to incite his wife to a lust equal to his own, the man was
harming her immortal soul by encouraging her to sin. In this, he again
parallels Hildegard of Bingen who, because of her understanding of
human physiology, believed that men were more prone to lustful urges than were women.[53] For Chobham, the marital relationship provided a perfect opportunity for men and women to complement each
other. A woman's compassion could balance a man's harshness, her
continence, his lust. Similarly, a man's intellectual abilities balanced a
woman's perceived simplicity. While integrating into his teaching the
notion of marriage as a hierarchical relationship, as understood by both
Aristotle and Paul, Chobham nevertheless mitigated the effects of
woman's subordination in daily life. Indeed, he saw marriage as providing men and women with the opportunity to balance each other's
natures and to help each other toward salvation.

Robert Grosseteste brought quite a different theoretical framework
to the understanding of gender he proposed in his pastoral works.
Grosseteste was one of the most remarkable figures of the Middle Ages.
He was a scholar and translator, teacher and pastor, administrator and
politician. As bishop of Lincoln (1235–53) he was particularly concerned
with clerical education and the *cura animarum*.[54] This interest, however, antedates Grosseteste's elevation to the episcopacy and many of
his pastoral manuals appear to have been written before 1235. Among
the treatises useful for a study of Grosseteste's understanding of gender are the *Templum Dei* (1220x1230) and the *Deus est* (c. 1239).[55] These
manuals present different approaches to the problem of how to discuss
the practical issues of pastoral care. Whereas Chobham illustrated his
points with relevant examples, in the *Deus est* Grosseteste preferred sim-

ple, logical but theoretical discussions. His strategy in the *Templum Dei* is quite different. Rather than being a prose discussion, this work is organized in the form of schematic diagrams. Consequently, information is presented in a shorthand form, without sustained and developed arguments. Despite these differences, both works clearly show a mature, independent, and sophisticated understanding of gender and human relationships.

Throughout his treatises Grosseteste remains faithful to the Pauline doctrine of the spiritual equality of women and men set out in Galatians 3. Most pastoral writers tended to use the universal "man" as the model penitent, with the occasional reminder that their advice or warnings applied also to women.[56] Grosseteste, however, chose to highlight the applicability of his advice for both women and men by using inclusive and reciprocal language. For example, in discussing the sin of insensibility, by which he denotes a lack of appropriate libido, he states that "married people commit this sin as when one or the other refuses to render the conjugal debt."[57] He also notes that for the unmarried (*non coniugati*) sexual relations are sinful but if the married (*coniugati*) engage in intercourse with the right intention, such as "for the sake of extinguishing lust in one or the other of them [*alterutro illorum*]," the sinfulness is removed.[58] Grosseteste also uses the plural to indicate inclusivity and mutuality where other manualists tended to use the masculine singular subject. For example, in the *Templum Dei* a diagram presents the licit reasons for which "the contracted" (*contrahentes*) may marry and includes the possibility that they may wish to live together in mutual chastity.[59] Grosseteste is consistent in his use of inclusive and reciprocal language, employing such terms as "the married," "the penitent," "parents," "one or the other," "each of them," and so on.

Grosseteste's treatment of the marital relationship stresses mutual support and partnership. The couple should observe each other and anticipate each other's sexual needs (*praevenire fervorem in alterutro*).[60] Either spouse might in fact wrongfully withhold the conjugal debt, a man because of anger or a dislike of women or sex, a woman because she loves another or dislikes her husband or because she fears childbirth or the burdens and possible poverty associated with childrearing.[61] Finally, a woman might find sexual intercourse disgusting and not think she is required to engage in something so distasteful.[62] This passage presents one of the most sustained and sympathetic discussions of a woman's perspective found in early pastoral manuals. Grosseteste's sympathy and respect for women are clearly indicated in this lengthy and thoughtful presentation of women's possible reactions to sexuality and childrearing.

Part of the explanation of Grosseteste's equitable interpretation of gender may be his adoption of Galenic medicine and its understanding of human physiology and reproduction. The Aristotelian theory of generation, which provided so much of the theoretical foundation for woman's inferiority, would not appear to have influenced Grosseteste. In the *Generation of Animals*, Aristotle wrote: "Thus, if the male is the active partner, the one which originates the movement, and the female *qua* female is the passive one, surely what the female contributes to the semen of the male will be not semen but material."[63] Grosseteste, however, based his ideas on a Christian interpretation of Galen's theory of generation, which characterized sexuality as reciprocal and complementary. Grosseteste wrote: "Matrimony is the sacrament which, if the Church were without it, it would be disposed to sin mortally, since it is necessary for the human species to multiply and it is not able to multiply except by the seminal propagation of human in human. For matrimony removes the sin which those not married contract from carnal pleasure in the effusion of semen."[64] Grosseteste believed that man and woman both contribute semen to the process of procreation, a belief that can be traced to Galen's understanding of reproduction. In *On the Usefulness of the Parts of the Body*, Galen wrote that "the female must have smaller, less perfect testes, and the sperm generated in them must be scantier, colder and wetter."[65] Later he concludes that "Besides contributing to the generation of the animal, the female semen is also useful in the following ways: It provides no small usefulness in inciting the female to the sexual act and in opening wide the neck of the uteri [*sic*] during coitus."[66] Thus, the emission of female semen not only facilitated intercourse but was also essential for conception.

Grosseteste may have encountered this theory in a number of ways. The Arabic abridgment of *On the Usefulness of the Parts of the Body* had been translated into Latin by Burgundio of Pisa in the mid to late twelfth century under the title *De iuvamentis membrorum*.[67] Grosseteste was certainly familiar with Burgundio's translation of John of Damascus and so might well have known other of his works.[68] This theory also appears in Galen's *De locis affectis*, which Burgundio translated from Greek.[69] The other possible source for Grosseteste's knowledge of Galenic thought is the *Salernitan Questions*, a number of which discuss the role of female semen in coitus and conception.[70] The earliest extant manuscript of the *Salernitan Questions* is found in a Bury St. Edmund's book dating from c. 1200. It was copied by a scholar in close contact with the scientific school at Hereford, which Grosseteste was also associated with at that time.[71]

This scientific belief in female sperm had a number of significant effects on the perception of sexuality and gender. The notion that female genitalia were the inverse of male genitalia meant that it was essential for women and men equally to experience sexual pleasure in order for conception to occur.[72] This notion of the inverse nature of male and female also gave material, physiological support to the Christian doctrine of spiritual equality. Given this theoretical framework, Grosseteste arrived at the logical conclusion that male and female are essentially equal. Neither is more nor less prone to sexual or any other kind of sin. Both have the same spiritual natures and are equally capable of moral perfection or failure.

The ideas of Thomas of Chobham and Robert Grosseteste thus reflect both the complexity and the diversity of medieval ideas about gender. Chobham, although influenced by Aristotelian and Pauline notions of hierarchy, nevertheless arrived at an interpretation of gender complementarity. He believed that man and woman are intrinsically different. He assigned to them different roles in marriage, placing man in the position of authority, woman in that of obedience, and agreeing with the old assumption that man is more intelligent, woman more emotional. Thus Chobham perpetuated the dichotomous understanding of gender while, like Hildegard, he sought to make it more nuanced. So, although tied to the hierarchical conception of gender relations that informed contemporary thought, he sought to mitigate the implications of this view for both domestic and social relations between women and men.

By using the notion of gender complementarity Chobham moderated the misogyny which was inherent in his scholastic education but which, as a theologian concerned with the pastoral care of the laity, he found problematic. And indeed, such a negative view of women and a rigidly hierarchical perception of marriage may not have harmonized with his personal observation of human relations and the interaction of women and men in daily life. Certainly, given the social and economic realities of medieval life, mutual dependence and cooperation between those in hierarchical relationships was well established and necessary for economic survival and individual well-being.[73] And Chobham was at pains to establish this interdependence on a domestic level, between wife and husband, as well.

Grosseteste did not present men and women in hierarchical relationship nor did he see them as complementary and balancing each other's defects. Rather, through his use of inclusive language, his scientific and medical understanding of sexuality and generation, and his theological understanding of spiritual equality, Grosseteste arrived at a doctrine of the equality of women and men which is less ambiguous and less dualist than that of Plato.

These authors of pastoral manuals did not perpetuate the misogynistic understanding of gender found in their authorities, whether ancient or contemporary, philosophical, theological, or canonical. Freed from the conventions of scholastic discourse and influenced by their personal knowledge of society and the interaction of women and men, they reflect a more complex and sophisticated understanding of gender than that articulated by the discourse of misogyny.

ᥱᴑ

In medieval thought, despite the superficial appearance of a monovocal, clerical discourse of misogyny, the evaluation of gender was in fact diverse and complex. It is essential that modern scholars be as open to these complexities as were their medieval predecessors, that they perceive the richness of this diversity, and become sensitive to the nuances of medieval discussions of gender. It may be easier to listen to a solitary voice, but in the process the richness and the sophistication offered by the chorus of complexities and divergent evaluations is lost. In the search for an understanding of gender it is imperative to reject the simplistic and monovocalic and instead to revel in the complex, competing, and frequently discordant chorus of medieval women and men.

Notes

I would like to thank Konrad Eisenbichler, Dyan Elliott, Robert Sweetman, and the anonymous readers of this essay for their invaluable comments and suggestions. Research for this paper was undertaken while I was a Canada Research Fellow and I am grateful to the Social Sciences and

Humanities Research Council of Canada, the University of Windsor Research Board, and the Centre for Reformation and Renaissance Studies (Toronto) for their support.

1. See the classic article by Gayle Rubin, "The Traffic in Women: Notes on the 'Political Economy' of Sex," in *Toward an Anthropology of Women*, ed. Rayna R. Reiter (New York, 1975), 157–210, esp. 165. See also Gayle Greene and Coppélia Kahn, "Feminist Scholarship and the Social Construction of Woman," in *Making a Difference: Feminist Literary Criticism*, ed. Gayle Green and Coppélia Kahn (London, 1985), 1–36; Gisela Bock, "Women's History and Gender History: Aspects of an International Debate," *Gender and History* 1 (1989), 7–30; Carole S. Vance, "Gender Systems, Ideology, and Sex Research: An Anthropological Analysis," *Feminist Studies* 6 (1980), 129–43; Joan W. Scott, "Gender: A Useful Category of Historical Analysis," *American Historical Review* 91 (1986), 1053–75; and Denise Riley, *"Am I That Name?" Feminism and the Category of "Women" in History* (Minneapolis, 1988).

2. Prudence Allen has surveyed the philosophical treatment of this question up to the thirteenth century. She promises a second volume which will survey the subsequent treatment of the question from the thirteenth to the twentieth centuries. See Prudence Allen, *The Concept of Woman: The Aristotelian Revolution, 750 BC–AD 1250* (Montreal, 1985). For a recent contribution to the debate see Anne Moir and David Jessel, *Brain Sex: The Real Difference between Men and Women* (Harmondsworth, 1989).

3. Theodore Zeldin has explored the benefits that accrue to the historical enterprise when the historian engages with the past rather than adopting the stance of "objective" observer ("Personal History and the History of the Emotions," *Journal of Social History* 15 [1981–82], 339–47). For a discussion of the role of and need for a feminist agenda in history see Judith M. Bennett, "Feminism and History," *Gender and History* 1 (1989), 251–72. For a reflection on some of the dangers inherent in feminist approaches to the Middle Ages see Barbara Newman, "On the Ethics of Feminist Historiography," *Exemplaria* 2 (1990), 702–6. For a wonderfully insightful exploration of how personal history can influence the medievalist and inform her understanding see Dyan Elliott, "The Historian and Her Past," *Exemplaria* 2 (1990), 706–11. The appeal of the idea of a medieval women's Golden Age is discussed by Judith M. Bennett, "'History That Stands Still': Women's Work in the European Past," *Feminist Studies* 14 (1988), 269–71.

4. Notable exceptions to this are *The Book of Margery Kempe*, ed. S. B. Meech and H. E. Allen (London, 1940; reprint, 1961) and the works of Christine de Pisan, especially *The Book of the City of Ladies*, trans. Earl Jeffrey Richards (New York, 1982).

5. R. Howard Bloch, "Medieval Misogyny. Women as Riot," *Representations* 20 (1987), 1–24. For criticisms of Bloch by a number of feminist scholars see "Commentary," *Medieval Feminist Newsletter* 6 (1988), 2–15, and his reply in 7 (1989), 7–12.

6. For examples of scholars who are beginning to surmount some of the problems inherent in studying societies for which virtually all texts are male-generated and reflect male experience see *Gender and Religion: On the Complexity of Symbols*, ed. Caroline Walker Bynum, Stevan Harrell, and Paula Richman (Boston, 1986).

7. Jo Ann McNamara, "*De quibusdam mulieribus:* Reading Women's History from Hostile Sources," in *Medieval Women and the Sources of Medieval History*, ed. Joel T. Rosenthal (Athens, Ga., 1990), 239.

8. See Scott, "Gender: A Useful Category," 1065–68; Sherry B. Ortner, "Is Female to Male as Nature Is to Culture?" in *Woman, Culture, and Society*, ed. Michelle Zimbalist Rosaldo and Louise Lamphere (Stanford, 1974), 67–87; and Nancy Jay, "Gender and Dichotomy," *Feminist Studies* 7 (1981), 38–56. F. Ellen Weaver and Jean Laporte have argued unconvincingly that binary opposition is a rhetorical device which indicates tension and balance rather than hierarchy ("Augustine and Women: Relationships and Teachings," *Augustinian Studies* 12 [1981], 115–16).

9. Caroline Walker Bynum, "'. . . And Woman His Humanity': Female Imagery in the Religious Writings of the Later Middle Ages," in *Gender and Religion*, 257.

10. See, for example, the unbroken litany of misogyny stretching from the early Church Fathers to the thirteenth century, presented by Marie-Thérèse d'Alverny, "Comment les théologiens et les philosophes voient la femme," *Cahiers de civilisation médiévale* 20 (1977), 105–29.

11. Caroline Walker Bynum, "In Praise of Fragments: History in the Comic Mode," in *Fragmentation and Redemption: Essays on Gender and the Human Body in Medieval Religion* (New York, 1991), 17.

12. Scott, "Gender: A Useful Category," 1067–68.

13. Bynum, ". . . And Woman His Humanity," 261–77.

14. Ibid., 277.

15. Ibid., 261–62.

16. Ibid., 277.

17. The Aristotelian and Platonic views of human nature and their medieval articulations are surveyed in P. Allen, *Concept of Woman* and in Ian Maclean, *The Renaissance Notion of Woman: A Study in the Fortunes of Scholasticism and Medical Science in European Intellectual Life* (Cambridge, 1980).

18. For a summary of Aristotle's ideas about dualities see Maclean, *Renaissance Notion of Woman*, 8.

19. Aristotle's philosophy of gender is summarized in Maryanne Cline Horowitz, "Aristotle and Woman," *Journal of the History of Biology* 9 (1976), 183–213; Maclean, *Renaissance Notion of Woman,* 8–9, 48–49; and P. Allen, *Concept of Woman,* 83–126. See, for example, Aristotle, *De generatione animalium, Physics,* and *Historia animalium.*

20. Christine Garside Allen, "Plato on Women," *Feminist Studies* 2 (1975), 131. See, for example, the varying ideas expressed in *The Symposium, Timeaus, The Republic,* and *The Laws.*

21. See P. Allen, *Concept of Woman,* 57–75, 79–81, and C. Allen, "Plato on Women," 135.

22. Jo Ann McNamara, *A New Song: Celibate Women in the First Three Christian Centuries* (New York, 1983; reprint, 1985), 23–29.

23. Numerous discussions both of women's dynamic role in early Christianity and of the process by which they were gradually excluded are available. See, for example, McNamara, *New Song;* Constance F. Parvey, "The Theology and Leadership of Women in the New Testament," in *Religion and Sexism: Images of Woman in the Jewish and Christian Traditions,* ed. Rosemary Radford Ruether (New York, 1974), 117–49; and Elizabeth Schüssler Fiorenza, "Word, Spirit and Power: Women in Early Christian Communities," in *Women of Spirit: Female Leadership in the Jewish and Christian Traditions,* ed. Rosemary Radford Ruether and Eleanor McLaughlin (New York, 1979), 29–70. For a discussion of women in Hellenistic Judaism see Dorothy Sly, *Philo's Perception of Women* (Atlanta, 1990).

24. All translations of the Bible are based on the New English Bible with modifications where it does not accurately reflect the Vulgate.

25. George H. Tavard, *Woman in Christian Tradition* (Notre Dame, Ind., 1973), 28. For varying interpretations of the Pauline doctrine and its influence see also the discussions by Constance Parvey ("Theology and Leadership of Women," 123–37) and Paul K. Jewett (*Man as Male and Female: A Study in Sexual Relationships from a Theological Point of View* [Grand Rapids, Mich., 1975], 50–61).

26. Jo Ann McNamara, "Sexual Equality and the Cult of Virginity in Early Christian Thought," *Feminist Studies* 3 (1976), 154.

27. Tertullian, *De Cultu Feminarum,* 1.1, PL 1:1419. For discussions of the Fathers of the Church see Peter Brown, *The Body and Society: Men, Women, and Sexual Renunciation in Early Christianity* (New York, 1988). A summary of early Christian and medieval views is provided by d'Alverny, "Comment les théologiens voient la femme." See also, Bernard P. Prusak, "Woman: Seductive Siren and Source of Sin? Pseudepigraphal Myth and Christian Origins," in *Religion and Sexism,* 89–116, and Rosemary Radford Ruether, "Misogynism and Virginal Feminism in the Fathers of the

Church," in *Religion and Sexism,* 150–83. For less critical studies of the development of medieval ideas about gender see Weaver and Laporte, "Augustine and Women"; Walter J. Wilkins, "'Submitting the Neck of Your Mind': Gregory the Great and Women of Power," *Catholic Historical Review* 77 (1991), 583–94; and Jean Leclercq, *Women and Saint Bernard of Clairvaux* (Kalamazoo, Mich., 1989), esp. 150–58.

28. The classic analysis of Aquinas's androcentric theology remains Kari Elizabeth Børresen, *Subordination and Equivalence. The Nature and Rôle of Women in Augustine and Thomas Aquinas,* trans. Charles H. Talbot (Washington, D.C., 1981), esp. 171–72, 315, 330. Børresen concludes that for Thomas the human being is a unitary substance, body and soul. Thus, since women's bodies are less perfect than those of men, their souls are proportionately less perfect as well (318–19). Prudence Allen describes the influence of Thomistic Aristotelianism as a revolution: "the Aristotelian Revolution is . . . understood as the first takeover of the western mind by a single theory of the concept of woman. It is, therefore, a revolution in the sense that it created a definitive context within which the subsequent development of thought about woman and man took place" (*Concept of Woman,* 1–2). Susan Mosher Stuard has placed this process about a century earlier. She discusses how in his *Decretum* Gratian suppressed the theological arguments for spiritual equality and retained the legal arguments for the subordination of women, thus arriving at an unambiguous assertion of women's inferiority, ("From Women to Woman: New Thinking about Gender c. 1140," *Thought* 64 [1989], 208–19).

29. Among the numerous studies of Hildegard's thought see in particular Prudence Allen, *Concept of Woman,* 292–315, and her "Hildegard of Bingen's Philosophy of Sex Identity," *Thought* 64 (1989), 231–41; Joan Cadden, "It Takes All Kinds: Sexuality and Gender Differences in Hildegard of Bingen's 'Book of Compound Medicine,'" *Traditio* 40 (1984), 149–74; Bernhard W. Scholz, "Hildegard von Bingen on the Nature of Woman," *American Benedictine Review* 31 (1980), 361–83; Sabina Flanagan, *Hildegard of Bingen, 1098–1179: A Visionary Life* (London, 1989); and Barbara Newman, *Sister of Wisdom: St. Hildegard's Theology of the Feminine* (Berkeley, 1987) and "Divine Power Made Perfect in Weakness: St. Hildegard on the Frail Sex," in *Medieval Religious Women,* vol. 2: *Peaceweavers,* ed. Lillian Thomas Shank and John A. Nichols (Kalamazoo, Mich., 1987), 103–22.

30. Newman, *Sister of Wisdom,* 255.

31. P. Allen, *Concept of Woman,* 312.

32. P. Allen, "Hildegard of Bingen's Philosophy," 232.

33. Bynum, ". . . And Woman His Humanity," 261–77.

34. A more cautious understanding of what "complementarity" actu-

ally signifies was made early on in the investigation of the position of women in the Middle Ages by Eleanor Commo McLaughlin. "The reader will pardon me if under every bush of 'complementarity' I espy this hierarchical cosmos, this Great Chain of Being, in which difference becomes rationalized subordination" ("Equality of Souls, Inequality of Sexes: Woman in Medieval Theology," in *Religion and Sexism*, 259–60).

35. The importance of the Fourth Lateran Council as an intellectual watershed has long been recognized by scholars. See, for example, Raymonde Foreville, "Les statuts synodaux et le renouveau pastoral du XIII siècle dans le Midi de la France," *Cahiers de Fanjeaux* 6 (1971), 119–50; Marion E. Gibbs and Jane Lang, *Bishops and Reform 1215–1272: With Special Reference to the Lateran Council of 1215* (London, 1962); Paul B. Pixton, "Watchmen on the Tower: The German Episcopacy and the Implementation of the Decrees of the Fourth Lateran Council, 1216–1274," in *Proceedings of the Sixth International Congress of Medieval Canon Law, Berkeley, Calif., 28 July–2 August 1980*, ed. Stephan Kuttner and Kenneth Pennington (Vatican City, 1985), 579–93.

36. There are many studies available on the development of the genre of pastoral manuals. See especially Leonard E. Boyle, "*Summae confessorum*," in *Les genres littéraires dans les sources théologiques et philosophiques médiévales: Définition, critique et exploitation* (Louvain-la-neuve, 1982), 227–37, and "The Summa for Confessors as a Genre, and Its Religious Intent," in *The Pursuit of Holiness in Late Medieval and Renaissance Religion*, ed. Charles E. Trinkaus and Heiko A. Oberman (Leiden, 1974), 126–30; Jean Longère, "Quelques *Summa de poenitentia* à la fin du XIIe et au début du XIIIe siècle," in *Actes du 99e Congrès national des Sociétés Savantes, Besançon, 1974. Section de philologie et d'histoire jusqu'à 1610*, vol. 1: *La piété populaire au Moyen Age* (Paris, 1977), 45–58; A. Murray, "Confession as a Historical Source in the Thirteenth Century," in *The Writing of History in the Middle Ages: Essays Presented to Richard William Southern*, ed. R. H. C. Davis and J. M. Wallace-Hadrill (Oxford, 1981), 275–322; Pierre Michaud-Quantin, "A propos des premières summae confessorum: théologie et droit canonique," *Recherches de théologie ancienne et médiévale* 26 (1959), 264–306; Michaud-Quantin, "Les méthodes de la pastorale du XIIIe au XVe siècle," in *Methoden in Wissenschaft und Kunst des Mittelalters*, ed. Albert Zimmermann (Berlin, 1970), 76–91; Michaud-Quantin, *Sommes de casuistique et manuels de confession au Moyen Age (XII–XVI siècles)* (Louvain, 1962); Thomas N. Tentler, *Sin and Confession on the Eve of the Reformation* (Princeton, 1977); and Tentler, "The Summa for Confessors as an Instrument of Social Control," in *Pursuit of Holiness*, 103–26. Boyle and Michaud-Quantin, in particular, stress the practical nature of these manuals.

37. Jean Gaudemet has discussed the usefulness for social history of

studying penitentials, the predecessors of the pastoral manuals under discussion here ("Les collections canoniques, miroir de la vie sociale," in *Mélanges en honneur de Jacques Ellul* [Paris, 1983], 243–53; reprinted in Jean Gaudemet, *Eglise et société en Occident au Moyen Age* [London, 1984], essay 13).

38. For example, McLaughlin, "Equality of Souls"; Georges Duby, *The Knight, the Lady and the Priest: The Making of Modern Marriage in Medieval France*, trans. Barbara Bray (New York, 1983), esp. chap. 3; and Tentler, *Sin and Confession*. A notable exception to this is the study of the treatment of love and morality in Thomas of Cantimpré's *De apibus* in Murray, "Confession as a Historical Source," 286–305.

39. I am grateful to Robert Sweetman for his observations on the role that convention played in perpetuating misogyny in scholastic discourse and for suggesting that a new genre, free from such expectations, might allow the same writer the freedom to reflect his own life experience, untainted by the expectations of institutionalized and conventionalized misogyny.

40. See the exchange between Leonard E. Boyle and Thomas N. Tentler in *Pursuit of Holiness*.

41. For a discussion of the role and influence of Peter the Chanter and his students and colleagues in stimulating investigation into pastoral theology see John W. Baldwin, *Masters, Princes and Merchants: The Social Views of Peter the Chanter and His Circle,* 2 vols. (Princeton, 1970).

42. Thomas of Chobham, *Thomae de Chobham: Summa Confessorum,* ed. F. Broomfield (Louvain, 1968). See also Thomas de Chobham, *Summa de arte praedicandi,* ed. Franco Morenzoni, Corpus Christianorum Continuatio Mediaevalis 82 (Turnhout, 1988), esp. the introductory discussion, vii–xxxviii.

43. "Proprie tamen potest dici coniungium, quia eque pertinet ad virum et ad feminam" (Chobham, *Summa confessorum,* 145).

44. ". . . si sacerdos iniungeret mulieri ieiunium, et vir eius preciperet ut comederet, teneretur magis obedire viro quam sacerdoti" (ibid., 363).

45. Eph. 5:22 quoted above.

46. ". . . virum inducat ut bonis conditionibus tractet uxorem suam et debitum honorem sicut parti corporis sui exhibeat, et si stulta est, moderate et decenter eam corripiat, et si opus fuerit castiget. Maiorem enim debet adhibere diligentiam circa uxorem suam custodiendam quam circa aliquam possessionem terrenam, quia nihil debet ei esse carius uxore sua" (Chobham, *Summa confessorum,* 375).

47. "Mulieribus tamen semper in penitentia iniungendum est quod sint predicatrices virorum suorum. Nullus enim sacerdos ita potest cor viri emollire sicut potest uxor. Unde peccatum viri sepe mulieri imputatur si per eius negligentiam vir eius non emmendatur. Debet enim in cubiculo

et inter medios amplexus virum suum blande alloqui, et si durus est et immisericors et oppressor pauperum, debet eum invitare ad misericordiam; si raptor est, debet detestari rapinam; si avarus est, suscitet in eo largitatem, et occulte faciat eleemosynas de rebus communibus, et eleemosynas quas ille omittit, illa suppleat. Licitum enim mulieri est de bonis viri sui in utiles usus ipsius et in pias causas ipso ignorante multa expendere" (ibid.).

48. Sharon Farmer has suggested that the increasing role of women in lay religious movements and perhaps their "more intense emotional and spiritual bonds" with confessors may account for why Chobham considers women morally responsible for men but not the opposite ("Persuasive Voices: Clerical Images of Medieval Wives," *Speculum* 61 [1986], 534).

49. Sharon A. Farmer, "Softening the Hearts of Men: Women, Embodiment, and Persuasion in the Thirteenth Century," in *Embodied Love: Sensuality and Relationship as Feminist Values,* ed. Paula M. Cooey, Sharon A. Farmer, and Mary Ellen Ross (San Francisco, 1987), 125.

50. Ibid., 128.

51. Pierre Payer, in his examination of the traditional presentation of Eve by medieval writers ("Eve's Sin, Woman's Fault: A Medieval View," *Atlantis* 2, no. 2 [1977], 2–14), concludes that it is "symptomatic of an attitude towards female nature as intellectually inferior, subordinate to man, easy prey to the suggestions of evil, which can turn man away from his superior position. For this reason it was believed good that woman be subject to man's dominance" (11).

52. "Unde qui ita delectantur vel in pulchritudine uxoris sue vel in suavitate carnis vel in blanditiis meretriciis vel adulterinis quod effundunt se in libidinem et tota nocte et die utuntur uxoribus suis quasi pro culcitra per oscula lasciva et per turpes amplexus peccant mortaliter. Et est eis gravis penitentia iniungenda, et ideo gravior quia uxoribus quas possunt habere ad necessitatem abuntur ad voluptatem. . . . et ostendendum est eis quod non debent provocare uxores suas ad libidinem sed ad sanctitatem" (Chobham, *Summa confessorum,* 335–36). See also John W. Baldwin, "Five Discourses on Desire: Sexuality and Gender in Northern France around 1200," *Speculum* 66 (1991), 797–819.

53. See the discussion in Cadden, "It Takes All Kinds," 157–59.

54. Numerous studies of Grosseteste's life, scholarship, and influence are available. See, in particular, Leonard E. Boyle, "Robert Grosseteste and the Pastoral Care," in *Pastoral Care, Clerical Education and Canon Law, 1200–1400* (London, 1981), essay 1; *Robert Grosseteste: Scholar and Bishop,* ed. Daniel A. P. Callus (Oxford, 1955); A. C. Crombie, *Robert Grosseteste and the Origins of Experimental Science: 1100–1700* (Oxford, 1953); James McEvoy, *The Philosophy of Robert Grosseteste* (Oxford, 1982); Maurice Powicke, "Robert Grosseteste, Bishop of Lincoln," *Bulletin of the John Rylands*

Library 35 (1952–53), 482–507; and R. W. Southern, *Robert Grosseteste: The Growth of an English Mind in Medieval Europe* (Oxford, 1986). A bibliography of Grosseteste's writings is provided by S. Harrison Thomson, *The Writings of Robert Grosseteste, Bishop of Lincoln, 1235–1253* (Cambridge, 1940).

55. Robert Grosseteste, *Templum Dei,* ed. Joseph Goering and F. A. C. Mantello (Toronto, 1984); and Siegfried Wenzel, "Robert Grosseteste's Treatise on Confession, '*Deus est*,'" *Franciscan Studies* 30 (1970), 218–93. Another treatise, the "*Perambulauit Iudas . . .*" (1200x1230), is not useful for the discussion at hand. It was written specifically for the pastoral care of monks and, while taking into account sins that could occur in the world before entry into the cloister, it is nevertheless exclusively masculine in perspective. Consequently, women are not discussed, either positively or negatively, and the manual has nothing to contribute to our knowledge of Grosseteste's evaluation of women or gender. An edition of the manual is found in Joseph Goering and Frank A. C. Mantello, "The '*Perambulauit Iudas . . .*' (*Speculum confessionis*) Attributed to Robert Grosseteste," *Revue Bénédictine* 96 (1986), 125–68. Another pastoral manual, the *De modo confitendi et paenitentias iniungendi* (1214x1225), is also of limited use for understanding Grosseteste's ideas about gender. This treatise, possibly the earliest of his pastoral works, is derivative, heavily dependent on the penitential canons in the *Decretum* of Burchard of Worms and in many ways perpetuates a traditional and anachronistic worldview. In this it is very different from the *Templum Dei* and the *Deus est,* which are more mature works that reflect Grosseteste's intellectual independence, free from the constraints of penitential and scholastic convention. For a discussion and edition of the *De modo confitendi* see Joseph Goering and F. A. C. Mantello, "The Early Penitential Writings of Robert Grosseteste," *Recherches de théologie ancienne et médiévale* 54 (1987), 52–112.

56. See the *Liber Poenitentialis* of Robert of Flamborough, which is written in the form of a dialogue between a confessor and a male penitent. From time to time Flamborough reminds the confessor that women too should be questioned. For example, in discussing the sin of *luxuria* he writes "Mollitiem autem dolose ab eo extorqueo, et de muliere similiter, sed modus extorquendi scribendus non est" (Robert of Flamborough, *Liber Poenitentialis,* ed. J. J. Francis Firth, 18 [Toronto, 1971], 4.8.224 [196–97]). For the limitations inherent in the notion of the universal "man" see Sandra Harding, "The Instability of the Analytical Categories of Feminist Theory," *Signs* 11 (1985–86), 645–64, esp. 646–47. Indeed, there is evidence that in the Middle Ages churchmen did not always understand the term "man" as universal and inclusive. For example, Gregory of Tours reports that at the Council of Mâcon (585) "There came forward . . . a certain

bishop who maintained that woman could not be included in the term 'man.'" Although the view of the other bishops, who argued on the basis of scriptural evidence that "man" did indeed include women, prevailed, nevertheless, this incident indicates that there was more ambiguity in medieval thought than many traditional scholars wish to admit. Gregory of Tours, *The History of the Franks,* trans. Lewis Thorpe (Harmondsworth, 1974), 8.20 [452]. For a related discussion see Maryanne Cline Horowitz, "The Image of God in Man—Is Woman Included?" *Harvard Theological Review* 72: 3–4 (1979), 175–206.

57. "Hoc peccato delinquunt coniugati, ut quando alter alteri debitum reddere negaverit" (Grosseteste, *Deus est,* 285–86).

58. "Aufert enim Matrimonium peccatum quod contrahunt non coniugati ex carnis delectatione in effusione seminis, si coeunt coniugati recta intentione, ut causa prolis procreandae vel causa libidinis in alterutro illorum extinguendae" (ibid., 246). Similar phrases using reciprocal language appear throughout both manuals, for example, "aut causa libidinis in se vel in alio extinguendae" (ibid., 254) or "Incestus: ut, si alter eorum coniunctus carnaliter fuerit eum consanguineis alterius" (*Templum Dei,* 60).

59. "Fines liciti inter contrahentes: Castitas: quando contrahunt ne impetantur uel sollicitentur ab aliis, set caste adinuicem simul uiuant," (Grosseteste, *Templum Dei,* 60). Similar uses of the plural are found throughout both manuals, for example, "quia non etiam coniugatis licet omni tempore coire," (*Deus est,* 284).

60. Grosseteste, *Deus est,* 284.

61. "Et fit quandoque causa irae, quandoque causa vilitatis coeundi, quandoque causa contemptus mulierum. Similiter et mulier, vel quia alium plus amat vel quia nequam est, debitum similiter prohibet, vel ne dolorem partus sentiat, vel ne paupertate gravetur, vel ne laboret nutriendo" (ibid., 286).

62. "[V]el quia taediosum est quod facere non tenetur" (ibid.).

63. Aristotle, *Generation of Animals,* trans. A. L. Peck, rev. ed., Loeb Classical Library (Cambridge, Mass., 1953), 729a25–34. For a discussion of Aristotle's ideas see Horowitz, "Aristotle and Woman," 192–201. Vern L. Bullough provides a comparision of various theories of generation current in the Middle Ages ("Medieval Medical and Scientific Views of Women," *Viator* 4 [1973], 487–95).

64. "Matrimonium est sacramentum, quo si careret ecclesia, affecta esset ad mortaliter peccandum, cum necesse est genus humanum multiplicari, nec multiplicari poterit, nisi per propagationem seminalem hominis in homine. Aufert enim Matrimonium peccatum quod contrahunt non coniugati ex carnis delectatione in effusione seminis" (Grosseteste, *Deus est,* 246).

65. Galen, *Galen on the Usefulness of the Parts of the Body*, trans. Margaret Tallmadge May, 2 vols. (Ithaca, N.Y. 1968), 2:631.

66. Ibid., 2:643.

67. Ibid., 1:6.

68. Southern, *Robert Grosseteste*, 199.

69. George Sarton, *Introduction to the History of Science*, vol. 2: *From Rabbi Ben Ezra to Roger Bacon*, 2 pts. (Baltimore, 1931; reprint, 1950, 1953), pt. 1, 348; Bullough, "Scientific Views," 495.

70. "Conceptio ex uno semine fieri not potest; nisi enim conveniant viri sperma et femine mulier non concipit" (*The Prose Salernitan Questions: Edited from a Bodleian Manuscript [Auct. F.3.10]*, ed. Brian Lawn [London, 1979], 6).

71. Brian Lawn, *The Salernitan Questions: An Introduction to the History of Medieval and Renaissance Problem Literature* (Oxford, 1963), xi. For Grosseteste's connections with Hereford see Southern, *Robert Grosseteste*, 65–66, 126, 130; and McEvoy, *Philosophy of Robert Grosseteste*, 4, 6.

72. For a discussion of Galen's influence on medieval anatomical and medical knowledge see Danielle Jacquart and Claude Thomasset, *Sexuality and Medicine in the Middle Ages*, trans. Matthew Adamson (Princeton, 1988), 7–38. For a discussion of Galenic medicine's influence on Grosseteste's theology see Jacqueline Murray, "Sexuality and Spirituality: The Intersection of Medieval Theology and Medicine," *Fides et Historia* 23 (1991), 20–36.

73. As Eleanor McLaughlin has stated, "in medieval society inequality was rationalized and perhaps even softened by a strong sense of mutual responsibility: God for the soul, lord for the serf, man for the woman" ("Equality of Souls," 256).

Rerouting the Dower:
The Anglo-Norman Life of St.
Audrey by Marie (of Chatteris?)

Jocelyn Wogan-Browne

 T IS A TRUISM TO SAY that Anglo-Norman women suffered a variety of gender-based restrictions, but equally a truism to say that rank and wealth could often cut across these restrictions for individual upper-class Anglo-Norman women. In the textual representation of the activities and capacities of women in the post-Conquest period, we cannot assume a direct relation between actual socioeconomic power and the conventions of representation, but there may be various kinds of interplay. Moreover, possible readings vary from one version of a text to another: the textual company kept by a given narrative in its various manuscript copies and the differing textual communities by which the manuscripts were used may well suggest different readings and uses. I want here to examine a relatively neglected account by an Anglo-Norman woman writer of one of the most extensively venerated and powerful figures of royal female sanctity in Britain, and to sketch out the kinds of readings this life might have received in the context in which we find it.

Among post-Conquest vernacular lives of women saints, reworkings of the *passio*-narratives of legendary virgin martyrs form the largest single category, followed by lives of repentant harlot figures such as Mary Magdalen and Mary of Egypt.[1] Dying for one's virginity (or repenting one's exercise of sexuality) is thus overrepresented in the female role models offered to Anglo-Norman women in hagiographic lives. There is however also a small group of lives of native British abbesses in either English or French or both.[2] Among these, the most important figure is Æthelthryth (Latin: Etheldreda) of Ely, about whom more medieval vernacular lives were composed in England than any other native female saint. The Latin sources for Etheldreda's cult and her foundation of Ely have been paid considerable attention in modern scholarship on ecclesiastical and hagiological history.[3] In her Anglo-Norman guise as Audrée, Etheldreda was also the subject of one of the three Anglo-Norman lives certainly by women writers, and this version of her legend has been relatively neglected.[4] Though it has been edited, *La vie seinte Audrée* has been little commented on until recently, partly because it has been considered too derivative from its principal source, the twelfth-century *Liber Eliensis,* to have anything to offer to historians.[5] On the other hand, for consideration as a literary text, it has fallen between specialists in medieval English and continental French vernacular literature. With recently increased awareness of the importance of translation in medieval literary theory and practice, however, demand for the historically irrelevant conception of "originality" ceases to be a barrier to the perception of the life's interest from a literary point of view. As the exemplary biography of a twice-married virgin, widow, and monastic foundress, a life written in all probability for a female community, and one of the rare post-Conquest works we know to have been composed by a woman in Britain, *La vie seinte Audrée* also has something to offer for the history of Anglo-Norman women, and medieval literary history in general.

Etheldreda, one of the saintly daughters of the seventh-century King Anna of the East Angles, secured lasting importance by virtue of the preeminence Bede gives her in his *Historia Ecclesiastica,* where she is his principal example of virginity. Though Etheldreda was twice married, first to Tonbert, prince of the South Gyrwe, and then, following his death, to Ecgfrith, king of Northumbria, she successfully preserved her virginity through both marriages and eventually persuaded Ecgfrith to release her to the religious life. After some time at the monastery of Coldingham, she used her first marriage's dower lands as the site of a large and successful foundation at Ely. Bede accepts the report of Bishop Wilfrid of York as authoritative testimony to Ecgfrith and Etheldreda's chaste cohabitation for twelve years; a still more authoritative sign is the incorruption of Etheldreda's body when translated to a new shrine by her sister Sexburga, sixteen years after her death.[6] Bede's treatment of Etheldreda emphasizes principally her virginity, her asceticism, and above all, her incorrupt dead body: in many ways the most important thing his Etheldreda does is to die and undergo translation. Etheldreda's enduring virginity is hymned, her asceticism praised as rigorous, and her incorrupt body extensively vouched for by Bishop Wilfrid and Etheldreda's physician Cynifrith, but Bede gives very little sense of Etheldreda's life from its principal protagonist's viewpoint. His narrative opens with Ecgfrith's marriage, and Etheldreda's biography is subordinated to an account of Ecgfrith and Wilfrid's relations (even though these, as Stephanie Hollis has argued, may have been the reverse of Bede's portrayal, with the queen being Wilfrid's most influential supporter with the king, rather than the bishop being an influential go-between from the king to the queen).[7]

Bede was followed by the Benedictine reformers of the tenth-century English church in making Etheldreda the most prominent native female saint. Her cult was developed in Winchester and southern England as well as in her East Anglian homeland.[8] She is the only native British woman included in Ælfric's small selection of female saints for his vernacular hagiographic writings, where she ranks alongside the universal virgin martyr and abbess saints of the church.[9] Lives continued to be rewritten and compiled in Middle English as they were in Latin, while the existence of an Anglo-Norman life, the mixture of Latin, Anglo-Norman, and English forms of the saint's name in calendars, narratives, and prayers in all three languages, and the existence of church dedications and iconographic representations suggests that, although her relative prominence declined in the later Middle Ages, Etheldreda remained a constantly commemorated and important saint in communities using either or both vernaculars.[10] Several of the versions of her life in later medieval England are associated with female religious communities.[11]

After the conquest, Norman churchmen did not ignore this powerful and well-known figure, but instead promoted her cult. The *Liber Eliensis,* which was put together between A.D. 1131 and 1174 and which incorporated earlier lives of the saint, is both the source for the Anglo-Norman life and the principal text of Etheldreda's post-Conquest cult.[12] A major concern of this later Ely Latin tradition is to assert continuity with the seventh-century foundation by stressing, as Ridyard says in her study of Anglo-Saxon royal saints, "the antiquity of the religious life at Ely and the continuity of St. Æthelthryth's own association with the isle." These aims, Ridyard shows, were as vigorously promoted by

Norman religious at Ely as by their tenth-century reforming English predecessors.[13] Vigor was needed since, as Miller writes in his history of the abbey, "the origin of the medieval lands and liberties of the church of Ely is to be sought in King Edgar's charter of refoundation. There is no direct link (possibly no link at all) between the region of the Southern Gyrwe [of whom Etheldreda's first husband was prince] and the medieval liberty of the Isle of Ely, or even between St. Etheldreda's dower and the endowment which King Edgar conferred upon the monastery of Ely. Between St. Etheldreda's abbey and the abbey which St. Ethelwold refounded there had been a break at least of a century."[14]

The *Liber Eliensis* not only had a vested interest in but probably was compiled largely in order to assert the continuity of monastic tradition at Ely. In post-Conquest England, following Ely's early support of Hereward's uprising, the abbey's relations with William the Conqueror had been uneasy, and the demands of land-hungry Norman barons did not cease. It is unsurprising that twelfth-century Ely should so strongly have reasserted its claims, or that these should have focused on Etheldreda.[15] As foundress and patron, Etheldreda was a crucial figure and her chief saintly attribute, virginity—a virginity manifested in the continuing presence of her incorrupt body at Ely—became the embodiment of the house's tradition and its custodianship of her lands. It is significant here that in her *vita* her powers are even greater once she is dead. Alive, the saint exerts control of herself and leadership of her community in mortification and ascetic practices: dead, she maintains and protects her own cult and lands, with vengeance miracles of protection and control making up a large proportion of the miracles attributed to her. On the power of her cult in part depended the abbey's power to enforce its claims and defend what it regarded as its own. For the monks of Ely, Etheldreda's incorrupt body, as Ridyard argues, "perpetuated [monastic] proprietorship and . . . provided it with a tangible symbol. . . . 'guardianship' of her relics conferred 'guardianship' of [her] church and lands" (191). Etheldreda's virginity was thus highly significant for the monks of Ely, not only as the embodiment of a doctrinal and behavioral ideal with its own powerful affective and psychological relevance for a professionally celibate community but for its divine testimony to intact property rights.

In the Latin source tradition, the representation of the saint thus encodes the needs of a wealthy monastic institution. It is not a portrait of female power as such. Etheldreda here functions rather like the "monumental" maidens studied by Marina Warner: for the monks of Ely she was an idea or a symbol rather than a biographical role model.[16] Reworked by a woman, and reworked, in all probability, for an audience of aristocratic nuns (some of whom may have been professed as widows or after annullment of their marriages), the life of this widowed virgin must have read with new power—and read rather differently than for the late twelfth- and thirteenth-century monks of Ely.

The single extant copy of *La vie seinte Audrée* is found in the thirteenth-century section of the "Welbeck" manuscript, a large collection of Anglo-Norman verse saints' legends used, according to the manuscript's own inscription, for reading at mealtimes in the Augustinian nunnery of Campsey Ash, Suffolk.[17] Like most other post-Conquest female foundations, Campsey did not have the rank of abbey, but it had at one point five chaplains, and it may well have been male clerics who compiled the manuscript.[18] It is however not impossible, although it may be unprovable, that the nuns themselves copied the texts and perhaps influenced their selection. The manuscript's text is not the original of the Anglo-Norman life (which may have been composed any time between the late twelfth and the mid-thirteenth century), but nothing is known of the circumstances of the life's composition apart from what can be inferred from the evidence of the text.[19]

At the end of her biography of Audrée, the author gives her name, Marie, "so that I may be remembered."[20] The most likely (but so far unproven) identity for her is that of a female religious in a community dedicated to Saint Etheldreda. Since it is still sometimes claimed that Marie was a member of a community at Ely, it is worth repeating the point (first made in this connection some time ago by M. Dominica Legge) that Ely was a male house from at least the tenth-century Benedictine reform onward.[21] Etheldreda's original seventh-century foundation was principally for women, but after her monastery's devastation by Danish raids in the ninth century and certainly at its refounding by Bishop Æthelwold in the tenth, it became a house for men only.[22] A more likely community for Marie is the neighboring Benedictine abbey of St. Mary at Chatteris, the possessions and feudal rights of which were given to Ely by Henry I in the early twelfth century.[23] One thirteenth-century abbess of Chatteris is named as Marie de St. Clare (though there is nothing to show that she wrote the *Vie seinte Audrée*).[24] The writer's identity remains as elusive as that of the more famous Marie "de France": she may have been an abbess, a nun, a novice, a laywoman vowed to chastity, perhaps even a lay patron of a religious house or a member of such a patron's family. The case for authorship and provenance rests on the assumption that a female religious community, especially a house dedicated to the saint, is the most likely place of production and reception for an Anglo-Norman life, and in the absence of other evidence, Chatteris is the best available candidate. Certainly the earliest known reception context, as evidenced by the Welbeck manuscript, is that of a text for reading aloud by women to other women in a female community.[25]

Bede, as already noted, begins his account with Ecgfrith and his marriage to Etheldreda, mentioning Tonbert only in parenthesis as a previous husband who had died soon after wedding Etheldreda. The Anglo-Norman life, following its immediate source in the *Liber Eliensis,* adds extra details and events to Bede's account of Etheldreda. It gives a much fuller account of Audrée's youth and first marriage, showing her descent, not only from King Anna but from a mother who was sister to St. Hild and was herself twice married, the producer of four saintly daughters, and who, "for the sake of the eternal crown" ("Pur la parmanable corone" [l. 620]), spent her widowhood as a professed nun at Chelles.[26] A portrait of Audrée as a child and adolescent shows her, like other exemplary virgin figures, as wise and demure from infancy, content to stay at home and to serve God (ll. 229–64). In adolescence, her beauty and worth make her much sought after, but however much she is courted by kings and princes, Audrée sighs only for her bridegroom Christ, to whom she has dedicated her virginity. She spends her days in prayer and in the mortification of her flesh (ll. 265–80). When her parents betroth her to Prince Tonbert of the South Gyrwe, she wishes to continue in the life she has undertaken and resists as far as she can, but eventually "on account of her father's prestige, and that of her relatives and her mother, she consented and was married . . . and dowered with the Isle of Ely" (ll. 299–306).[27]

Tonbert, however, proves to be agreeable to a chaste marriage and they live on the pattern of Joseph and Mary, committed to chastity and almsgiving, while Audrée continues her martyrdom of fleshly mortification. Not only do the Virgin and Joseph provide a pattern for leading one's married life "without becoming besmirched" ("sanz suillier" [l. 402]) but others have achieved this: a story from the *Verba seniorum* illustrates surpassing virtue in a chaste shepherd and his wife who donate a third of what they have to the poor and another third to hospitality and who sleep separately on sacks at night (ll. 413–58).[28] However amicable her own marriage, Audrée is very pleased, when she becomes a young widow, to be free of marriage's yoke and worldly cares. She determines not to remarry: "from the tribulation of the world, which blinds and confuses people, the virgin intended to be free and to live all her life without marriage" (ll. 371–74).[29] She goes to her dower island of Ely, and finds it to be an ideal site for her purposes; being difficult of access, but with plenty of water and trees, it offers sustainable solitude. Here, with more joy in serving her creator than in any earthly honor, she leads a life of holy silence while a community of like-minded people develops around her (ll. 744–73). She conquers every carnal desire, only to have the reputation of her virginity and goodness attract King Ecgfrith of York (ll. 774–87).

Audrée's second marriage is also given in more detail than in Bede and with some significant additions. Bede presents Ecgfrith as devout and noble, and mentions only his dealings with Bishop Wilfrid and his eventual consent to Etheldreda's desire for a religious life. In *La vie seinte Audrée,* as in the *Liber Eliensis,* the second marriage is narrated in chronological sequence and, in the vernacular life, very much more from Audrée's point of view than Ecgfrith's. It is the viewpoint of someone who experiences his offers as a harassing distraction from her own prior commitment to God: "she was burdened by his suit, and oppressed by his offers" (ll. 792–93).[30] Ecgfrith consults her relatives (especially her uncle, her father now being dead), who once again prevail and have her married off "without her heart's consent" ("Sanz volenté de son curage" [l. 803]). At first Audrée and Ecgfrith lead a holy and beautiful life, together with their bishop, Wilfrid. His advice is useful in their good works, such as Audrée's foundation of a double monastery at Hexham ("Augustaldeus" [l. 886]). Ecgfrith is initially astonished and finally enraged at Audrée's steadfastness: she spends her nights in prayerful vigil, and, protected by the Holy Spirit, can be neither attacked in her body nor ravished in her heart (ll. 943–94). When he sees that he will never win a private victory over her "in her chamber" ("en sa chambre" [l. 968]), he solicits Bishop Wilfrid's influence, but Audrée will not relinquish her vow of virginity. As she conquered her first husband, so too she is victorious over her second, and she preserves her virginity for twelve years. A second portrait shows her at this stage of her life as "kind to everyone, and sweet, and pious, and helpful; she loved righ-

teousness, and she held to it, conducting herself with righteousness.
. . . the life of this queen was a model for many people. Nature brought
her forth good, her [own] will kept her a virgin, and the grace of God
which was lodged in her heart protected her" (ll. 1115–28).[31]

Audrée eventually persuades Ecgfrith to let her take the veil at Wilfrid's hands, and to enter the abbey of Ecgfrith's aunt, Ebba, at Coldingham (ll. 1179–87). Only now when she is free of the tribulations of
marriage and has adopted the career of a queen of heaven does she feel
herself truly royal, crowned (like her mother) with an enduring crown
(see ll. 620, 1210). However Ecgfrith soon regrets his decision and comes
along to throw Audrée out of his aunt's convent, so that she has to flee
to her dower island (ll. 1295–96). Cornered by Ecgfrith en route on
"Goldeborch" (l. 1332), Audrée and her two handmaidens are saved by
the sea which miraculously surrounds the headland and cuts them off
from Ecgfrith.[32] For some time, they live on this desert rock, surviving by God's grace and the miraculous opening of a spring in the rock
in answer to Audrée's prayer (ll. 1385–1402). Ecgfrith complains to
Wilfrid (now archbishop of York), but eventually accepts that he cannot "obtain St. Audrée" ("sainte Audree porchacier" [l. 1381]), and takes
Ermenborg as his wife instead. Audrée now founds a double monastery on her dower land and institutes a female spiritual and genealog-
ical dynasty, with her sister, niece, and great-niece succeeding as abbesses. Her death (in A.D. 679 [ll. 2003–6]) is saintly, and further proof of
her virginity appears sixteen years later, when, at the translation insti-
gated by her sister, Sexburga, and Bishop Wilfrid, her body is found
to be incorrupt (ll. 2234–37). The governance of the abbey passes from
Sexburga to Sexburga's daughter, Ermenhild, and thence to Ermenhild's
daughter, Werburga, and Ely continues in virtuous tranquillity until
the invasions of the pagan Danes, Ingvar and Ubbi. Attempted viola-
tion of Audrée's shrine by a marauding Norseman is punished by blind-
ness and death (ll. 2426–39), as is a later failure in reverence by clerks
and priests at the shrine (ll. 2440–55, 2484–2627). With the advent of
King Edgar and Bishop Æthelwold, Ely is restored. A recapitulatory
portrait of Audrée stresses her voluntary poverty, asceticism, and miraculous help from God in establishing her religious life (ll. 2782–95).
In her virgin and hence angelic life ("vie angeliel" [l. 2799]), Audrée
has become kin to the angels of heaven (ll. 2796–99).[33] The remaining
two thousand lines of the life recount Audrée's shrine miracles and her
visionary appearances to suppliants up to the late twelfth century.

The Anglo-Norman life and the *Liber Eliensis* thus develop Bede's narrative by more detailed accounts of both marriages. Marie usually follows the order of events in the Latin source very closely. Nevertheless, however little altered the basic narrative *dispositio* of the Latin *vita* as found in the *Liber Eliensis, La vie seinte Audrée* is a narrative in a wholly different *koiné*. The Anglo-Norman text's alterations of diction, register, and emphasis, as well as its choices in retention and omission from the Latin source, effectively recompose the *vita* into a narrative of new priorities and perspectives. Thus, for instance, where the *Liber Eliensis* sees at Audrée's second marriage "the virgin daughter of Syon . . . led to the city of Babylon yet not in the least touched by the burning of its furnace" (p. 20), the Anglo-Norman text sees, in "this virgin, St. Audrée" ("cele virge, seinte Audree" [l. 857]), a female protagonist, rather than a type of virginity. She is not a series of rhetorical *loci* (as in Thomas of Ely's "Syon" and "Babylon") but a protagonist with a viewpoint, and one which is being constrained by the demands of others: "she would gladly oppose [the marriage] if she dared and if she could" (ll. 859–60).[34] Having escaped from this second marriage, Audrée in the Anglo-Norman life "clearly perceived within a single year" that she had had "less trouble and distress [A-N *haan*]" from a harshly ascetic life of religion than "from suffering existence with her husband" (ll. 1239–42).[35] This echoes the clerical topos of the "woes of marriage" (*molestiae nuptiarum*) and is close to Thomas of Ely's "within a year she understood that the Lord's yoke is gentle and and its burden lighter for her" in the *Liber Eliensis* (p. 26). It is, however, written from the point of view of a female protagonist who has experienced marriage as tribulation, and reads in its context with personal as well as rhetorical immediacy. The vernacular life's author and audience may well have experienced comparable difficulties in their own lives.

For the monks of Ely, Etheldreda's first marriage to Tonbert is not an embarrassment, as it had been to Bede (in whose narrative it is quickly glossed over), but the necessary means of associating the patron saint and the land of their house. It is important that Etheldreda remains virgin (the chief qualification for female sanctity) and that her dower remains incontestably valid and uncontestedly hers. An amicable chaste marriage suits both these requirements. A second chaste marriage underlines both virginity and property, and confirms the maintenance of Etheldreda's sanctity and virginity under duress. Ecgfrith is presented as noble and devout in Bede and does not pursue

Etheldreda into Coldingham and to Ely, but in the *Liber Eliensis* and the Anglo-Norman life he is moved toward the role of the insistent pagan tyrant of the contemporary virgin-martyr *passio*.[36] Rather than the torture and dismemberment faced by the virgin martyr, Audrée has to resist persuasion, harassment, and a failed kidnapping, but her resistance is no less crucial. Had either husband raped her, she would not, regardless of her own unwillingness in the matter, have been allowed to become a consecrated virgin.

In theory, contemporary canon law required the free assent of both parties in marriage, but, as is suggested in both the *Liber Eliensis* and the Anglo-Norman life, constraint could be brought to bear on women for purposes of dynastic exchange and affiliation.[37] The role of consummation in confirming a marriage (and hence in locking women into careers as wives and mothers) shifted in the twelfth and thirteenth centuries. Whereas, in the early twelfth century, Hugh of St. Victor had argued betrothal to be a complete sacrament in itself, Peter Lombard and others later argued that consummation completed and could even constitute marriage, so that it became much harder to dissolve a consummated marriage.[38] Vowed virginity could constitute a prior marriage to Christ, as Thomas Head has argued, but consummation with a subsequent earthly bridegroom, even for an unwillingly affianced woman, could confirm marriage and make it impossible for the validity of the prior contract as bride of Christ to be maintained and publicly accepted.[39] *La vie seinte Audrée* is one of many lives of virgin spouses from the twelfth and thirteenth centuries in which these issues are represented with varying emphases (other examples of special importance in insular hagiography include St. Alexis, St. Cecilia, Edward the Confessor, and his queen, Edith).[40]

The new inflection of virgin martyr conventions signaled in the *Liber Eliensis* and the *Vie seinte Audrée*'s handling of Ecgfrith is important in their treatments of marriage, but significant in rather different ways for the Latin and the Anglo-Norman versions. The dower associated with the saint's first marriage is important to the monks of Ely as the entitlement to the lands of their virgin foundress, but in the Anglo-Norman life, Audrée's dower lands are even more importantly a refuge and the basis for her independent life. On marriage, the property brought by a woman (dowry) came under the control of her husband, but provision for her widowhood was made out of his wedding gift to her (dower). To this, or, in some cases, to part of it, she retained her rights. Dower (not dowry) is thus critical in the context of Anglo-Norman female independence: legally it is the part of a married woman's property over which, as a widow, she could expect to have some control.[41] With her virginity and her dower intact, Audrée's unconsummated second marriage allows Ecgfrith to marry someone else, and permits Audrée the freedom of a widow and the career prerogatives of a consecrated virgin whose first and unsullied commitment had been to Christ. Here, in recalling Audrée's claim to her lands, virginity becomes the sign of personal and socioeconomic autonomy, the foundation of a female religious career. Incorruption signifies intact property rights in the Latin tradition of Ely's cartularies and chronicles, and virginity certified in death is the most resonant fact about Etheldreda. Once the Anglo-Norman text creates a female protagonist's viewpoint, however, virginity comes to signify freedom of volition and the possibility of a life lived according to choice. Marie's rewriting of the *vita* produces a model of less immediate relevance to the monks of Ely and of greater relevance to the concerns of Anglo-Norman noblewomen.

Although Audrée's religious career is largely defined by the fact of her foundation of Ely, it includes a number of stages and styles of female religious life which can be found in both historical record and literary representation in Anglo-Norman England. Though martyrdom (the favored destiny for the virginal hagiographic heroine) is not her fate, Audrée's rigorous asceticism functions instead to procure her a martyrdom "without iron": "Although she was not put to death, she took on her flesh the cross upon which Christ suffered death when Longinus struck him. In fasting, vigils and weeping, she tormented her body night and day. . . . Without shedding blood, she was a martyr in vigils, weeping, longing, in hunger, thirst and nakedness" (ll. 1469–74, 1489–91).[42] She also exemplifies the sanctity of the chaste spouse, and of the abbatial foundress. Audrée's posthumously exercised miraculous powers (in which protection of her observances and rights and vengeance for their infringement are especially prominent) may have offered precedents and inspiration to contemporary abbesses and noblewomen, since the management and protection of territorial and other rights is a feature common to the exercise of power by dead saints and by living abbesses and noble householders.[43] In her retreat to the Isle of Ely between her marriages, as in her flight from Ecgfrith to the rock of "Goldeborch," Audrée exemplifies the eremitic and anchoritic spirituality especially prevalent in insular culture, and especially undertaken by women in the twelfth and thirteenth centuries.[44]

The chief point of Audrée's sanctity is her virginity, but she is twice married, once widowed, and once separated before becoming a monastic foundress, patron, and leader. As an exemplary figure, Audrée speaks to the concerns not only of the technically intact but of wives and widows in those other female "estates of the flesh," chastity and marriage. Her vernacular life suggests the range of female experience and aspiration which can be modeled on the ideal of virginity, both as recommended to and as taken up by women. Motherhood, the only role not literally experienced in Audrée's life, is spiritually available to her, since her status as virgin foundress and abbess enables her to propagate a spiritual lineage of successors while occupying a maternal spiritual role toward her nuns and handmaidens. Female identity and experience (whether of saint, writer, or audience) is only very inadequately labeled by the term "female religious." Medieval categories of virginity, chastity, and biological motherhood, and the corresponding occupations—nuns, widows, and wives—by which women were chiefly identified in estates theory, are not just categories stably inhabited by different women but potentially, and in many cases actually, stages of experience in a single lifetime. Moreover, however firmly convents may have been defined as enclosed communities in the theories and representations of the churchmen responsible for them, lay and professed women in practice moved in and out of them. Women entered and sometimes reentered communities at different stages of their lives for different reasons, not always as professed religious. The post-Conquest female community was very likely at any one time to include virgins, wives, and widows, women professed in youth for life, young women kept in temporary enclosure pending marriage, women entering on vidual corrodies and pensions late in life, or women visitors who might themselves have some kind of religious life, such as that of the chaste widow or vowess, and so on.[45] An Anglo-Norman female community such as that of Campsey Priory (in whose manuscript collection for mealtime reading *La vie seinte Audrée* is extant) will have included many members whose experience of marriage and widowhood would have made Audrée's biography resonant hearing. The audience of the Audrée manuscript may well have included, for instance, Maud de Ufford, countess of Ulster, who entered Campsey in 1347. She brought with her the revenues of her extensive dower lands in England for a year (to be followed, when part of the dower reverted to her son, by less munificent but still ample financial arrangements). In October of 1347 Maud secured a licence for a perpetual chantry of five priests at Campsey to care for the welfare of the souls, among others, of her two previous husbands, William de Burges, earl of Ulster, and Ralph de Ufford, and of her two daughters by these husbands, Elizabeth and Maud.[46]

As well as functioning as career choices or refuges for women with vocations or with objections to marriages arranged for them by their families, nunneries served the interests of the families of patrons, donors, and clients whose daughters were recruited to them. They could function as *gynacea* for surplus women or safekeeping for women whose dynastic potential was to be held in reserve and they also provided a cheaper alternative to the costs of a marriage portion.[47] Families remained important in the founding and staffing of post-Conquest nunneries, so that the pattern established for the royal Anglo-Saxon nunneries was frequently repeated in noble and gentry Anglo-Norman foundations. In her important study of post-Conquest foundations, Sally Thompson finds that "a significant number of women entered a nunnery founded by a member of their family" and further argues that "practical considerations of providing a refuge for a widow or unmarried daughters should not be dismissed as irreligious . . . the entrance of family members into the new community could be an illustration of the link between the nunnery and its founder, and a further testimony to the spiritual purpose of the foundation as a retreat from the world and a focus of prayer for the living and the dead. . . . a dual purpose [in the establishment of nunneries] would not necessarily involve tension between the spiritual and the secular."[48] In St. Audrée, the Anglo-Norman life presents a consecrated virgin who, as a princess and queen, also occupies roles familiar to secular Anglo-Norman noblewomen. The sharpness of our own conceptual opposition of secular and sacred may incline us to discount the links and interchanges between these realms of experience, but *La vie seinte Audrée,* while most probably composed in a religious community, would apply in many of its concerns and emphases to women in a range of secular and religious lives.

La vie seinte Audrée's interest in issues of status, lineage, and class fits well with the milieu of post-Conquest nunneries.[49] Concern with such matters is signaled by Marie after she has used the more conventional themes of the hagiographic prologue: "I have begun to make this book for St. Audrey the queen, in whom goodness never fails or is lacking.

Here it behoves me to tell and relate the lineage from which she was born, and how she was twice married. Before I speak of her marriage, I must describe her lineage" (ll. 29–36).[50] Audrée's lineage is duly traced in some detail from the first Angles mentioned in Bede (ll. 57–228). Her exemplary readiness to abandon her prerogatives is also a theme of the prologue (ll. 17–28), but Audrée's rank is constantly reinscribed in the life: the whole point of her humility is that it is exercised from so great a height. Audrée's virginity is, appropriately, "queen over all the virtues which are present in those who live in this world" (ll. 2801–3).[51] When she is finally able to make her profession at Coldingham, great stress is laid on her influence (hearing of her profession, people in many regions decide to flee the world and turn to religion themselves [ll. 1198–1204]) and on her renunciation of the riches and dignities of rank (her royal robes, adornments, and the gold and silver she possesses are donated to Coldingham [ll. 1217–22]). She is praised for her exemplary humility (l. 1245) and for her cultivation of holiness: "this queen was perfect in the service of God" (ll. 1223–24). It is nonetheless the combination of her East Anglian "descent from the noble English" ("Engleis" [l. 1630]) and her "noble holy life" (l. 1632) which induces so many people to send their daughters to her (ll. 1629–36) once her legal possession is established at Ely ("sa lige possession" [l. 1601]). One of Audrée's miracles attracts the participation of Henry I's queen, Matilda: Brustan, a Chatteris man wrongfully imprisoned in London, is miraculously freed by St. Audrée and St. Benedict; the queen commands celebration of the miracle in London and accompanies Brustan back to Ely to deposit his miraculously broken chains at Audrée's shrine (ll. 3218–37).[52] Audrée's lineage goes forward into the future as well as creating her initial status: in the peculiar radicalism of the virgin body, at once the denial and the perfection of human generation, the virgin foundress simultaneously disrupts direct biological lines of filiation and creates spiritual genealogies. She thus both evades and reinscribes the contours and constraints of family lineage, and does so in a matrix of kinship and family connections affecting the status and property of her house. By lines of spiritual and biological filiation the motherhouse of Ely passes to Audrée's sister, Sexburga, and to her niece, while Sexburga perpetuates the memory and presence of Audrée for future generations by translating her body to a richer shrine. Female spiritual community and a founding family's connections and influence in a major religious house are both perpetuated here.

In the range of Anglo-Norman social groups for whom *Audrée*'s account of virginity, marriage, dower, and autonomy may have had special pertinence, aristocratic and gentry widows, whether professed or lay, seem an especially appropriate audience. As women with the greatest property rights and powers in post-Conquest Britain, their concerns and activities were similar to those dealt with in the vernacular life.[53] Both as wives and widows, but particularly as widows with dower property, Anglo-Norman noblewomen were notable patronesses and foundresses. Some women, whether or not they preferred what *La vie seinte Audrée* calls "the spouse who cannot die" ("l'espous ky ne peust morir" [l. 1166]), resisted remarriage and/or paid large sums to avoid it, and some are known to have become vowesses.[54] Although royal foundations were less prominent in the post-Conquest period, aristocratic widows carried out contemporary versions of Audrée's achievements, founding Elstow, Godstow, Stixwould, Lacock, Marham, and Canonsleigh (there are other probable cases where complete documentation is lacking).[55] The status of such foundations is also significant: the great majority of post-Conquest nunneries had only the rank of priory, but of the nine which were abbeys, five were the foundations of noblewomen. Some post-Conquest nunneries were founded by widows who later remarried: "even for those who stayed in the world, founding a nunnery may well have seemed the best way of crystallizing a measure of independence."[56]

Audrée's life is just possibly the inspiration of an imitative piece of patronage. One woman who may have been influenced by the cult of St. Etheldreda and who certainly rerouted some dower property in the interest of women is Matilda (or Maud) de Clare, countess of Gloucester. Matilda's father, the earl of Lincoln, offered Henry III five thousand marks for permission to marry her to the sixteen-year-old Richard de Clare, heir of the enormous Gloucester estates. They were married in 1237 and Richard died in 1262.[57] Like many medieval noblewomen, Matilda had a wealthy and vigorous widowhood, in her case of over twenty-five years' duration. During this time, till her death in 1289, she held one-third of the de Clare estates in dower.[58] In 1284 she successfully turned out the Augustinian canons from the priory of Canonsleigh in Devon and replaced them with canonesses.[59] Matilda had earlier tried to restaff an existing male priory at Sandleford with forty enclosed nuns under the rule of Augustine accompanied by ten Fontevrault priests, but despite a generous endowment and a papal

mandate of 1274 directing the fulfillment of her intentions, the Sandleford project did not come to fruition.[60] Eventually, again providing for
forty canonesses, Matilda was successful at Canonsleigh or rather Myn-
chenlegh (i.e., "Nuns"-leigh) as it comes to be called in later medieval
documents.[61] She also gave her new house a very interesting version of
a Rule—the manuscript containing (in all probability) the author's
autograph revisions of *Ancrene Wisse,* Cotton Cleopatra C.vi.[62] This
famous thirteenth-century guide for women was written in the West
Midlands, probably near the Welsh Marches in Mortimer and de Braose
territory (families intermarried with the de Clares).[63]

After the battle of Evesham in 1265, Matilda had spent time in Cambridgeshire with her pluralist son Bogo annexing further monastic
houses from the rebels.[64] It is tempting to think that she took away some
ideas from this heartland of Audrée's cult, for, though many early
churches were dedicated to the saint, only one religious house apart
from Ely itself had Etheldreda as dedicatee—Matilda's own at Canonsleigh. Previously dedicated to the Virgin and St. John the Evangelist,
Canonsleigh seems to have added Etheldreda after Matilda had changed
its personnel.[65] Whether or not a connection ever existed between
Marie's life of Audrée and Matilda de Clare's foundation, both Matilda and Audrée suggest the contained but often potent influence of
Anglo-Norman noblewomen.[66] These women were not less important
in the distribution of both texts and lands than the figure of Etheldreda was to the monks of Ely in their house history and the retention of
their property. Certainly for a noblewoman like Matilda (or any of the
Anglo-Norman noblewomen who were connected in various ways with
hagiographic production and reception in the period), a narrative such
as Audrée's was hardly remote: in a life of dynastic marriage, virginity
or its cognate, chastity, offered as an ideal the control of oneself, one's
spouse, and one's property. Where one could be disposed of as a piece
of property, one riposte was to dispose of property oneself: in a system
where virginity was exchanged for dower property, the use of dower
property for a life of consecrated virginity forms a suggestive example
of the ways in which power could be rerouted. Marie's text presents the
life of a female community not only as offering a refuge from unwant-
ed marriages but as having more realizable personal power than was the
lot of women who had not, through legal separation or widowhood,
resumed their dower. It can usefully remind us that the lives of abbess-
saints, particularly in the vernaculars, may be perceived in their differ-

ent versions and textual communities not only as providing institutional identity and ideas to think with for medieval religious and clerical men but as offering representations of powerful and independent women. In the hagiography written for Anglo-Norman women, and written by women as well as men, destinies outside marriage embraced a wider range of female achievement than that of dying in defence of one's chastity.

Notes

I am grateful to the British Academy for a travel grant to the conference in Toronto where this paper was first given in February 1990; to the editors of the present volume for their thoughtful and meticulous work; and to Professor Jill Mann of Girton College, Cambridge, for helpful information on the early cult of Etheldreda.

1. The corpus of Anglo-Norman verse lives includes eight traditional virgin martyrs (some, notably Catherine and Margaret, the subjects of numerous different versions): these are Agatha, Agnes, Catherine, Christine, Faith, Juliana, Lucy, and Margaret. There are three penitent harlots (Mary of Egypt, Mary Madgalen, and Thaïs). Married women with children are represented only by Nichole Bozon's late thirteenth- or early fourteenth-century life of Elizabeth of Hungary. Holy women close to Christ are further exemplified by his life of Martha. See further the list in Jocelyn Wogan-Browne, "'Clerc u lai, muïne u dame': Women and Anglo-Norman Hagiography in the Twelfth and Thirteenth Centuries," *Women and Literature in Britain 1100–1500,* ed. Carol M. Meale (Cambridge, 1993), n. 4 (75–78), to which should be added "The Life of Saint Melor," ed. A. H. Diverres, in *Medieval French Textual Studies in Memory of T. B. W. Reid,* ed. Ian Short, Anglo-Norman Text Society Occasional Publications Series 1 (London, 1984), 41–53.

2. For a preliminary account of early hagiographic vernacular lives of abbesses in medieval England, see Jocelyn Wogan-Browne, "Queens, Virgins and Mothers: Hagiographic Representations of the Abbess and Her Powers in Twelfth- and Thirteenth-Century Britain," *Women and Sovereignty,* ed. Louise Fradenburg (Edinburgh, 1992), 14–35. Anglo-Norman lives and editions are included in the list referred to in n. 1 above.

3. See, for example, Susan J. Ridyard, *The Royal Saints of Anglo-Saxon England* (Cambridge, 1988), 53–56, 176–210; Simon Keynes and Angus Kennedy, *Anglo-Saxon Ely* (Woodbridge, forthcoming).

4. The other lives certainly by women are from Barking: Clemence of Barking, *The Life of St. Catherine,* ed. William MacBain, ANTS 18 (Oxford, 1964); Östen Södergård, ed., *La vie d'Edouard le confesseur: Poème anglo-normand du XIIe siècle* (Uppsala, 1948).

5. *La vie seinte Audrée, poème anglo-normand du XIIIe siècle,* ed. Östen Södergård (Uppsala, 1955). Citations in this essay are from this edition by line number. Södergård himself signals the interest of the text for literary historians: "Marie . . . utilisa le texte latin avec une grande liberté et en retint les éléments qui étaient concrets, narratifs et parfois dramatiques. Le style de Marie ne s'attache donc pas servilement au canevas latin" (36). For historians of the Latin tradition, the Anglo-Norman life has seemed understandably irrelevant: nevertheless, the fact that it is often not even mentioned in Latin-centered scholarship provides an instance of how easily entire (vernacular, female) historical textual communities have been elided in modern historiography.

6. See *Bede's Ecclesiastical History of the English People,* ed. Bertram Colgrave and R. A. B. Mynors (Oxford, 1969; reprinted with corrections, 1991), book 4, chap. 19 (390–96), and, for the encomium on virginity in which Etheldreda is Bede's native English example, 396–400. In this article, the name "Etheldreda" is used for the saint as perceived by Bede, Thomas of Ely, and the monks of Ely; "Audrée" is reserved for the saint in the vernacular life.

7. Stephanie Hollis, *Anglo-Saxon Women and the Church: Sharing a Common Fate* (Woodbridge, 1992), 65–74, esp. 70.

8. For Æthelwold's use of her cult see Wulfstan of Winchester, *The Life of St. Æthelwold,* ed. Michael Lapidge and Michael Winterbottom (Oxford, 1991), 38–40.

9. See Walter W. Skeat, ed., *Ælfric's Lives of the Saints,* EETS o.s. 76 and 82 (London, 1881–85; reprinted in 1 vol., 1966), 432–40.

10. Middle English lives of Etheldreda are listed by Charlotte d'Evelyn and Frances A. Foster, "Saints' Legends," in *A Manual of the Writings in Middle English 1050–1500,* gen. ed. J. Burke Severs (New Haven, Conn., 1970), 584, s.v. *Etheldreda, Audrey, Abbess of Ely. The South English Legendary* includes a Middle English life of which texts exist in London, British Library, MS. Egerton 1993, fol. 163r; Oxford, Bodleian Library MS. Eng. poet. a.1 (the Vernon manuscript), fols. 33r–33v; and MS. Bodley 779, fol. 279v. (For descriptions of these manuscripts see Manfred Görlach, *The Textual Tradition of the South English Legendary* [Leeds, 1974], 75–77, 80–81, 102–4.) This life follows the *Liber Eliensis* narrative order, beginning with the saint's marriage to Tonbert. Like some other lives of abbess saints in the *South English Legendary,* Etheldreda's life does not appear in the principal modern edition (*The South English Legendary,* ed. Charlotte

d'Evelyn and Anna J. Mill, EETS o.s. 235, 236 [London, 1956]), since it is not in the base manuscript there selected. For the later Middle English life in quatrains extant in British Library MS. Cotton Faustina B.iii, fols. 265 ff., see C. Horstmann, ed., *Altenglische Legenden,* new series, 2 vols. (Heilbronn, 1881), 2:292–307. The rhyme royal life by Bradshaw listed by d'Evelyn and Foster is not strictly a life of Etheldreda but forms part of Bradshaw's life of Etheldreda's great niece Werburga: it nonetheless contains a substantial account of the saint.

At least twelve church dedications to Etheldreda are known (see Francis Bond, *Dedications and Patron Saints of English Churches* [London, 1914], 17), and she is omnipresent in insular calendars and litanies (see Francis Wormald, *English Kalendars before A.D. 1100,* Henry Bradshaw Society (hereafter HBS) 72 [London, 1934]; ibid., ed., *English Benedictine Kalendars after A.D. 1100,* 2 vols., HBS 77 and 81 [London, 1934–46]; and Michael Lapidge, ed., *Anglo-Saxon Litanies of the Saints,* HBS 106 [London, 1991]). Variant spellings of her name in Latin calendars include "Aeþeldryþe" (Hyde calendar, early eleventh century, printed in Wormald, *English Benedictine Kalendars,* vol. 1, 119), "Aeðeldryþe" (ibid., 133); "Etheldride" and "Eteldride" (*The Gilbertine Rite,* ed. Reginald Maxwell Woolley, HBS 60 [London, 1922], 8, 76); "Etheldrithe" (*Missale ad usum ecclesie Westmonasteriensis,* ed. John Wickham Legg, HBS 1, 5, 12 [London, 1891–97], 1:x [the manuscript dates from 1388]); and "Etheldrede" (*The Ordinale and Customary of the Benedictine Nuns of Barking Abbey,* ed. J. B. L. Tolhurst, HBS 66 [London, 1928], 240). In vernacular notices the French form of her name is prevalent by the late Middle Ages: in a French and Latin Amesbury manuscript of the fourteenth century (Cambridge University Library, MS. Ee.vi.16, fol. 16v) she appears as "Audree" in the calendar, though in the same manuscript's hierarchically ordered litany, she appears, at fol. 66r, as "Edeldreda"; in Whytford's *The Martiloge in Englysshe* for Syon (printed by Wynkyn de Worde in 1526) she is both "saynt Etheldrede a virgyn 7 quene" with a marginal note "Saynt Audre," and "saynt Awdre a virgyn 7 a quene" (ed. F. Procter and E. S. Dewick, HBS 3 [London, 1893], 98 and 164), while in the list of foundresses in the late satire on nunneries, "Why I can't be a nun," she heads a list of Anglo-Saxon royal foundress saints as "seynte audre" (ed. F. J. Furnivall, "Early English Poems and Lives of Saints," *Trans. Phil. Soc.* [Berlin, 1862], 148, l. 389). The Anglo-Latin form survives in the *South English Legendary* texts, as "aþildrede" in Oxford, Bodleian MS. 779, fol. 279v (early fifteenth century), and as "Aeldrede" and "Aldrede" in Oxford, Bodleian MS. Eng. poet. a.1 (the Vernon MS), fol. 33r (see A. I. Doyle, ed., *The Vernon Manuscript: A Facsimile of Bodleian Library, Oxford, MS. Eng. poet.a 1* [Woodbridge, 1987]). It is also present in the fifteenth-century quatrain life (ed. Horstmann, see above) and in the late medieval Latin nationalizing legendaries by Tynemouth and Capgrave (ed. C. Horstmann, *Nova Legenda Anglie,* 2 vols. [London, 1902], 2:424-29) and their English versions by Pynson (*Kalendre of the New Legende of Englande,* 1516, British Library, STC 4602, xxxi, where Pynson adds an explanatory "comenly callyd Seynt Awdry"). Given the French form's eventual predominance (and contribution of the word "tawdry" to the English language [OED, s.v. *tawdry*]), the propagation of the cult in Anglo-Norman seems to have been as important as its English diffusion.

11. In addition to the Anglo-Norman life in the Welbeck manuscript (see below, n. 17), the *South English Legendary* Middle English text is found in the Vernon manuscript, which is generally agreed to have been compiled for a female community (see Doyle, *Vernon Manuscript,* 14). The quatrain life was thought by Horstmann (*Altenglische Legenden*) to come from Wilton, in view of its appearance in the same manuscript as a life of St. Edith of Wilton; N. R. Ker confirms Wilton ownership of the manuscript (*Medieval Libraries of Great Britain,* 2d ed. [London, 1964], 198) and Michael Benskin confirms Wilton origin (though not Wiltshire dialect or a holograph manuscript) and proposes a copyist, possibly one of the nuns of Wilton, working at the abbey but not herself a native of Wiltshire ("In Reply to Dr Burton," *Leeds Studies in English* n.s. 22 [1991], 246–51). The other two manuscripts of the *South English Legendary* text (Oxford, Bodleian MS. 779, fol. 279v; and London, British Library, MS. Egerton 1993, fol. 163r) are unprovenanced, but cannot be assumed to belong to male houses, since other comparable manuscripts belonged to nunneries; for instance, London, British Library, MS. Lansdowne 436, an extensive (Latin) legendary with a special focus on British saints and abbesses which belonged to Romsey (see Ker, *Medieval Libraries,* 164); Oxford, Bodleian MS. Douce 372, a manuscript of the *Gilte Legende* left to the London Augustinian priory of Holywell (see Richard F. S. Hamer, *Three Lives from the Gilte Legende* [Heidelberg, 1978], 27–28); and Cambridge, Cambridge University Library MS. Dd. 8.2, fol. 11v, where, in a list of gifts to the priory of Kington St. Michael, "A boke of seynte lyves yn Englishe" is mentioned.

12. See E. O. Blake, ed., *Liber Eliensis,* Camden 3d ser., 92 (London, 1962); the earlier sources are discussed on xxviii–xxxiv. Citations from this edition are henceforth referenced by page number in the text.

13. Ridyard, *Royal Saints,* 209.

14. Edward Miller, *The Abbey and Bishopric of Ely: The Social History of an Ecclesiastical Estate from the Tenth Century to the Early Fourteenth Century* (Cambridge, 1951; reprint, 1969), 15.

15. See further Ridyard, *Royal Saints,* 196–210 (henceforth cited by page number in the text).

16. See Marina Warner, *Monuments and Maidens: The Allegory of the Female Form* (London, 1985; 2d ed., 1987). Warner does not discuss abbess saints specifically as a category of "monumental maiden," but her study is nonetheless suggestive for them.

17. The manuscript (formerly MS. Welbeck IC1) is now British Library MS. Additional 70813. On fol. 265v a medieval inscription specifies that the book belongs to Campsey and that it is "de lire amengier." For an account of the manuscript's contents, see *St. Modwenna,* ed. A. T. Baker and Alexander Bell, ANTS 7 (Oxford, 1947), xi–xii.

18. On Campsey, see *The Victoria History of the County of Suffolk,* ed. William Page, vol. 2 (London, 1907), 112–15.

19. On the date of *Audrée's* manuscript and composition, see *Vie seinte Audrée,* 37 and 55, and M. Dominica Legge, *Anglo-Norman Literature and Its Background* (Oxford, 1963; reprint, Westport, Conn., 1978), 264–65. The Anglo-Norman text cannot have been completed before 1189, since, as Legge points out (264), a miracle from the time of Bishop Geoffrey Ridel (d. 1189) is included, but it may have been written at any time up to about sixty years later.

20. "Ici escris mon non Marie, / Pur ce ke soie remembree" (*Vie seinte Audrée,* ll. 4619–20; henceforth cited by line number in the text).

21. In her *Anglo-Norman in the Cloisters: The Influence of the Orders upon Anglo-Norman Literature* (Edinburgh, 1950), M. Dominica Legge speculates (on unnamed grounds) that Marie may have been from Barking but points out that she could not have been a Benedictine nun of Ely (50–51).

22. See Wulfstan's *Life of St. Æthelwold,* 38–40.

23. Although Etheldreda was widely venerated in Anglo-Saxon and medieval England and had multiple church dedications, only one other religious house apart from Ely was dedicated to the saint (see n. 65 below, and see Alison Binns, *Dedications of Monastic Houses in England and Wales 1066–1216* [Woodbridge, Suffolk, 1989], 19, 70). Chatteris was first suggested as the possible context for the writing of the life by Legge (*Anglo-Norman Literature,* 264). This nunnery was approximately ten miles from Ely and was given to Ely by Henry I (*The Victoria History of the County of Cambridge and the Isle of Ely,* ed. L. F. Salzman, vol. 2 [London, 1948], 220).

A possible indication of interest in Chatteris, if not of Chatteris origin, is Marie's particular mention of this house (unnoted by Legge or Södergård):

> En cest maries [around Ely] est Rameseie
> Et l'abbeie de Thorneie,
> Plusurs autres ke jeo ne puis
> Nomer, si cume escrit le truis.

Chateriz est en ydle de Ely,
Ceste matere lais issi,
Kar revertir voil a l'estoire
Dont en romanz fas la memoire.
(ll. 313–20)

("As I find written, Ramsey is in this marshland, and the abbey of Thorney, and several others I cannot name. Chatteris is in the isle of Ely: I leave this matter here, for I want to return to the story, a record of which I am making in the vernacular.") It is hard to see why, if she is writing elsewhere than in one of these three religious houses, Marie should stress their connection with Audrée's foundation site, and Ramsey and Thorney were male Benedictine houses. Chatteris was founded between A.D. 1006 and 1016 by Ednoth, first abbot of Ramsey after the death of Ramsey's founder Ailwin, and Ednoth's sister Ælfwen (wife of King Athelstan and Chatteris's first abbess). A female community in this locality could not but be aware of the larger communities at Ramsey and Thorney.

The passage from the vernacular life quoted above elaborates the *Liber Eliensis*'s "sicut scriptum repperitur, insulam Elge ab eodem sponso eius accepit in dotem" ("as is found in the deed [i.e., a written document], she received the island of Ely in dower from her husband": a written source, which if it indeed existed, is unknown, see Blake, *Liber Eliensis,* 15, n. 2). Although she usually follows the Latin ordering of material, Marie may here be summarizing from the *Liber Eliensis*'s prologue description of the abbey's property as understood in the twelfth century, where it is mentioned that "Nominatur etiam ad predictam insulam Chateriz, ubi abbatia est sanctimonialium, et pagus Withleseia atque abbatia monachorum de Torneia ("Also named within the previously mentioned island is Chatteris, where there is an abbey of nuns, and the district of Wittlesea and the abbey of monks of Thorney" [Blake, 3]) shortly after Bede's explanation of Ely's name as derived from the plentifulness of eels in the marshes is cited ("dicimus autem Ely Anglice, id est a copia anguillarum" ["however, we say Ely in English, that is, from the abundance of eels," Blake, 2]); compare *Vie seinte Audrée,* ll. 307–10: "Pur la plenté k'a ou mareis / D'anguillies et de peissons freis / Fu cest, ydle nomé issi; / De ales en engleis dist hom Ely" ("this island was so named because of the abundance of eels and fresh[water] fish that there is in the marsh; from the English for 'eels,' one says Ely"). Since the question of the continuity of Ely Abbey's rights in the island is the crucial one for the *Liber Eliensis,* and the absence of continuity between Etheldreda's and Æthelwold's foundations what most needs obscuring in asserting the post-Conquest rights of the abbey, it is not surprising that Marie's work reflects a certain amount of vagueness here

about just what is and is not included in Etheldreda's dower lands. Marie
may conceivably have had access to the mysterious deed or other written
source mentioned in l. 316 of her text, but the *Liber Eliensis* gives no further information concerning this source and she may be simply following
its "sicut scriptum repperitur" (Blake, 15). She does not seem to have used
Geoffrey of Ely's poem on Etheldreda or Alcuin's on Ely; see Pauline A.
Thompson and Elizabeth Stevens, "Gregory of Ely's Verse Life and Miracles of St. Æthelthryth," *Analecta Bollandiana* 106 (1988), 333–90. The
importance and political sensitivity of the precise contents of the dower
may explain why a community at Chatteris should need to be reminded
that it is in the Isle of Ely.

The passage could, of course, be read quite differently, as pointing to
origin outside the Isle of Ely. It would be odd, however, for an Ely com-
pilation to be reworked in such detail and length for a female community *without* any connections with the Isle of Ely, though once written, a
saint's life might well be copied for other houses, as in the case of the
Welbeck manuscript.

Although this passage in the Anglo-Norman life may appear abrupt,
Marie seems to have been alert and precise in her handling of Ely and its
meaning for Audrée. The *Liber Eliensis* repeats its account of Ely when
dealing with Etheldreda's occupation of her dower lands. The etymology
from eels reappears and a sacred etymology is added whereby Ely unites
two Hebraic words, "el" meaning God and "ge" meaning land, hence "land
of god" ("quoniam dicitur 'el' Deus, 'ge' terra, quod simul 'Dei terra' sonat"
[Blake, 32]). In dealing with this passage, Marie omits the repetition of
the eel etymology which she had herself earlier used:

> Cist Edli ou la dame fu
> Si cum nos avom entendu,
> Elge si fu primes nomez
> Et ore est Ely apellez.
> Elge est un non en hebreu,
> En la glose dist la terre Dieu.
> (ll. 1615–20)

("This Ely where the lady was, as we have heard, was first named Elge and
is now called Ely. Elge is a Hebrew name and is called the 'land of God'
in the gloss.") It is just possible that this could be accounted for by Marie's
use of a source manuscript with variant readings, but it seems more likely
that she is consciously selecting here, using the secular etymology at the
first mention of the dower lands in ll. 307–10, and, in the later passage at
ll. 1615–20, focusing on the sacred etymology at the point of Audrée's occupation of the land for spiritual purposes.

24. The abbess so named dates before 1265; see W. Dugdale, *Monasticon Anglicanum,* ed. J. Caley, H. Ellis, and B. Bandinel (London, 1846), 3:614. This is rather early for St. Clare (canonized A.D. 1255) and is certainly before the arrival of the first minoresses at the convent of Waterbeach near Ely (A.D. 1294). Conceivably it is an error for Marie de Clare.

25. Though they are most frequently found in manuscripts associated with religious communities, saints' lives do appear in the books of gentry households in both Anglo-Norman and Middle English. For the social and generic mix of insular manuscripts in the post-Conquest period, see John Frankis, "The Social Context of Vernacular Writing in Thirteenth Century England: The Evidence of the Manuscripts," in *Thirteenth Century England I,* ed. P. R. Coss and S. D. Lloyd (Woodbridge, Suffolk, 1986), 175–84; and, for an example of gentry patronage, Ian Short, "The Patronage of Beneit's *Vie de Thomas Becket,*" *Medium Aevum* 56 (1987), 239–56. Felicity Riddy has argued that the early fourteenth-century Auchinleck manuscript (Edinburgh, MS. 19.2.1), an early example of a manuscript with a generic mix inclusive of English saints' lives, was produced for the women of a London merchant family ("The Auchinleck Manuscript a Woman's Book?" paper delivered at the Bristol Conference on Romance in England, Easter 1992, to form part of her forthcoming study of medieval English female subcultures). The greater proportion of Anglo-Norman manuscript copies of hagiographic lives with known provenance are largely, though not exclusively, associated with religious communities. For a discussion of the pertinence they may nonetheless have had for women who were not professed religious see pp. 38–39 above.

26. Blake, *Liber Eliensis,* 13, 18; *Vie seinte Audrée,* ll. 141–228, 613–24. Hereswitha's daughters were Sexburga, married to Erconbert of Kent, foundress and abbess of Minster-in-Sheppey, and subsequently Audrée's successor at Ely; Ethelburga, nun and abbess of Faremoutier-en-Brie; Withburga, solitary at Holkham and East Dereham; and Saethryth (Hereswitha's daughter by another husband), abbess of Faremoutier-en-Brie. Bede says that Hereswitha became a nun at Chelles and that it was her example that inspired Hild as abbess (Colgrave and Mynors, *Bede's Ecclesiastical History,* book 4, 23 [406]). Bede is the source of the *Liber Eliensis's* information that there were not many monasteries in Britain in Etheldreda's mother's time, and that young noblewomen were sent to foreign religious houses "to be taught in them and to be betrothed to their heavenly Bridegroom" (Colgrave and Mynors, *Bede's Ecclesiastical History,* book 3, 8 [238]). For brief modern accounts and bibliography of the daughters, see the entries under their names in David Hugh Farmer, *The Oxford Dictionary of Saints* (Oxford, 1978; reprint, 1982).

27. "Pur l'auctorité de son pere, / De ses parens et de sa mere / Assenti

et fu mariee. . . . Et de l'ydle de Ely douee." Although "auctorité" can mean "power, prerogative," it seems in context here more likely to allude to the standing and prestige of Audrée's kin groups as the reason for the pressure to marry. The *Liber Eliensis* gives "Sed vincit parentum auctoritas" at this point (Blake, 14).

28. See Blake for the identification of this story from what the *Liber Eliensis* calls *"Collationes Patrum"* (16, and *Audrée,* "collaciun des peres," ll. 411–12) as that in PL 73:1006.

29. "De l'enpechement del mond / Ke la gent avuegle et confund / Kydoit la virge estre delivre, / Toz jurz sanz mariage vivre."

30. "De sa requeste fu chargee / Et de ses offres ennuyee."

31. A tote gent ert amiable
E duce e pie et revoable.
Dreiture ama, dreiture tint,
Dreiturelement se contint.
. . . .
La vie de ceste roine
Fu a meinte gen discipline.
Nature bone l'enfanta,
Volenté virge la garda.
La grace Deu la garda
Ke en son quer se herberja.

32. "Goldeborch" is probably St. Ebb's head ("Coldeburcheshevet, quod Latine caput Coldeburci dicitur," see Blake, *Liber Eliensis,* 27).

33. On virginity as the *vita angelica,* see Bella Millett, ed., *Hali Meiðhad,* EETS 284 (London, 1982), xxviii–xxx.

34. "Volontiers li constresteut, / Si ele osast et si ele peut."

35. "Bien entendi en un seul an / Ke menor peine et meins de haan / Out el jeu de religion / Ke suffrir l'estre ou son baron."

36. For an attempt to relate the conventions of virgin martyr *passio* to women's lives in post-Conquest Britain, see Jocelyn Wogan-Browne, "Saints' Lives and the Female Reader," *Forum for Modern Language Studies* 27 (1991), 314–32. In the later English quatrain life in the Wilton manuscript (see nn. 10 and 11 above), the treatment moves back toward Bede and Ecgfrith becomes more tractable again.

37. See further John T. Noonan, Jr., "Power to Choose," *Viator* 4 (1973), 418–34; Michael M. Sheehan, "Choice of Marriage Partner in the Middle Ages: Development and Mode of Application of a Theory of Marriage," *Studies in Medieval and Renaissance History* n.s. 1 (1978), 1–33.

38. A. Esmein, *Le mariage en droit canonique,* 2 vols. (Paris, 1929–35), 1:99–211; Marc Glasser, "Marriage in Medieval Hagiography," *Studies in Medieval and Renaissance History* n.s. 4 (1981), 3–34, esp. 20–22; Janet

Coleman, "The *Owl and the Nightingale* and Papal Theories of Marriage," *Journal of Ecclesiastical History* 38 (1987), 517–68, esp. 535–39.

39. Thomas Head, "The Marriages of Christina of Markyate," *Viator* 21 (1990), 75–101, esp. 93.

40. On chaste marriage see Glasser, "Marriage"; André Vauchez, *Les laïcs au Moyen Age: Pratiques et expériences religieuses* (Paris, 1987), 203–9; and Dyan Elliott, *Spiritual Marriage: Sexual Abstinence in Medieval Wedlock* (Princeton, 1993). For discussion of Anglo-Norman and French examples, see Janice M. Pindar, "The Intertextuality of Old French Saints' Lives: St Giles, St Evroul and the Marriage of St Alexis," *Parergon* n.s. 6A (1988), 11–21. St. Cecilia's life is, famously, retold by Christina of Markyate to her bridegroom to avert consummation (see C. H. Talbot, ed. and trans., *The Life of Christina of Markyate: A Twelfth Century Recluse* [Oxford, 1959; reprint, 1987], 50); for a further example which includes the point of view of the bride, see the discussion of the nun of Barking's life of Edward the Confessor in Wogan-Browne, "Clerc u lai, muïne u dame," 68–73.

41. Janet Senderowitz Loengard, "'Of the Gift of Her Husband': English Dower and Its Consequences in the Year 1200," in *Women of the Medieval World: Essays in Honor of John H. Mundy*, ed. Julius Kirshner and Suzanne F. Wemple (Oxford, 1985), 215–55; Michael M. Sheehan, "The Influence of Canon Law on the Property Rights of Married Women in England," *Mediaeval Studies* 25 (1963), 109–24, esp. 113–14. For estimates of the proportions of households headed by widows and for discussion of the late twelfth-century register of widows and heirs (Rotuli de Dominabus) see John S. Moore, "The Anglo-Norman Family: Size and Structure," *Anglo-Norman Studies* 14 (1991), 153–96, esp. 157–67, 185.

42. Ja soit iceo ke ele ne fust occise,
   Si out ele sur sa char mise
   La croiz ou Jhesu Crist sueffri
   La mort, quant Longis le feri.
   En jonne, en veillie et en plur
   Tormentoit son cors nuit et jur.
   . . . .
   Senz sanc espandre fu martir
   En veillie, en plur et en desir,
   En feim, en soif et en nuesce.

43. Audrée's miracles (ll. 2782–4620) are of interest; their inclusion in the Anglo-Norman version strengthens the grounds for provenance from near the Ely area, while their presence in the Welbeck manuscript exemplifies the transmission of miracles beyond the immediate cult area and suggests that these could be perceived as part of an exemplary biography

and not just as shrine or house history. I have explored this question in early abbesses' lives in a preliminary way in "Queens, Virgins and Mothers" (cited in n. 2 above, see esp. 27–30) and in two papers, "The Body of the Abbess: Corporate Culture and Representation" and "Administratrix: Medieval Abbess Biographies," toward a forthcoming study. For lack of space the miracles are not studied in detail here, but the power and authority represented in them, especially in Audrée's vigorous defence of her rights and observances, are striking.

44. See Ann K. Warren, *Anchorites and Their Patrons in Medieval England* (Berkeley, 1985), 20, table 1.

45. Evidence of informality and the presence of laywomen is omnipresent in visitations and bishops' registers. For instance, in 1298, the nuns of Chatteris protested the bishop of Ely's nomination of a laywoman as a nun, and when he insisted on their accepting her as a choir nun, fed and clothed her as a lay sister; at Ickleton Priory, in 1278, the archbishop's vicar-general forbad the reception of married laywomen for holidays, and enjoined that secular women should not stand in the choir during the singing of the canonical hours or while Mass was celebrated (see *VCH, Cambridge,* 2:220, 224).

46. *VCH Suffolk,* 2:113. The Welbeck manuscript is dated from the thirteenth century with (it has been argued) the addition of eight folios to the beginning of the manuscript in the early fourteenth century (*Vie seinte Audrée,* 37), so it is unlikely to be associated with Maud's creation of what became the only known instance of "a small college of secular priests . . . actually established within the precincts of a nunnery" (*VCH Suffolk,* 2:113); the manuscript may well have been in Campsey when Maud was received into the priory.

47. On religious dowry, marriage portion, and social origin see the case study by Kathleen Cooke, "Donors and Daughters: Shaftesbury Abbey's Benefactors, Endowments and Nuns c. 1086–1130," *Anglo-Norman Studies* 12 (1989), 29–45. I am very grateful to Dr. Sally Thompson for drawing my attention to this article.

48. Sally Thompson, *Women Religious: The Founding of English Nunneries after the Norman Conquest* (Oxford, 1991), 181. See also 161, n. 2, for Anglo-Saxon nunneries founded by royal widows.

49. On the class mix of English nunneries, see Eileen Power, *Medieval English Nunneries c. 1275–1535* (Oxford, 1922), 4–14.

50. Pour sainte Audree la roine
    Cui bien ne faut ne decline
    Hay comencé ce livre a faire.
    Ici m'estuet dire et retraire

De quel linage ele fu nee
Et com deus foiz fu mariee.
Ainz ke paroil dou mariage,
M'estuet moustrer de son linage.

These lines are preceded by topics more commonly found in hagiographic prologues (reflections on the use of time and the worthlessness of worldly
riches [ll. 1–16]).

51. "Ke virginité est roine / Sur tutes les vertuz ki sont / En ceus qui
habitent en mond."

52. See Blake, *Liber Eliensis,* 266–69, and also the account of the same
miracle by Orderic Vitalis (*The Ecclesiastical History of Orderic Vitalis,* ed.
Marjorie Chibnall [Oxford, 1969–80], 3 [1972], 346–58), where it is clear
that Brustan is an English speaker (he is reported as saying, "That wat min
lauert Godel mihtin that ic sege soth" [350]).

53. On the property rights of widows, see the works listed in n. 41 above,
and for discussion of thirteenth-century widows, see Linda E. Mitchell,
"Noble Widowhood in the Thirteenth Century: Three Generations of
Mortimer Widows 1246–1334," in *Upon My Husband's Death: Widows in
the Literature and Histories of Medieval Europe,* ed. Louise Mirrer (Ann
Arbor, 1992), 169–90.

54. For examples of women paying for the right not to remarry, see
Loengard, "Of the Gift of Her Husband," 233–37. Examples of vowesses
include Eleanor, sister of Henry III and widow of William, earl of Warwick (d. 15 Apr. 1231), who took *Benedictio viduae* vows in January, 1238,
witnessed by Edmund of Abingdon, archbishop of Canterbury, and Richard, bishop of Chichester (both of whom subsequently protested against
her later marriage to Simon de Montfort, for which in the event a dispensation had to be procured from Rome). Vows were still being taken by
aristocratic women in French in the later fourteenth century; in August,
1360, Philippa, widow of Guy, eldest son of the earl of Warwick (d. April
1351) vowed "purement & des queor & voluntee entierement, avow a Dieu
& seint Eglise, & a la benure Virgin Marie, & a tout le bel compaigne
celestine, & a vous reverent Piere en Dieu, Sir Reynaud per le Grace de
Dieu Evesque de Wircestre, que jeo ameneray ma vie en chastitee defore
en avant, & chaste ferra de mon corps a tout temps de ma vie" (Frederick
J. Furnivall, ed., *The Fifty Earliest English Wills in the Court of Probate,
London,* EETS o.s. 78 [London, 1882], "Additions and Corrections," 3–4,
note to p. 135). For further, later, examples see Charles Henry Cooper, "The
Vow of Widowhood of Margaret, Countess of Richmond and Derby . . .
with Notices of Similar Vows in the 14th, 15th, and 16th Centuries," *Com-
munications Made to the Cambridge Antiquarian Society* 1 (1859), 71–79.
Mary C. Erler gives further bibliography on vowesses in her "Margery

Kempe's White Clothes," *Medium Ævum* 62 (1993), 78–83, see 82, n. 3 (I am very grateful to Professor Erler for making a copy of this article available to me).

55. Thompson, *Women Religious*, 172. Only Lillechurch, the refoundation of Amesbury, and Burnham are allowed as certain royal foundations by Thompson, see 166–67. For foundations by widows, see 167–72.

56. Thompson, *Women Religious*, 177; see also 175.

57. Michael Altschul, *A Baronial Family in Medieval England: The Clares, 1217–1314* (Baltimore, 1965), 34.

58. Ibid., 36.

59. On Canonsleigh see George Oliver, *Monasticon Dioecesis Exoniensis* (London, 1846), 224; Thompson, *Women Religious*, 171–72.

60. *The Victoria History of Berkshire*, ed. P. H. Ditchfield and William Page, vol. 2 (London, 1907), 86–88; Thompson, *Women Religious*, 131, 172 n. 84.

61. Charles Spencer Perceval, "Remarks on Some Early Charters and Documents Relating to the Priory of Austin Canons and Abbey of Austin Canonesses at Canonsleigh in the County of Devon," *Archaeologia* 40 (1865), 417.

62. See E. J. Dobson, ed., *The English Text of the Ancrene Riwle*, EETS o.s. 267 (London, 1972), xxv–xxix. The thirteenth-century text of *Ancrene Riwle* in English is followed, among pen trials and scribbles, by Latin verses to Etheldreda and devotional directions and verses in French (xxii–xxix).

63. It has been argued that Mortimer and de Braose women were involved in the dissemination of *Ancrene Wisse* (see E. J. Dobson, *The Origins of Ancrene Wisse* [Oxford, 1976], 307–10). The problems with the Wigmore affiliation of *Ancrene Wisse* recently demonstrated by Bella Millett ("The Origins of *Ancrene Wisse*: New Answers, New Questions," *Medium Aevum* 61 [1992], 206–28) make this connection purely speculative however (though the unfixing of *Ancrene Wisse* from Wigmore Abbey does not necessarily rule out the involvement of noble and gentrywomen from the West Midlands and the Welsh borders with this text). I am very grateful to Dr. Millett for making, with characteristic generosity, an early copy of this article available to me.

64. On Bogo (who for a while had Leverington, the richest living in Cambridgeshire) see *VCH Cambridge*, 2:147 and Altschul, *Baronial Family*, 35, 176–87, esp. 183–84. A Clare from an earlier generation was abbot of Ely (Richard fitz Richard de Clare, d. 1107), see Blake, *Liber Eliensis*, 225–34, 413–14; Jennifer C. Ward, "Royal Service and Reward: The Clare Family and the Crown, 1066–1154," *Anglo-Norman Studies* 11 (1988), 261–78, esp. 268–69.

65. The first written evidence of the new dedication to Etheldreda is from A.D. 1308 (see Perceval, "Remarks on Some Early Charters," 426).

66. I give the case of Matilda here obviously not as a proven reader or patron of the life but as a specific example of the kind of audience whose interests were well met by, and who had at least the possibility of connection with, the vernacular life. Other possibilities may well be uncovered by further research into the manuscripts and patronesses of nunneries in the southwest (especially the Fontevrault houses), or among the east coast houses where the extant manuscript of *Audreé* is located, or even by new information on the biography of Marie de France. (For an alignment of all the post-Conquest texts with a narratorial figure named as Marie, see Jocelyn Wogan-Browne, "Wreaths of Thyme: Anglo-Norman Hagiographic Translation and the [Female] Clerkly Narrator," in *The Medieval Translator*, 4, ed. Ruth Evans and Roger Ellis (Exeter, 1994), 46–65. The valuable study by William MacBain, "Anglo-Norman Women Hagiographers" in *Anglo-Norman Anniversary Essays,* ed. Ian Short, appeared while this and the present essay were in press (Anglo-Norman Text Society Occasional Publications Series 2 [London, 1993], 235–50).

Juette of Huy, Recluse and Mother (1158–1228): Children and Mothering in the Saintly Life

Jennifer Carpenter

EDIEVAL MOTHERHOOD was an intricate and ever-changing network of ideas and practices. Medieval people's experience and understanding of motherhood was naturally influenced by the values of contemporary Christian culture, while at the same time mothering provided metaphors and narrative structures for experiencing and describing aspects of Christian practice.[1] The present essay seeks to investigate some aspects of the interaction between understandings of motherhood and the perfect Christian life by exploring the relationship between motherliness and sanctity in the life of Juette of Huy, a widow, recluse, and mother of three children. Since institutions and ideas are both reproduced and changed by those who live within them, my essay will discuss, as far as possible, the ways in which Juette of Huy herself experienced, and by her own actions negotiated, the constraints and powers involved with motherhood.[2] Before we turn to Juette's life, however, a brief consideration of the ideological and historical context for her role as a holy mother is appropriate.[3]

A powerful ambivalence toward family obligations for those striving for the perfect Christian life is evident from the earliest period of Christianity. From the earthly mission of Christ onwards, ties to the family might be, and often were, powerful obstacles to be valiantly overcome on the path toward God.[4] The antagonism of monastic life to the family has often been noted, and the theme of parental opposition to a saintly career is an ancient and potent one. Family may very strongly symbolize the world that pulls the holy person away from his or her vocation.

Furthermore, late antique Christianity developed a particular emphasis on the holiness of virginity, especially in women. Virginity became an important and established element in society's understanding of female sanctity.[5] The problem of children in this context is clear: they were living reminders of the saint's failure to remain virginal, and were solid links to the earthy, mundane aspects of human existence. Only the Virgin Mary, whose cult was to grow in importance in the high Middle Ages, would be able to offer a model which combined the virtues of motherhood and virginity.[6]

These ancient and deep-rooted features of the Christian model of religious perfection ensured that there were few models of saintly motherhood, and a limited tradition from which to shape a narrative about a saintly mother. One group of holy mothers who nevertheless gained a lasting place in Christian tradition were the influential mothers of sons who became important Christian figures. St. Helena, the mother of Constantine, and St. Monica, the mother of St. Augustine, are early examples of this group, which would later include St. Aleth, the mother of St. Bernard of Clairvaux, and St. Joan of Aza, the mother of St. Dominic.

During the early Middle Ages, most of the saintly mothers whose lives are recorded were aristocrats, like most of the female saints of their time. These women were able to command religious authority and gain recognition for their sanctity largely as a result of the powerful position of their families.[7] Typically they were noble widows, such as St. Monegund, St. Ita, St. Rictrude, and St. Waudru, who gave up their high place in society to enter religious life after their children had been raised, or royal mothers, such as St. Clothild, St. Ethelburga, and St. Sexburga, whose support of the church and influence over their husbands and families made their personal piety of public significance.[8] The *vitae* of these holy widows and queens did not always emphasize their role as mothers, but childbearing was understood to be an important duty of women of their rank.[9]

The eleventh and twelfth centuries produced significantly fewer female saints than the previous five centuries, and this decrease was matched by a sharp drop in the numbers of mothers who attained a reputation for sanctity.[10] During these centuries, when the church focused much attention on reforming and strengthening the clergy and the prelacy by an insistence on clerical celibacy and on ecclesiastical freedom from lay control, as well as on reforming monasticism, the religious models of the church and people were typically powerful reforming bishops and abbots. Women in general, and mothers in particular, had few opportunities to demonstrate their saintly dedication to the ideals of the Gregorian or monastic reform, and so achieve sainthood.[11] However, in the long run, as the reforms of the church deepened in the twelfth century, and as the ramifications of the ideal of a holy and pastoral church unfolded, the increased expectations of the religious life of the clergy and laity alike were to be of great benefit to religious women.

Recent studies have described the increase in the opportunities which began to appear during the high Middle Ages for women who wished to choose a heightened form of religious life. More women were able to find, or create, a space for themselves in the new monastic or mendicant orders, as recluses, or in more loosely defined areas, such as beguine communities, semireligious hospital communities, confraternities, or heretical groups.[12] A marked democratization and laicization of religious life made specialized religious roles and practices available to a broader section of society. At the same time, the greater emphasis in late medieval piety on such spiritual accomplishments as a humble life of poverty, service, or suffering, or the presence of mystical gifts, gave women who were not virgins other areas within which to aspire to saintliness.[13] These changes meant an increasing willingness to accept as saintly lives which at one stage included marriage and children, and indeed, the proportion of women saints, including women saints who had borne children, rose considerably in the thirteenth century.[14] The women who appear to have most clearly benefited from the religious opportunities of the late Middle Ages were lay women as a whole and lay and religious women from the urban middle classes in particular, and it is to these groups that many of holy mothers of the late Middle Ages belong.

The acceptability to society of a saintly mother is, of course, related to the value placed by that society on mothering as a role, and in turn to the value placed on the children who are to be mothered. This brings us to the elusive problem of the social norms and moral standards concerning parental duties which were endorsed by medieval society. What kinds of obligations did Christian parents have toward their children, and what sort of upbringing and education were parents who wished to be obedient to the church expected to give their children? What kinds of behavior toward children would have been incompatible with a holy life? These issues are one aspect of the larger problem of the history of ideas about children, to which social historians have drawn our attention in recent years.[15]

თ

Juette of Huy, the subject of this study, was born in 1158, in the town of Huy, situated in the bishopric of Liège, in what is now southern Belgium, and she died in 1228, at the age of sixty-nine.[16] The religious ardor of Juette's life should be seen in the context of the thriving religious culture of the southern Low Countries in the twelfth and thirteenth centuries, two of whose most notable fruits were the beguine movement and a flourishing tradition of hagiography, which took as its subject local, contemporary saints.[17] Juette's *vita* is one of twelve *vitae* about local female saints, known as the *mulieres religiosae*, whose lives were recorded by their contemporaries in the thirteenth century.[18]

The *vita* which records Juette's life was written in the generation after her death by Hugh of Floreffe, a canon at the Premonstratensian abbey of Floreffe, at the request of Hugh's superior, Abbot John of Huy.[19] The Premonstratensians were an order of Augustinian canons regular, which had had from its inception a strong commitment to the pastoral care of its neighboring community.[20] The abbey of Floreffe had firm links to the leper community of Huy, amongst whom Juette was to find her religious vocation, through the priests it supplied for two benefices there.[21] Hugh of Floreffe, who was himself Juette's friend and sometime confessor, insists on the authoritativeness of his account of Juette's life, and claims two impeccable sources: the abbot for whom he was writing, who had been Juette's last confessor, and Juette's female companion of many years, with whom she had shared many aspects of her spiritual life.[22]

While I am always aware of the impossibility of equating Juette's feelings and words directly with those attributed to her by her biographer (though these are of course interesting in themselves), I nevertheless feel that more can be gained from an attempt to discern Juette behind the words of her biographer than from a position of absolute skepticism about the possibility of recovering anything of Juette's own life. In the case of the *Vita Juettae*, I have found the analyses used in source criticism to be appropriate and useful. The sources of very many of the stories in the *Vita Juettae* are either indicated in the text, or can be reasonably inferred from the context. Apart from the numerous passages in which the author's voice is most clearly apparent, usually defending himself or Juette, the information in the *vita* can be divided into that which Hugh of Floreffe owed to his abbot, John of Huy, and that which he heard from sources close to Juette's own circle of companions and sympathizers.

The abbot's information about Juette appears in the *vita* still in the form of the questions and answers of her last confession. It is possible that John of Huy already had in mind the idea of Juette's *vita,* which he commissioned, at the time of Juette's last confession, and may have made a written record of her words. The abbot probed the more mystical, theological aspects of Juette's religious life, asking her about her mystical knowledge of heaven, the Trinity, and Christ.[23]

In contrast to the material provided by his abbot, Hugh also included much information which is shaped into discrete stories, each of which has a firm narrative structure. Many of these stories, particularly those which describe Juette's encounters with visitors, are probably traceable to the other main source mentioned by Hugh, the servant woman who shared Juette's cell. Almost all of the events of Juette's geographically very limited life could easily have been known to the servant.[24] Other stories in the *vita* may have come directly from their main protagonists, mostly spiritual friends, other members of the leper community or townspeople sympathetic to Juette.[25]

These stories would have circulated within Juette's group of companions, and would finally have passed to Juette's biographer in oral form. They often represent everyday situations in which Juette or sometimes other protagonists are brought to a dramatic climax of emotional struggle. The chief causes of distress and spiritual turmoil are sexual desire and avarice, and this gives the stories a somewhat novelistic tone. This is in contrast to the *vitae* of the other *mulieres religiosae* of the southern Low Countries, which seldom depict scenes with such a clear dramatic structure, tend not to feature scenes of temptation, and are also much more reticent in their description of the emotional power of sexual and economic motives.

I would argue that in the case of the *Vita Juettae,* these distinctions between the different kinds of material in the *vita* allow us to make hesitant steps toward the life and feelings of Juette herself. To begin with, we can be reasonably confident of the main outlines of the public, external activities of Juette and her family, such as their entry into religious communities. These events would have been public knowledge, and may be given greater credence than, for example, the details of Juette's stated motives for her actions. But I would go further and argue that we can also attach some importance to the emotional content of the stories told by those in Juette's circle because it is reasonable to assume that their perceptions were close to Juette's own understanding of her life.

Before turning to the *vita*'s narrative of Juette's life as a mother, I would like to explore Juette's own experience of being mothered. Juette's mother is a shadowy figure in the *vita*, who seems to have died not long after Juette's marriage.[26] However, we can gain some understanding of how Juette experienced and depended upon the motherliness of others by looking at her passionate relationship with the Virgin Mary. Juette was unusual amongst the *mulieres religiosae* for the intensity and intimacy of her devotion to the Virgin, as the spirituality of the other holy women was ardently Christocentric.[27] Juette's interest in Mary may be related to her own identity as a mother; certainly, she was the only mother amongst the *mulieres reliogiosae,* all of whom, except for the childless Marie d'Oignies, were virgins.

Mary's special maternal relationship with Juette was established in a dramatic vision in which Juette saw herself condemned by Christ to harsh punishment for her sins.[28] Juette desperately begged Mary to intervene on her behalf, and Mary responded by prostrating herself in front of Christ and asking her son to remit Juette's sin to her.[29] Christ, said to be unable to deny his mother, acceded to Mary's request, and then presented Juette to Mary as her daughter: "Mother, behold your daughter. I commend her to you as your own, as your special handmaid forever. Keep, protect, and guide her as your own."[30]

Mary fulfilled the role of protector given to her by Christ when she responded to Juette's anguished entreaties and defended her against the amorous approaches of a young man,[31] and when she responded to Juette's plea for help with a difficult and deceitful cleric in her community by causing him to be transferred to another area.[32] And finally, at the end of Juette's life, Mary appeared as a guide for Juette's journey to heaven. For her part, Juette fulfilled the role of Mary's servant by acting in cooperation with Mary in seeking repentance from and, failing that, revenge against the perpetrators of offenses against Mary.[33]

Juette's experience of the motherliness of the Virgin Mary, the perfect mother, was one of protection and guidance. In Juette's experience,
Mary was fearless in her efforts to secure the salvation of those who
dedicated themselves to her, even if it meant sharing the burden of sin
borne by them. Mary was also known to Juette as a mother who was
able to influence her son, Christ, because of her relationship to him.
All these qualities are pertinent to Juette's own relationship with her
children. She too felt that her ties to her sons, even after she no longer
lived with them, were strong and permanent; she too was confident of
her ability to influence her sons; she too would exert herself to ensure
their salvation.

The special closeness of the bond between mother and son is also
stressed in the *vita*'s description of the relationship between Christ and
Mary. Juette is described as being concerned that her devotion to, and
dependence on, Mary might involve her in neglect of Christ. Her biographer then assures his readers that Christ and Mary are so closely
associated that devotion to one is devotion to the other.[34] In particular
Hugh stresses the close connection of shared flesh which binds Christ
to Mary:

> For the mother cannot be honored worthily or truly loved without
> the son, nor the son without the mother. Indeed they are one in feel-
> ing, one in purpose, one in flesh, one in spirit, one in grace, one in
> glory, according to their humanity, I say, one and the same, flesh and
> blood, mother and son, Christ and Mary. . . . The one and the same
> having been conceived, born, and suffered, rising again from the
> dead, conveyed the flesh which he had received from Mary, above
> the stars to the right hand of God the Father, honoring every hu-
> man and especially maternal nature.[35]

Again, this kind of understanding may have had strong resonances with
Juette's understanding of her own role as mother, and the corporeal ties
that bound her to her children. The passage also demonstrates Hugh's
interest in using the example of the Virgin to present a positive picture of human motherhood. But athough the Virgin Mary was a powerful model for Juette of a perfect mother whose saintliness was expressed without ambivalence in motherly concern and protection, Juette
herself would find the Virgin's calm certainty about her role as a mother
difficult to emulate.

We meet Juette in the first chapter of the *vita* as a thirteen-year-old

daughter who was already rejecting the world by resisting her imminent marriage. Juette's parents had consulted with their friends and
relatives about the marriage of their daughter, but Juette already knew
of the heavy responsibilities of marriage and wished to avoid them. This
aspect of Juette's reluctance to marry is stressed, rather than the more
common desire to remain a virginal bride of Christ:

> But the girl, prudently noticing what she had not yet learned by ex-
> perience, that the law of marriage, the disagreeable burdens of the
> womb, the dangers of birth, the education of children were a heavy
> yoke, and considering, besides all these things, the unsteady fortunes
> of husbands, the care of the family and household and especially the
> labor of daily responsibility, she refused every marriage and she urged
> by what means she could, now her father, now her mother, supplicat-
> ing them, that they might allow her to remain without a husband.[36]

Juette was not able to resist the combined insistence of her parents
and the townspeople and was married.[37] She could not, however, for-
get the liberty of her unmarried life, and growing to hate married life
in practice as much as she had feared she would, she began to detest
every coupling with her husband.[38] Hugh of Floreffe's description of
Juette's unhappiness and despair at this time in her life seems to point
to considerable emotional disturbance. Juette focused her unhappiness
on her dislike of sex, and her desire to be free of her husband, who did,
in fact, die at that time: "From the violence of continual sorrow in her
spirit she began to grow weary of her life and falling thus into a certain torpor of mind, she began to have so great a hatred for the payment of the conjugal debt, that, in order that she could be free from
her husband, she seemed voluntarily to desire her husband's death, and
truly so it was."[39] Juette was later to experience great remorse over her
desire for the death of her husband, which she only slowly came to
understand as a sin of great magnitude.[40] At the time of her husband's
death, after five years of marriage, eighteen-year-old Juette had given
birth to three boys, one of whom had died.[41] Although the *vita* does
not mention Juette's children in connection with her depression, it is
not difficult to imagine that the changes and hardships brought to her
life by the birth of her children, especially since one of them seems to
have died during the period of her marriage, contributed to Juette's dark
feelings toward her husband and her nostalgia for her own childhood.[42]

If we look at the progression of Juette's religious and emotional life in a schematic way, we can point to a small number of clear turning points and stages of development. The death of Juette's husband was one such point, and was the occasion for her first turning toward God. After becoming a widow, Juette gradually distanced herself from her solid social position in her community by refusing to remarry and by impoverishing herself through almsgiving. In the most dramatic moment of her life, she took up a liminal position by leaving her family and giving up her social status to live in the marginal world of a leper community on the periphery of her town. Thereafter, Juette was drawn back from the margins toward the center, not by returning to her town but by attracting society to herself in the leper community. This movement was marked by Juette's enclosure in the institutionalized marginality of the life of a recluse.

The first of Juette's movements toward her religious life was her refusal to remarry after the death of her husband. Juette's father wanted her to marry again in order to continue the family line and inheritance.[43] She, however, is said to have been visited at this time by the Lord, who began his work of grace in her, and "she was suddenly changed into another woman."[44] Her steadfast refusal to marry induced her father to bring her before the bishop of Liège in the hope that he might convince her otherwise.[45] However, Juette's wise speech, in which she related that she had vowed herself to widowhood and, wishing to keep her vow, sought not to enter into any pact which would do injury to her prior agreement with Christ, persuaded the bishop, who then took her side against her father.[46] Juette's confrontation with authorities who wished to stand in the way of her desire for chastity, and her courageous speech defending her aspirations, link her to a long line of hagiographical heroines who followed the example of the early virgin martyrs who spoke defiantly to their pagan judges and executors.[47] The description of Juette's defence is notable for the details it gives of her emotional state during her ordeal: on arrival, she was confused and terrified by the multitude of officials and soldiers at the bishop's palace; while the bishop was persuading her gently and intimately to accept a second husband, she uttered a desperate prayer to God to help her keep her resolve; she confessed her agreement with Christ humbly and modestly.

After her successful confrontation with her father and her bishop, Juette also had to guard her chaste widowhood from attack from another direction, the solicitous and then amorous attentions of one of her husband's relatives. When it became clear to Juette that this man's concern for her had grown into passion, she spoke to him with great sympathy, but thereafter denied him her company. But one night, while they were both guests in the house of mutual friends, he tried to approach her bed and was only prevented by a visitation of the Virgin.[48] In addition to her involvement in this detailed story of thwarted passion and temptation, Juette stands alone among the *mulieres religiosae* of the thirteenth-century Low Countries in being described as having done battle with sexual temptation in the form of erotic thoughts, which she fought by castigating her body.[49] Sexual temptation is an important theme in the *vita,* which contains several stories in which Juette encourages others to continue in the celibacy to which they had committed themselves, warns them of coming sexual temptation, or admonishes them to repent of their present sexual sins.[50]

It seems clear that the rejection or patient endurance of marriage and the desire for chastity were, for Juette no less than for the large majority of lay female saints and those who wrote about them, important ways of constructing her struggle against the world. If we may see marriage and family as the heaviest of a woman's burdens in secular life, the responsibilities of domestic life are inseparable from, and symbolized by, the burden of the conjugal debt. The attitudes toward marriage, husbands, sex, and second marriage expressed in Juette's *vita* do nothing to weaken the power of the ideal of chastity for women. And yet it remains a fact that in presenting as saintly a woman who is not a virgin, and who is troubled by sexual temptation, Juette's biographer does present a sanctity which is not solely based on sexual purity.[51] At the same time, we must remember that the initiative for these changes came from those women whose desire to live a heightened religious life thrust them into the limelight, whose confidence in poverty, humility, suffering, and charitable activity as routes to sanctity demanded attention, and eventually, new attitudes toward the content of female sanctity.

It is certainly true that Juette's biographer is very much concerned to counter the kind of criticisms which might be made of Juette, and indeed of him, for imagining her life fit to record. Hugh's prologue describes how his reluctance to write was overcome by his conviction of the worth of Juette's life, and later in the *vita,* he defends vigorously both himself and Juette against those who consider sanctity impossible in a local, contemporary figure.[52] Hugh is careful to defend Juette's holiness when describing her temptations and lapses into sin, and takes pains to demonstrate the sufficiency and efficacy of her penance, and to present evidence of her heavenly forgiveness.[53]

Turning our attention again to Juette's early widowhood, we learn that Juette remained in the town of Huy as a widow for about five years "having responsibility for the house and for her sons, whom she certainly brought up as zealously as she was able in all fear of the Lord."[54] She raised her two surviving children until they had passed beyond the boundaries of "infantia,"[55] at which point she gave up one to the study of letters and the other, too young to study, she kept at home with her.[56] She was aided in her duties by at least one other woman, a servant who remained with Juette through her life.[57]

During this time, three incidents occurred that highlight the impediments to Juette's spiritual progress arising from her condition as a mother. Firstly, we are told of Juette's great charity for the poor, to whom she gave whatever she could, even pieces torn from her household linen, despite the fact that in so doing she was taking from her own children. This did not escape the notice of her father, who was afraid that the children might be dispossessed by this charity, and "indeed he took the sons away from her for some time so that she would have less control of affairs and would not be able to sell their right of inheritance without his knowledge, for he seemed to look after them as his own children."[58] The children were, however, returned to Juette after a short while, since she could not be without them for long, "because she loved them tenderly."[59]

Secondly, in another struggle resulting from the need to provide for her children, we are told that fearing "as much for her children as for herself, and wishing to take care for the future" Juette followed her father's advice and invested some money with local businessmen.[60] This was apparently a common practice, and Juette was unaware that she was committing the sin of usury.[61] She was distraught on discovering her wrongdoing, and her biographer takes care to explain why God allowed her to fall unknowingly into this sin.[62]

These conflicts of economic priorities, together with the subtler interplay of conflicting emotions, are also found in the story of Juette's rejected suitor, mentioned earlier.[63] The story gains new significance as an example of the conflict between the domestic and the religious life when we read that the young man, her husband's relative, developed his friendship with Juette through the children: "He, on the pretext of earlier familiarity, or pretending to care for the children and the widowed mother, used to visit her, and to speak with her as if to help her with her and her sons' family affairs; he used to show that he cared for them like a next-of-kin."[64] He became so indispensible in domestic matters that he was like "her right hand,"[65] until his disguised lust for Juette became apparent and caused her to banish him from her company. This story further demonstrates how Juette's responsibility for her children could seem to be a liability since it made her vulnerable to this kind of temptation and danger.

In all three episodes, the implicit message is that children are part of the pressure of the world which forces those who strive for perfection into compromise. These stories elaborate the theme already prominent in the preface of the *vita*, that Juette was indeed saintly because she was able to escape the traps set for her by the devil: temptations of the world or of the flesh, as found in the domestic sphere.[66]

Juette's remorse at having sinned through her usurious business dealing on behalf of the children prompted her to give alms even more generously than before. She also opened her house to strangers and pilgrims, and fed the hungry: pious work that she could carry out in the world, and yet all the time she was unsatisfied with the extent of her spiritual commitment.[67] Juette remained in the world for five years after her husband died, all the time wanting to be free and knowing it was not possible to perfect herself unless she left the world.[68] Finally, unable to delay her spiritual growth any longer, she went to live with and to serve the leper community that was situated outside the town of Huy:

> Therefore, when she had made arrangements for all her affairs and her house and her sons, and although all her friends and her father (for her mother had already departed from her righteous life a long time ago) were against it, she took herself to the above-mentioned place [the leper community]. As she did this, all the inhabitants of the whole town marveled that a youthful woman, who seemed to be in a better position in life, wealth, and age, according to the world, having spurned worldly glory, desired such great misery, even misery heavier than all miseries, namely to serve and to live with the lepers.[69]

Juette's biographer emphasizes the fact that her decision was made before leper communities had been transformed, through the work of such people as herself, into established religious communities; when

Juette made her startling decision, no healthy person lived with the lepers. By her actions, Juette created a religious life and space for herself outside traditional monastic communities, and her life is a testimony to the growth in opportunities for institutional religious expression for laypeople, and especially women, during this period. Juette may have felt that entry into a monastic community, given her family situation, was impossible or unappealing.[70] But she was also moving away from her family, as part of the established world which she pushed aside in seeking the liminality of the leper community, and indeed her separation from the social ties of the family would have contributed to her marginal status. It is rather poignant to think that Juette's journey to the periphery of society only took her as far as the edges of her own town. Perhaps she was not able or did not need to go further.[71]

The fate of Juette's children on her departure for the leper community is unclear, and one may be sure that concern for them formed part of the objection of Juette's father to her plan. Juette was now twenty-three. If she had had her first child at the age of fourteen, he was now nine years old, and if her last was born when she was eighteen, he was now five. The elder boy was probably already living away from home when his mother moved to the leper community. The passage quoted suggests that Juette left her children behind, perhaps with their grandfather.[72] There is no suggestion that Juette kept her children with her, and no discussion of the arrangements made for their welfare.

The little-explored issue of parental responsibility, or what may indeed be conceived of as children's rights, is pertinent here. We are aware of the debts that medieval spouses, joined by a sacramental bond, owed their partners, particularly that they were unable to forsake them for the religious life without permission. The position of children, however, is less clear. Studies on the child in canon law have concentrated on the delineation of the parents' rights vis-à-vis their children. It is evident that parents had the duty of baptizing their children, and that children of the age of reason (variously defined) in the high and later Middle Ages had access to confirmation, the eucharist, confession, and extreme unction.[73] The duty of parents to raise their own children, and the minimal duties that a parent had toward a child, beyond baptism, were not explicit convictions or concerns of the canonists.[74]

We are told that Juette served the leper community where she settled for about eleven years, eating and drinking with them, washing them and their bedclothes, and washing herself in the same bathwater which they had used. Juette was entering into a new life as a mother, with its own very maternal tasks. She identified with those she helped to such an extent that she wished that she could become a leper herself.[75] During this time a community of men and women gathered itself around her, whom she instructed with teaching and encouragement.[76] Having sought out the margins of society, Juette now became the center of a new community of her own.

The next step in Juette's religious life was her enclosure as a recluse.[77] This new move to a stricter religious life is made by the biographer to parallel her earlier withdrawal from family life to service in the leper community. Hugh of Floreffe reintroduces Juette's family into his narrative in order both to emphasize her freedom from obligations to worldly life and to construct the sanctity of Juette's new life through contrast with her former life as a laywoman. The place of the family is reasserted so that it may be denied once again.

The reappearance of Juette's family begins with her father. The biographer writes that God heard Juette's prayers and illumined the eyes of her father, so that he sought to amend his life. He entered a community of canons regular outside Huy,[78] but finding the discipline too lax, and that he was given too much honor from the other brothers, he took counsel from his daughter, and having obtained permission from the superior of his monastery, he built a cell in the side of the little church in the leper community where his daughter lived. He was never enclosed in the cell, however, as he then remembered a pilgrimage vow he had made and journeyed to Santiago. On his return, he entered a Cistercian monastery, again following the advice of his daughter, and after a time died there.[79]

Juette's biographer states that her father and the son who died in infancy were now no longer her responsibility. Nor, we are told, was her elder son, now aged about twenty, who had become a Cistercian at Orval in the archdiocese of Trier.[80] The biographer continues: "the devoted woman, feeling as if she were freed from all the cares of the present life, decided to serve the Lord under a program of a still stricter vow, and leaving off the service of Martha gave herself entirely to the part of Mary, which is the best, and had herself enclosed in the little cell which had been built next to the church for her father."[81]

The fact that there is no mention of her younger surviving son among those who are no longer a burden for Juette is ominous, and indeed, this prodigal son, now at least sixteen years old, turns up several chapters later, and his conversion, brought about through the prayers and tears of his mother, forms the most detailed and moving account of the mother-son relationship in the *vita*.

The biographer begins the story by stating that the devil, as he could not make any progress with Juette, sought to draw her from her prayers by working on her son.[82] The son, from the time of "infantia," had given himself up to a reprobate and frivolous life, and spent his time with youths of his own age, who were equally frivolous.[83] The prayers of his mother, however, saved him from greater harm.[84] Juette came to hear about the deeds of her son, and was distraught: "the mother wished that he had died or that she had never borne him before such a life should be reported to her concerning him. Yet she pressed on in her prayers, made herself wet with tears, prostrated her body, humiliated her soul, beat her breast, plucked at her hair, was twisted inside and out, an innocent mother for a guilty son: proposing two things, she desired one of the two, either death for herself, or life for her son."[85] The theme of Juette's horror at hearing bad reports of her son is quite marked: it is clear that those people who reported the son's actions to Juette felt that she bore some kind of responsibility for them, and that she also felt the burden of this.

Juette then asked all the friends who came to console her to pray for her son devoutly, and asked him to come to her cell to see her.[86] After she had rebuked him and cried over him, the son expressed remorse for his past life, but seems to have been mostly anxious to prevent the punishment that he feared would come upon him if his deeds affected the holiness of his mother's life. This sentiment is an interesting representation of the ambivalence a rebellious son felt, or was thought to have felt, toward the holy mother he both resented and revered. The son consoled his mother, and attributed his wicked life "partly to his youthfulness and partly to the partners of his crimes" and saying to her that she would henceforth only hear good reports of him, he "departed from her as an unhappy Cain from the face of the Lord."[87]

The son, however, returned to his old friends and ways, and hearing this from her friends, Juette was again greatly concerned: "tears came again to her cheeks, though the previous ones were not yet wiped away."[88] At this stage, Juette called her son to her cell, and ordered him to leave the province if he could not reform his ways; his obedience to her in this was a sign of her authority over him.[89]

The turning point in the son's life came while he was in Liège on the first leg of his journey into exile. He had a vision in which he saw himself judged to be fit only for hell, where his torturers attempted to drag his soul from his body by means of pitchforks and flame-vomiting tongs. The son was only saved when his torturers were ordered to stop by a messenger who revealed that the son had received a truce of three years from God. This dispensation, which is granted on account of the merits of his mother, is an extraordinary expression of the ways in which blood ties were perceived to be intertwined with spiritual ones.[90] The next day, he encountered a woman telling him to go to his mother. The young man "was changed into another man," his conversion echoing his mother's earlier experience, and immediately he returned to his mother's cell, and telling her all these things, announced that he wished to do her will.[91]

Convinced now of her son's conversion, Juette, weeping, raised her eyes and hands to the heavens: "thanks be to you, good Father, since you have heard the voice of your handmaiden and you have not wanted to disappoint me of the desire of my heart before I should die. Behold, now I shall die happy because the son of my womb has turned to you, my God, and will be left behind in your grace."[92]

On Juette's advice, the son joined the Cistercian monastery of Trois-Fontaines, not, however, before returning to school to learn to read. He soon attained the rank of priest, and died in the monastery after a long and praiseworthy life of penance.[93]

The story of Juette's prodigal son illustrates the kinds of close ties that bound mothers to their children, which both made holy mothers responsible for the moral lives and ultimate destiny of their children and made it possible for the sanctity of a mother to benefit her children. Similar stories, in which a holy mother is described as suffering for her wayward son, who is finally brought to salvation through her efforts, are told of the mother of Guibert of Nogent, of Birgitta of Sweden, and of Margery Kempe.[94] Suffering was increasingly a defining feature of sanctity, and helped make the role of motherhood, which could easily include vicarious suffering for a child, acceptable in a saint.[95] As Clarissa Atkinson has written, "Instead of blocking access to the sacred, motherhood made it available through sorrow and suffering, permitting women to share the tears of Mary and the pains of Christ."[96]

Further information about Juette's relationship with her adult sons as monks is found in the one near-contemporary reference to Juette outside her *vita*. The *vita* of Abundus of Huy (born c. 1189) records an incident in which Juette's ties to her sons are emphasized. When he was still a young layman, Abundus of Huy visited Juette, described as a recluse of great piety, in order "to converse about the good things of the Lord and about the salvation of his soul."[97] Juette understood that Abundus wanted to join a Cistercian monastery, and gave him this advice: "My son, if you desire to be a monk, behold I propose two monasteries to you, the first Trois-Fontaines, and the second Orval; choose one of the two and I promise you, in charity which is not false, that I will make your concern most certainly succeed with the abbot of Trois-Fontaines, especially since I am confident of the goodwill of the abbot toward me, and my sons who became monks, one in the monastery of Trois-Fontaines, the other in the monastery of Orval, ought to offer you their help, along with me."[98] This passage indicates how Juette's connections in the monastic world were formed through her sons. She is proud to recommend the abbeys of her sons, and feels confident that her relationships with the abbot of Trois-Fontaines and her two sons will assist Abundus with his desire to become a monk.

Juette's older surviving son was to be the only member of her family to survive her, and until her death she continued to express her concern for him. As she felt death to be approaching she sent for her son so as to be able to advise him: "And she also had her elder son, who as we have said was at that time the abbot of Orval, ordered through a messenger to come to her, wishing to persuade him before her death to be willing to resign his administrative office, because the authority held by her son had for a long time been very burdensome for him, although no one knew the cause of the trouble."[99] Juette's son was not able to come in time to see his mother alive, or even to attend her funeral, though her burial was delayed for three days or more in the hope that he might be able to come.[100] He arrived after the funeral, and was hardly able to visit her grave before being recalled by his superior. But heeding his mother's advice to resign from the office of abbot, he asked to be released from his duties, and obtained permission.[101]

In reading Juette's *vita* for evidence of her relationships with her children, it is impossible to ignore the numerous places in which her motherly affections and concerns for young people who are not her children are expressed. She had found new monastic families for her own children, now she was finding a new "spiritual" family for herself.

The main group of Juette's spiritual daughters were the other women, some of whom were still girls, who gathered around Juette in cells of their own. We are told that when Juette foresaw her own death, she "began to be anxious and to be more solicitous concerning her daughters, whom she had acquired as profit from Christ, each of whom she had, up to that time, nurtured very gently in the instruction of the Lord."[102] One of these girls Juette had adopted as her own: "There was indeed among the other virgins whom she educated in Christ, a certain young virgin, whom she loved, instructed, and exhorted in a unique way, above all the rest, because she had adopted her as a special daughter from her years of infancy long ago."[103] The girl, often referred to as "filia," is saved from sin by the prayers of Juette.

We have already seen that Juette was the person that the young Abundus of Huy came to see when he wanted advice about his vocation. It may be that Abundus had been a regular visitor to Juette's cell as a schoolboy. A story in the early thirteenth-century *vita* of Arnulf (d. 1228), a conversus who was Abundus's confrere at Villers, offers us some insight into the kind of relationship Juette and Abundus may have had: we are told of a schoolboy who visits a female recluse (his "magistra et mater") every day, and doesn't mind missing his lessons in order to learn of the "way of Life" in her "school."[104]

Young monks were also given motherly attention. Concerned about "a certain brother of the Premonstratensian Order, a young man who was commended specially to this saint as a spiritual son from his infancy,"[105] she spoke to him and "as a wise materfamilias, with the wine of harsh correction she mixed the oil of benign consolation."[106] Juette counsels "amicably and secretly" another young monk, who was a friend of hers because they were related, about his involvement with a young woman outside the monastery.[107] Perhaps Juette's friendships with these young people were seen as the "hundredfold" return of spiritual relationships promised by Jesus in return for his followers' withdrawal from worldly kinship ties; this is certainly suggested by Hugh's description of Juette as having acquired her spiritual daughters "as profit" from Christ.[108]

In conclusion, it is clear that Juette's attitude toward the condition of motherhood and toward her children as revealed in the *vita* was highly ambivalent. Certainly, Juette's children are represented as contributors to the temptation of the world which she had to overcome in order to achieve progress in her spiritual life. The biographer creates a context from her conquests over the temptations of her worldly life as a wife, and then as a mother for the spiritual victories which lead Juette toward her life as a recluse. For the writer of the *vita* and presumably for its audience, refusing to conform to the normal behavior of a mother and abandoning even quite young children for the religious life could be evidence of heroic virtue.

And yet the very fact that Juette's children could be the occasion of temptation for her was only possible if she had feelings of responsibility and affection toward them: there is no virtue in separating oneself from something that is not attractive. Motherliness, as the example of the Virgin in Juette's own life showed, need not be rejected quite as fully as wifeliness, and there is evidence of Juette's continuing affection and concern for her sons in the *vita*. This is particularly seen in Juette's anxiety over her younger son's soul, and her desire to see and advise her elder son before her death. The authority with which Juette advised and directed the lives of her children and her father was considerable: the power inherent in Juette's dual role as mother and holy woman was to prove irresistible even to family members who were at first recalcitrant.

Even such maternal concern as is communicated in the *vita* is not, however, without its own ambiguity. Juette's deepest expression of maternal love was in her desire to guide her children's souls to safety: that is, into the new spiritual families of monasteries.

Yet looking in another direction, Juette was able to retain aspects of her motherly role in her relations with her spiritual associates: motherhood in the world might have been far from a blessing, but as a recluse, Juette was able to exercise motherly concern and authority over the lives of her spiritual "children" to great effect. The practical condition of motherhood was a worldly burden for Juette, but spiritual motherhood held possibilities of blessedness.

Thus the life of Juette, as told by Hugh of Floreffe, gives us some insight into the phenomenon of the saintly mother, and allows us to explore the place of children and motherhood in the perfect Christian life. From a wider study of women such as Juette, a deeper understanding of the nature of late medieval lay sanctity and the attitudes and perceived obligations held toward children may be expected. In a broader perspective, the power of both Juette's rejection of the role of motherhood, and conversely the power available to her in the role of a mother, may be seen as further indications of the deep ambiguity of motherhood in the lives of women.

Notes

I would like to thank all those who have read and contributed to this paper, especially the late Father Michael Sheehan CSB, in whose graduate seminar at the Pontifical Institute of Mediaeval Studies it was first presented, and Professor Joseph W. Goering, my thesis supervisor at the University of Toronto, Robert Sweetman, Isabelle Cochelin, and Father Martinus Cawley OCSO.

    1. For an example of the use of maternal imagery, see Caroline Walker Bynum, *Jesus as Mother: Studies in the Spirituality of the High Middle Ages* (Berkeley, 1982), 110–69.

    2. Motherhood has been an issue of great importance and controversy in feminist writing of the twentieth century. Mothering has been seen variously as the source of the oppression of women, the source of the liberation of women, and finally the locus of the formation and continuation of the patriarchy. For example, Simone de Beauvoir, in *The Second Sex,* ed. and trans. H. M. Parshley (New York, 1953), and Shulamith Firestone, in *The Dialectic of Sex: The Case for Feminist Revolution* (New York, 1970), both presented reproduction and mothering as fundamental causes of women's oppression. Haunani-Kay Trask may be cited as representative of the cultural feminists who have found in mothering the source of women's beneficial and indeed potentially revolutionary contribution to society (*Eros and Power: The Promise of Feminist Theory* [Philadelphia, 1986]). Nancy Chodorow has argued for the social reproduction of mothering as greatly significant in the creation of our gendered society (*The Reproduction of Mothering: Psychoanalysis and the Sociology of Gender* [Berkeley, 1978]).

    The above writers tend to emphasize the universality of their understanding of motherhood, and so overlook the history of the institution. This essay is a contribution to the study of motherhood as an ever-changing historical institution, a project to which Adrienne Rich made a pioneering contribution in *Of Woman Born: Motherhood as Experience and Institution* (New York, 1976).

    3. For a valuable overview of the ideas which informed medieval motherhood, see Clarissa W. Atkinson, *The Oldest Vocation: Christian Motherhood in the Middle Ages* (Ithaca, N.Y., 1991).

    4. Three important gospel passages in which spiritual duties are placed above those owed to the family are Christ's promise that all who leave their families for his sake will receive a hundredfold reward and shall possess life everlasting (Matt. 19:29), Christ's warning that those who love their families more than him are not worthy of him (Matt. 10:37), and

his affirmation of the ties of spiritual relationships over blood ties (Mark 3:31–35).

5. The importance of sexual purity in the attainment of a holy reputation and eventual saintly status for women is illustrated in the statistical analysis of Donald Weinstein and Rudolph M. Bell, *Saints and Society: The Two Worlds of Western Christendom, 1000–1700* (Chicago, 1982), 97–99. Marc Glasser's article, "Marriage in Medieval Hagiography" (*Studies in Medieval and Renaissance History* n.s. 4 [1981], 3–34), confirms the importance of virginity as a saintly virtue, particularly in the early Middle Ages, while at the same time arguing for a relative increase in the acceptance of married women as saints in the later Middle Ages. For background to the high regard in which virginity was held, see Peter Brown, *The Body and Society: Men, Women and Sexual Renunciation in Early Christianity* (New York, 1988); and Jo Ann McNamara, "Sexual Equality and the Cult of Virginity in Early Christian Thought," *Feminist Studies* 3–4 (1976), 145–58. John Bugge discusses the feminization of the ideal of virginity in the Middle Ages in *Virginitas: An Essay in the History of a Medieval Ideal* (The Hague, 1975), 80–110.

6. See R. W. Southern, *The Making of the Middle Ages* (London, 1953), for the transformation of the image of the Virgin from a queenly symbol of dominion to a realistic model of devoted, tender motherhood (238–40); he also notes the intimacy and availability of the figure of Mary in the Marian miracle story which developed from the late eleventh century (246–54). See also Penny Schine Gold, *The Lady and the Virgin: Image, Attitude, and Experience in Twelfth-Century France* (Chicago, 1985), for the renewed interest in Mary seen in the iconography of the twelfth century (43–75), and for a general history of Mary during the same period, see Hilda Graef, *Mary: A History of Doctrine and Devotion*, 2 vols. (London, 1963), 1:210–64.

7. See Suzanne Fonay Wemple, *Women in Frankish Society: Marriage and the Cloister 500 to 900* (Philadelphia, 1981), esp. 97–106, 150–54, and 183–85; Jane Tibbetts Schulenburg, "Sexism and the Celestial Gynaeceum—From 500 to 1200," *Journal of Medieval History* 4 (1978), 117–33; and her "Female Sanctity: Public and Private Roles, ca. 550–1100," in *Women and Power in the Middle Ages,* ed. Mary Erler and Maryanne Kowaleski (Athens, Ga., 1988), 102–25.

8. Rombaut Van Doren, "Monegonda, vedova, santa," *Bibliotheca Sanctorum,* 12 vols. (Rome, 1961–69), 9: cols. 544–45; Albert D'Haenens, "Ita, monacha a Nivelles, santa," *Bibliotheca Sanctorum,* 7: col. 988; Émile Brouette, "Valdetrude, santa," *Bibliotheca Sanctorum,* 12: cols. 881–82; Rombaut Van Doren, "Rictrude, santa," *Bibliotheca Sanctorum,* 11: cols. 181–82; Alfonso Codaghengo, "Clotilde, regina dei Franchi, santa," *Bibliotheca Sanctorum,* 4: cols. 64–66; Filippo Caraffa, "Etelburga di Lyminge, santa,"

Bibliotheca Sanctorum, 5: col. 120; Hugh Farmer, "Sexburga, badessa di Ely, santa," *Bibliotheca Sanctorum,* 11: cols. 1007–8. For English translations of the *vitae* of Clothild, Monegund, Rictrude, and Waudru (Waldetrude), see now *Sainted Women of the Dark Ages,* ed. and trans. Jo Ann McNamara and John E. Halborg with E. Gordon Whatley (Durham, N.C., 1992).

9. Patrick Corbet has emphasized the value placed on maternity in the *vitae* of saintly Ottonian queens and aristocrats (*Les saints ottoniens: Sainteté royale et sainteté féminine autour de l'an mil* [Sigmaringen, 1986], 200–203, 262–63).

10. For the decline in female saints during the eleventh and twelfth centuries, see Weinstein and Bell, *Saints and Society,* 220–21; and Schulenburg, "Sexism and the Celestial Gynaeceum," 122. Of the eleventh- and twelfth-century women included in Weinstein and Bell's master list of saints, I have only been able to confirm that two women, St. Aleth, the mother of St. Bernard of Clairvaux, and St. Joan of Aza, the mother of St. Dominic, were mothers (*Saints and Society,* 252–76).

11. Weinstein and Bell, *Saints and Society,* 220–25. Schulenburg, drawing on the analyses of Jo Ann McNamara and Suzanne Fonay Wemple, links the decrease in the numbers of female saints during the central Middle Ages to the decline in opportunities available to aristocratic women within the family during the eleventh and twelfth centuries ("Female Sanctity," 119–21; Jo Ann McNamara and Suzanne Wemple, "The Power of Women through the Family in Medieval Europe, 500–1100," in *Women and Power,* 83–101; and Suzanne F. Wemple, "Sanctity and Power: The Dual Pursuit of Early Medieval Women," in *Becoming Visible: Women in European History,* ed. Renate Bridenthal, Claudia Koonz, and Susan Stuard, 2d ed. [Boston, 1987], 131–51; cf. Weinstein and Bell, *Saints and Society,* 223–24).

12. Caroline Walker Bynum, *Holy Feast and Holy Fast: The Religious Significance of Food to Medieval Women* (Berkeley, 1987), 13–30; and Herbert Grundmann, *Religiöse Bewegungen im Mittelalter: Untersuchungen über die geschichtlichen Zusammenhänge zwischen der Ketzerei, den Bettelorden und der religiösen Frauenbewegung im 12. und 13. Jahrhundert . . .* (Berlin, 1935; reprint, Darmstadt, 1970), 170–354.

13. André Vauchez, *La Sainteté en Occident aux derniers siècles du Moyen Age: D'après les procès de canonisation et les documents hagiographiques,* 2d rev. ed. (Rome, 1981), 427–48, 450–78; and his *Les Laïcs au Moyen Age: Pratiques et expériences religieuses* (Paris, 1987), 189–275; Atkinson, *Oldest Vocation,* 144–93.

14. Weinstein and Bell, *Saints and Society,* 220–25; Vauchez, *Sainteté,* 402–10, 427–48; Michael Goodich, *Vita Perfecta: The Ideal of Sainthood in the Thirteenth Century* (Stuttgart, 1982), 173–85.

15. These questions can only be answered by attention to medieval conceptions of parental duties in and of themselves. Much of the literature on attitudes toward children has been concerned with describing the progress toward modern ideas of childhood, and modern norms of the treatment of children. Some medievalists have argued that the evidence suggests an increasingly conscious interest in and concern with the socialization of children from the twelfth century onwards. See, for example: David Herlihy, "Medieval Children," in *Essays on Medieval Civilization,* ed. Bede Karl Lackner and Kenneth Roy Philp (Austin, Tex., 1978), 109–41; his *Medieval Households* (Cambridge, Mass., 1985); and Mary Martin McLaughlin, "Survivors and Surrogates: Children and Parents from the Ninth to the Thirteenth Centuries," in *The History of Childhood,* ed. Lloyd deMause (New York, 1974), 101–81. The above authors often link these changes to "progress" in the humane treatment and affectionate concern for children.

In contrast, Stephen Wilson in "The Myth of Motherhood a Myth: The Historical View of European Child-Rearing" (*Social History* 9 [1984], 181–98), has argued against what he sees as a "largely unsubstantiated orthodoxy among historians from widely different backgrounds, the 'indifference and neglect' thesis" (184), and urges that norms and behavior surrounding children and child-rearing practices be investigated in their social context and compared over time. Shulamith Shahar, in her *Childhood in the Middle Ages* (London, 1990), while arguing that changes have occurred in child-rearing and issues relating to children, denies that it is possible to chart parental concern and affection as progressing toward the modern situation (see esp. 3).

16. Hugh of Floreffe, *De B. Juetta sive Jutta, vidua reclusa, Hui in Belgio,* in *Acta Sanctorum quotquot toto orbe coluntur . . . ,* 3d ed., 70 vols. (Paris, 1863–1940), Jan., 2 (Jan. 13), 145–69, hereafter cited as *Vita Juettae.* A full discussion of the context of Juette of Huy's lay piety is found in Isabelle Cochelin, "Sainteté laïque: l'exemple de Juette de Huy (1158–1228)," *Le Moyen Age,* 95, 5th ser., vol. 3 (1989), 397–417. Another important discussion is in Alcantara Mens, *Oorsprong en Betekenis van de Nederlandse Begijnen- en Begardenbeweging: vergelijkende studie: XIIde–XIIIde eeuw* (Louvain, 1947), 384–402. Mens sees Juette as the prototypical beguine. Her life in the leper community, later to become a community of recluses, is for him an important indication of the origins of the common life of the beguines. See also Patricia J. F. Rosof, "The Anchoress in the Twelfth and Thirteenth Centuries," in *Medieval Religious Women,* vol. 2: *Peaceweavers,* ed. Lillian Thomas Shank and John A. Nichols (Kalamazoo, Mich., 1987), 138–41; Brenda M. Bolton, "*Vitae Matrum:* A Further Aspect of the *Frauenfrage,*" in *Medieval Women,* ed. Derek Baker (Oxford, 1978), 253–

73; and P. Norbert Backmund, *Die Mittelalterlichen Geschichtsschreiber des Prämonstratenserordens* (Averbode, 1972), 221–24. On Juette's name, see Elisée Legros, "Pour sainte Juette," *Annales du cercle hutois des sciences et beaux-arts* 24 (1951), 13–21.

As this bibliography suggests, there are many contexts within which to place Juette of Huy, all of which add to our understanding of her life. My aim in this essay is to explore what the life of Juette can tell us about mothering in the saintly life, rather than to suggest that my approach offers the key to understanding Juette herself, or that Juette's status as mother determined the shape of her religious life.

17. The groundbreaking works on the early beguine communities in the Low Countries, and on the spiritual milieu from which they arose, remain fundamental. See Joseph Greven, *Die Anfänge der Beginen: Ein Beitrag zur Geschichte der Volksfrömmigkeit und des Ordenswesens im Hochmittelalter* (Münster, 1912); Mens, *Oorsprong en Betekenis;* and Ernest W. McDonnell, *The Beguines and Beghards in Medieval Culture: With Special Emphasis on the Belgian Scene* (New Brunswick, N.J., 1954; reprint, New York, 1969).

On the hagiography written in the thirteenth century in the diocese of Liège, see Simone Roisin, *L'hagiographie cistercienne dans le diocèse de Liège au XIIIe siècle* (Louvain, 1947); and now Michel Lauwers, "Expérience béguinale et récit hagiographique," *Journal des savants* (1989), 61–103; and his "Paroles de femmes, sainteté féminine: L'église du XIIIe siècle face aux beguines," in *La critique historique à l'épreuve,* ed. Gaston Braive and Jean-Marie Cauchies (Brussels, 1989), 99–115.

18. Bibliographical information for *vitae* of the *mulieres religiosae* may be found under their entries in the *Bibliotheca Hagiographica Latina:* Marie d'Oignies (d. 1213), *BHL* 5516–17; Christina Mirabilis (d. c. 1224), *BHL* 1746–47; Ida of Nivelles (d. 1231), *BHL* 4146–47; Margaret of Ypres (d. 1237), *BHL* 5319; Lutgard of Aywières (d. 1246), *BHL* 4950; Alice of Schaerbeek (d. 1250), *BHL* 264; Juliana of Cornillon (d. 1259), *BHL* 4521; Beatrice of Nazareth (d. 1268), *BHL* 1062; Elizabeth of Spalbeek (fl. 2d half 13th c.), *BHL* 2484; Ida of Leeuw (d. c. 1260), *BHL* 4144; Ida of Louvain (fl. mid-13th c.), *BHL* 4145.

19. *Vita Juettae,* Prologus, par. 5 (146). Since Abbot John of Huy was in office at the time when the prologue to Juette's life was written, the end of his term of office in 1239 sets the *terminus ante quem* for the *Vita Juettae.* See *Gallia christiana,* 1st and 2d ed. (Paris and Rome, 1856–76), 3: cols. 611–12; *Monasticon Belge,* ed. Ursmer Berlière et al., 6 vols. (Maredsous and Liège, 1890–1976), 1:183; P. Norbert Backmund, *Monasticon Praemonstratense,* 3 vols. (Straubing, 1949–56), 2:373–78. On the abbey of Floreffe during the tenure of John of Huy as abbot, see V. Barbier, *Histoire de*

l'abbaye de Floreffe de l'ordre de Prémontré, 2 vols., 2d ed. (Namur, 1892), 1:109–21.

The *Vita Juettae* does not survive in any known medieval manuscript. A seventeenth-century manuscript containing the *vitae* of Juette of Huy, Lutgard of Aywières, Elizabeth of Spalbeek, and Christina Mirabilis is still extant as Stadtbibliothek Trier MS. 1179. The first edition of the *Vita Juettae* is found in *Lilia Cistercii sive sacrarum virginum Cisterciensium origo, instituta et res gestae,* ed. Chrysostomus Henriquez, 2 vols. (Douai, 1633), 2:6–83. The Bollandists published their edition in 1642 in the January volume of the *Acta Sanctorum.* Henriquez and the Bollandists used the same codex as a basis for their editions (*Acta Sanctorum,* Jan., 2 [Jan. 13], 145). That codex, now lost, had been lent to the editors by its owner, the Belgian savant Aubertus Miraeus, who recorded that it contained the *vitae* of Ida of Nivelles and Ida of Leeuw as well as that of Juette (Aubertus Miraeus, *Ordinis Praemonstratensis Chronicon* [Cologne, 1613], 171–72). The *Vita Juettae* was also included in a collection of saints' lives, no longer extant, listed as belonging to the library of the Benedictine abbey of St. Trond in 1638. The list records the "Vita Juttae inclusae Huyensis" in the same entry as a number of other thirteenth-century *vitae* from the Low Countries (S. Bormans, *Bulletin de la société des bibliophiles liégeois* 4 [1888–89], 38; Brussels, Bibliothèque des Bollandistes MS. 98, fol. 345v.). It should be noted that this manuscript history demonstrates the close relationship, at least in transmission, between the *Vita Juettae* and other *vitae* of the *mulieres religiosae.*

20. The interest of Premonstratensian abbots of the southern Low Countries in the pastoral care of religious women is demonstrated by the decision of the chapter general of the order, meeting in 1221, to delegate to John of Huy, abbot of Floreffe, and also to the abbots of the nearby Premonstratensian abbeys of Averbode and Tongerloo, the responsibility of incorporating an informal community of religious women into the Premonstratensian order (Barbier, *Histoire de Floreffe,* 1:109–10). Presumably, these women were themselves attracted to the Premonstratrensian order. Indeed, Carol Neel has argued that the active, charitable way of life followed by the lay sisters of the Premonstratensian order in the twelfth century was a precursor to the life of the beguines in the thirteenth century ("The Origins of the Beguines," *Signs* 14 [1989], 321–41). See also A. Erens, "Les soeurs dans l'ordre de Prémontré" (*Analecta Praemonstratensia* 5 [1929], 5–26), for an account of the Premonstratensian sisters based on the legislative sources of the order.

21. In 1226, Margaret, a religious from the leper community, used the alms of the faithful to establish two benefices, the patronage of which was given to Floreffe by the bishop of Liège, Hugh of Pierrepont, with the

consent of the prior and the religious of the leper community (Barbier, *Histoire de Floreffe*, 1:112). Margaret is probably the same woman mentioned in the *Vita Juettae* as leading a delegation to the bishop of Liège concerning the financial state of the leper community (chap. 55, par. 125 [168]). A dispute between Floreffe and the leper community concerning these benefices was mediated with the help of town officials in 1236 (Barbier, *Histoire de Floreffe*, 2:91).

22. *Vita Juettae*, Prologus, par. 7 (146).

23. *Vita Juettae*, chap. 22, par. 67 (158); chap. 23, pars. 68–71 (158–59).

24. *Vita Juettae*, chap. 21, par. 60 (157). Examples of the kind of story which the servant woman would have witnessed include those which give prominence to visitors to Juette's cell (*Vita Juettae*, chap. 30, pars. 88–89 [161–62], and chap. 31–32, pars. 90–94 [162–63]).

25. Examples of such material in the *Vita Juettae* include: a story which is told of a woman still alive in the leper community (chap. 24, par. 79 [160]); the story of a young monk, a relative of Juette, who held her in great reverence and commended her to others (chap. 35, pars. 97–98 [163]); and the story of a woman who was prominent in the leper community after Juette's death (chap. 55, par. 125 [168]). Hugh of Floreffe tells us he himself learned about the vision related in *Vita Juettae*, chap. 34, par. 96 (163), when hearing Juette's confession.

26. Juette's mother is mentioned at the time of Juette's marriage (*Vita Juettae*, chap. 2, par. 9 [147]), but she has died by the time of Juette's departure for the leper community (*Vita Juettae*, chap. 10, par. 34 [152]). By contrast, considerable place is given to Juette's relationship with her father and to his search for an appropriate religious life.

27. See Martinus Cawley, "Our Lady and the Nuns and Monks of XIII-Century Belgium," *Word and Spirit* 10 (1988), 94–128. Cawley discusses the *vitae* of Christina Mirabilis, Alice of Schaerbeek, Beatrice of Nazareth, Ida of Nivelles, Ida of Leeuw, Lutgard of Aywières, and Marie d'Oignies. His observation of the preference for Christocentric piety amongst those women also holds true for Margaret of Ypres, Juliana of Cornillon, Elizabeth of Spalbeek, and Ida of Louvain. None of these women share the warmth of Juette's enthusiasm for the Virgin.

28. *Vita Juettae*, chap. 15, pars. 44–47 (154). Juette's biographer opines that the sin for which she deserved grave punishment was her desire for her husband's death (*Vita Juettae*, chap. 15, par. 47 [154]).

29. Compare the vision in which Margaret of Ypres was assured by the Virgin Mary that her sins had been forgiven by Mary's Son. See *Vita Margarete de Ypris*, chap. 11, in G. Meersseman, "Les Frères prêcheurs et le mouvement dévot en Flandre au XIIIe s.," *Archivum Fratrum Praedicatorum* 18 (1948), 111.

30. "Mater, inquiens, ecce filia tua: hanc tibi commendo, velut propriam, velut ancillam perpetuo peculiarem, hancque ut tuam custodi, protege, et guberna" (*Vita Juettae,* chap. 15, par. 46 [154]). The passage echoes Christ's command from the cross that Mary take John as her son, and John take Mary as his mother (John 29:26–27).

31. *Vita Juettae,* chap. 8, par. 24 (149–50).

32. *Vita Juettae,* chap. 22, pars. 62–64 (157–58).

33. *Vita Juettae,* chap. 48–49, pars. 118–19 (167). Two of these offenses involved clerics fornicating in the collegial church of St. Mary at Huy (*Vita Juettae,* chap. 26, pars. 81–82 [160–61]; chap. 27, pars. 83–84 [161]; chap. 32, pars. 91–94 [162–63]).

34. A similar point about the interchangeability of devotion to Mary and Christ is made in the *vita* of Margaret of Ypres, though in her case it is Mary who is in danger of neglect (*Vita Margarete,* chap. 32, in Meersseman, "Frères prêcheurs," 121).

35. "Non enim mater sine filio, nec filius sine matre honorari digne potest aut vere diligi. Unum quidem sunt in affectu, unum in effectu, unum in carne, unum in spiritu, unum in gratia, unum in gloria, secundum hominem dico unum et idem, caro et sanguis, mater et filius, Christus et Maria. . . . Ipse idemque conceptus, genitus, et passus, resurgens a mortuis, carnem quam de carne Mariae suscepit, super astra ad Patris Dei dexteram transvexit, honorans omnem humanam naturam et maxime maternam" (*Vita Juettae,* chap. 22, par. 65 [158]).

36. "At puella prudenter animadvertens, quod nondum experimento didicerat, grave jugum legem esse matrimonii, fastidiosa onera ventris, pericula partus, educationes liberorum; et praeter haec omnia, casus virorum dubios, curam familiae reique familiaris, insuper et laborem quotidianae sollicitudinis attendens, renuebat omne conjugium: instabatque quibus modis poterat nunc patri, nunc matri supplicans, ut eam manere absque viro dimitterent" (*Vita Juettae,* chap. 2, par. 9 [147]). This passage is reminiscent of the antimarriage rhetoric found in the letters of St. Jerome, as in, for example, his letter to Eustochium (Letter 22, *Sancti Eusebii Hieronymi Epistulae,* ed. Isidorus Hilberg, Corpus Scriptorum Ecclesiasticorum Latinorum, 54 [Vienna, 1910] part 1, 145–46). See also Letter 54, to Furia (*Sancti Eusebii,* part 1, 468–69).

37. *Vita Juettae,* chap. 2, par. 9 (147).

38. *Vita Juettae,* chap. 2, par. 10 (147).

39. "Ex vehementia siquidem moeroris continui, coepit animum ejus taedere vitae suae, et sic in quamdam mentis acediam deveniens, tanto solutionem conjugalis debiti odio habere coepit, quod ut libera fieri posset a viro, viri mortem ultro videbatur optare, et vere sic erat" (*Vita Juettae,* chap. 3, par. 11 [147]). The *vita* of the seventh-century saint Waudru

(or Waldetrude), which was written in the southern Low Countries in the thirteenth century (but which may have derived from an earlier source), provides an interesting parallel to the *Vita Juettae* at this point. Waudru is a matron who also, like Juette, "began to have a great horror of the very coupling of the flesh" ("coepit ipsam carnis copulam valde perhorrescere"), and she "prayed . . . that she might be freed by God's will" ("ut nutu Dei solveretur . . . exorabat") from her marriage. Waudru's crisis is a noticeably calmer one than Juette's, and is more calmly resolved: Waudru's husband is filled with divine inspiration and decides to enter a monastery, thus dissolving the marriage. Waudru's *vita* is found in *Acta Sanctorum,* Apr., 1 (Apr. 9), 828–33; see chap. 1, par. 4 (829) for the extracts quoted.

40. *Vita Juettae,* chap. 15, pars. 46–47 (154).

41. *Vita Juettae,* chap. 5, par. 13 (147).

42. Compare Juette's situation with that of the women in Patricia Paskowicz's study of twentieth-century mothers who no longer lived with their children. Paskowicz's work suggests that these "absentee" mothers were more likely than other mothers to have experienced emotional and psychological illness, to have had unsatisfactory marriages, to have given birth to their children at short intervals, and to have had male children. As a group they were also characterized by a low degree of personal self-awareness and self-realization during the time they lived with their children (*Absentee Mothers* [Totowa, N.J., 1982], 125–37).

43. "Qui, ut posteritatis suae lineam protenderet, coepit pulsare animum filiae monitis quibus poterat, instans opportune, importune, ut nuptiis consentire, et per hoc amicorum suorum consiliis et voluntati acquiescere vellet" (*Vita Juettae,* chap. 6, par. 15 [148]).

44. "Subitoque mutata est in feminam alteram, et deposito vetere homine cum actibus suis, renovata est in agnitione ejus, qui creavit eam" (*Vita Juettae,* chap. 4, par. 12 [147]); see also, *Vita Juettae,* Praefatio in vitam, par. 2 (146). On Juette's refusal to remarry, see *Vita Juettae,* chap. 6, pars. 15–17 (148).

45. The bishop is said to have been well disposed toward Juette's father because of his position within the bishop's household as the collector of episcopal revenues, or "cellerarius," in the town of Huy. For further information on this office, see A. Joris, *La ville de Huy au Moyen Age: Des origines à la fin du XIVe siècle* (Paris, 1959), 421–22.

46. *Vita Juettae,* chap. 6, par. 16, (148). Randulfus of Zähringen was bishop of Liège from 1167 or 1168 till his death in 1191 (*Gallia christiana,* 3: cols. 875–76; É. de Moreau, *Histoire de l'église en Belgique,* 5 vols. [Brussels, 1945–52], vol. 3: *L'église féodale 1122–1378,* 677).

47. See, for example, Alison Goddard Elliott, "The Power of Discourse: Martyr's Passion and Old French Epic," *Medievalia et Humanistica* n.s. 11

(1982), 39–60. Juette's defence of her chosen life of chastity recalls similar scenes in the *vita* of the twelfth-century recluse Christine of Markyate. Christina explains to Fredebert, prior of Huntingdon, then to Robert Bloet, bishop of Lincoln, and finally to her betrothed Burthred, about the vow of virginity which binds her to Christ in a marriage which must take precedence over all others (*The Life of Christina of Markyate: A Twelfth Century Recluse*, ed. and trans. C. H. Talbot [Oxford, 1959], 58–73). See also Thomas Head, "The Marriages of Christina of Markyate," *Viator* 21 (1990), 75–101.

48. *Vita Juettae*, chap. 8, pars. 20–24 (149–50).

49. *Vita Juettae*, chap. 14, par. 43 (153–54).

50. See *Vita Juettae*, chap. 22, pars. 62–67 (157–58); chap. 24, pars. 72–79 (159–60); chap. 26–27, pars. 81–84 (160–61); chap. 32, pars. 91–94 (162–63); chap. 35, pars. 97–98 (163); chap. 40, pars. 105–6 (164–65).

51. See Clarissa W. Atkinson, "'Precious Balsam in a Fragile Glass': The Ideology of Virginity in the Later Middle Ages" (*Journal of Family History* 8 [1983], 131–43) for a discussion of the decreasing importance given to physical virginity in the later Middle Ages as greater emphasis was placed on the "spiritual" content of virginity. See also Glasser, "Marriage in Medieval Hagiography," for a description of the newly positive models of marriage which are being used by hagiographers after the twelfth century.

52. *Vita Juettae*, Prologus, pars. 5–7, (146); chap. 41, pars. 107–9 (165).

53. For examples of Hugh's defence of Juette, see *Vita Juettae*, chap. 9, pars. 27–32 (150–52) and chap. 18, pars. 50–51 (155); for an example of Juette's penance, see *Vita Juettae*, chap. 16, par. 48 (155). For episodes in which Juette receives assurance that her sins are forgiven, see *Vita Juettae*, chap. 15, pars. 44–47 (154); chap. 33, par. 95 (163); and chap. 43, par. 112 (166). Both the Virgin Mary and Mary Magdalen act as mediators between Juette and Christ: perhaps she felt that they, as role models for her own life as a saintly mother and a saintly former sinner, would be well able to understand her problems and anxieties.

54. "Sedit autem post obitum viri sui vidua in oppido annis circiter quinque, curam habens domus, et filiorum, quos utique educabat quanto studiosius poterat in omni timore Domini" (*Vita Juettae*, chap. 9, par. 26 [150]).

55. The term "infantia" is used twice in the *Vita Juettae* in reference to Juette's sons: here, to describe the point to which Juette raised her children (*Vita Juettae*, chap. 5, par. 13 [147]), and later, when Juette's younger son is described as having been frivolous from the time of "infantia" (*Vita Juettae*, chap. 19, par. 53 [156]). In the first case, the end of "infantia" seems to indicate the end of Juette's responsibility to her children, and in the second, the end of Juette's influence and control over her children. The

use of the term in canon law describes not the young child who cannot yet speak but the child of up to seven years (René Metz, "L'enfant dans le droit canonique médiéval: Orientations de recherche," in _La femme et l'enfant dans le droit canonique médiéval_ [London, 1985], 39–42, 46). This conception of "infantia" as the first stage of childhood, ending at about seven, was also held by many other writers. See Shahar, _Childhood in the Middle Ages,_ 21–31. The author of the _Vita Juettae_ may have this upper limit in mind as a point after which a child moves beyond the realm of the mother.

Juette is also described as nurturing three of her spiritual friends and companions "ab infantia." See _Vita Juettae,_ chap. 21, par. 60 (157); chap. 24, par. 72 (159); chap. 30, par. 88 (161).

56. "Susceperat autem ex eo tres liberos, quorum unum in albis Deo reddidit; duosque reliquos enutrivit, donec infantiae limites praetergressos, unum litteralibus addixit studiis, altero secum retento domi quia junior erat, nec studii laborem sufferre poterat aetas adhuc infirma" (_Vita Juettae,_ chap. 5, par. 13 [147–48]). Abundus of Huy, a close contemporary of Juette's children, and from the same town, was also sent to school "when he had attained the limit of the years of infancy" ("cum infantilium metam annorum attigisset"), in the first instance to learn enough to help in his father's business. Abundus first attended a school next to the collegial church of St. Mary at Huy, and then, at his mother's insistence, was sent to a school next to Neufmoustier, the community of canons regular just outside Huy (_Vita Abundi,_ edited in A. M. Frenken, "De Vita van Abundus van Hoei," _Cîteaux_ 10 [1959], 11–33; Abundus's schooling is discussed in chap. 2 [13–14]). See below for further discussion of Abundus.

57. _Vita Juettae,_ chap. 33, par. 95 (163).

58. ". . . abstulit quidem ei filios aliquamdiu, ut rerum minus esset compos ipsa, nec vendere posset jus hereditatis ipsorum absque conscientia, qui quasi pueros mamburnire videbatur" (_Vita Juettae,_ chap. 9, par. 25 [150]). In _The Domestic Life of a Medieval City: Women, Children, and the Family in Fourteenth-Century Ghent_ (Lincoln, Neb., 1985), David Nicholas considers the practice of appointing guardians for children who have suffered the loss of one parent amongst citizens of fourteenth-century Ghent (109–29). These guardians were normally nominated by the clan of the deceased parent, and were usually male. A mother could become a guardian only with the approval of her husband's clan. The guardian had the right to manage the child's property, its share of the dead parent's estate, and even to take it out of the custody of its mother if the circumstances demanded it.

This discussion is of interest for the role played by Juette's father in the life of her children. It seems that he is the most likely candidate for guardian of her children, either at her husband's death or when she leaves the world. If he was guardian at her husband's death, this would make it his duty to concern himself with the financial situation of his wards, and his right to take custody of the children. We do know that Juette's children received inheritance portions from their mother, because her younger son is given a sum over and above this amount by his mother so that he can leave the province (*Vita Juettae,* chap. 19, par. 56 [156]), but when this inheritance was divided and when it became available to the sons is unclear. Nicholas's demonstration of the considerable influence of the dead husband's family in the cases he has investigated helps to explain the story of the relative of Juette's husband who became closely involved with her household affairs (see discussion following).

59. "Quos tamen ei in brevi post restituit, eo quod diutius sine eis mater esse nollet, quia tenerrime eos diligebat" (*Vita Juettae,* chap. 9, par. 25 [150]).

60. ". . . metuens tam sibi, quam filiis cavere volens in posterum, de voluntate et consilio patris consensit in hoc, ut pecunia quae sibi proveniebat ex substantiola sua, publicis negotiatoribus accommodaretur" (*Vita Juettae,* chap. 9, par. 26 [150]).

61. *Vita Juettae,* chap. 9, par. 26 (150). Compare Juette's actions with the practice discussed by David Nicholas in which fourteenth-century citizens of Ghent would invest money for a surviving child at interest after the death of one parent (Nicholas, *Domestic Life of a Medieval City,* 111, 130–32). Nicholas suggests that the argument which justified the avoidance of usury restrictions in this case was that "children were incapable of increasing the value of their property themselves and that as 'innocents' they were not responsible to God for the sins committed on their behalf" (111). Juette, however, is described as having taken full responsibility for her own action after she had learned it was sinful.

62. *Vita Juettae,* chap. 9, pars. 26–30 (150–51). This incident took place in about 1180, at the time when the clerical campaign against usury, which was so marked at the beginning of the thirteenth century, was being prepared. By the time Hugh of Floreffe was writing in the 1230s, the issues involved would have been more clearly defined. See John W. Baldwin, *Masters, Princes and Merchants: The Social Views of Peter the Chanter and His Circle,* 2 vols. (Princeton, 1970), 1:296–311. The career of Fulk of Neuilly, who preached against usury in northern France and in the Low Countries from about 1195, gives us some indication of how the growing clerical sensitivity to the practice of usury was disseminated (Milton R. Gutsch, "A Twelfth Century Preacher—Fulk of Neuilly," in *The Crusades and Other Historical Essays: Presented to Dana C. Munro by His Former Students,* ed. Louis J. Paetow [New York, 1928], 183–206). On usury and

religion in the Middle Ages, see Jacques Le Goff, *Your Money or Your Life: Economy and Religion in the Middle Ages,* trans. Patricia Ranum (New York, 1988).

63. *Vita Juettae,* chap. 8, pars. 20–24 (149–50).

64. "Hic praetextu familiaritatis pristinae, curam se habere simulans filiorum et matris viduae, frequentare eam solebat, et colloqui ei quasi pro utilitate rerum necessariarum ejus et filiorum, quos intime se diligere ostendebat quasi proximus" (*Vita Juettae,* chap. 8, par. 20 [149]).

65. ". . . quasi pro rebus domesticis multiplicibusque causis, in quibus exhibebat se velut manum dexteram ejus" (ibid.).

66. *Vita Juettae,* Praefatio in vitam, par. 4 (146).

67. Juette's biographer states that she wanted to reconcile herself to God, who had been offended by her usurious business transactions, by first restoring to God, in his presence amongst the poor, anything which she feared was not rightfully hers. Only then did she proceed to offer hospitality and distribute food (*Vita Juettae,* chap. 9, par. 30 [151]).

68. ". . . coepit concupiscere aliquem solitudinis locum, ubi reliquum vitae suae tempus redimeret" (*Vita Juettae,* chap. 9, par. 32 [151–52]).

69. "Dispositis ergo rebus, domo, et filiis, invitis amicis omnibus et patre, quia mater jam dudum ejus religiosa vita discesserat, ad memoratum se locum transtulit admirantibus universis totius habitatoribus villae, mulierem juvenculam, quae in meliori statu consistere secundum seculum videbatur vitae, divitiarum, et aetatis, spreta mundana gloria, tantam appetere miseriam, et miseriam omnibus miseriis graviorem, videlicet servire, et cohabitare leprosis" (*Vita Juettae,* chap. 10, par. 34 [152]).

70. There was a great increase in the foundation of leper communities throughout France and the Low Countries during the second half of the twelfth century and the thirteenth century (Françoise Bériac, *Histoire des lépreux au Moyen Age: Une société d'exclus,* 151–79). These communities provided not only opportunities for almsgiving and charitable service to the laity but also opportunities for semiregular religious life. On the leper community of Huy, see Joris, *Ville de Huy,* 388–89.

71. Cochelin, in *Sainteté laïque,* points out the position of the leper community ensured Juette's continued contact with the citizens of Huy (398), and that in choosing the leper community, Juette chose a place outside ecclesiastical control, under lay authority (400).

72. Brenda M. Bolton in "*Vitae Matrum*" concludes that Juette "handed her young family over to her father and opened a hostel for pilgrims and guests" (258 and n. 39), although there is no evidence for this in the text. She is followed in this by John Boswell, in *The Kindness of Strangers: The Abandonment of Children in Western Europe from Late Antiquity to the Renaissance* (New York, 1988), 285, n. 44, and by Atkinson, in *Oldest Profession,* 165.

73. On the responsibilities spouses had to each other, see Elizabeth M. Makowski, "The Conjugal Debt and Medieval Canon Law," *Journal of Medieval History* 3 (1977), 101–2; for the duties a parent had toward a child in canon law, see Metz, "Enfant dans le droit canonique," 59, 61–66.

74. John Boswell's study of the abandonment of children in the Middle Ages emphasizes the general lack of moral or canonical censure of those parents who abandoned their children, suggesting an underlying absence of the conviction that parents had a particular obligation to raise their natal children (*Kindness of Strangers*, 331–35, 428–30). Thomas Aquinas focuses on the responsibility of parents to make adequate arrangements for the children they are leaving, rather than their duty to bring up their own children, when he objects to parents leaving their children for the religious life if they have not made provision for the children's upbringing (*Summa Theologiae* 2–2.189.6 resp.; cf. 2–2.101.2.ad 2).

75. *Vita Juettae*, chap. 11, par. 36 (152).

76. *Vita Juettae*, chap. 11, par. 37 (152).

77. The difficulties faced by widows in their attempts to find a suitable form of religious life, and the opportunities that the role of the recluse could offer, are discussed in Nicolas Huyghebaert, "Les femmes laïques dans la vie religieuse des XIe et XIIe siècles dans la province ecclésiastique de Reims," *I laici nella "Societas Christiana" dei secoli XI e XII*, Miscellanea del Centro di Studi Medioevali, 5 (Milan, 1968), 346–89.

On the phenomenon of the urban recluse in the late Middle Ages, see Paulette L'Hermite-Leclerq, "Le reclus dans la ville au bas Moyen Age," *Journal des savants* (1988), 219–258. L'Hermite-Leclerq points out that recluses were commonly associated with leper communities ("Reclus," 229).

78. Juette's father entered Neufmoustier, a priory of canons regular of St. Augustine, founded around 1101 (*Gallia christiana*, 3: col. 1002; de Moreau, *Histoire de l'église en Belgique*, 3:429–30).

79. *Vita Juettae*, chap. 13, pars. 39–41 (153). The Cistercian monastery was Villers in the diocese of Liège, which was founded in 1146 and often visited by St. Bernard (de Moreau, *Histoire de l'église en Belgique*, 3:400–409). Juette had a strong attachment to the Cistercian order, which both her sons and her father eventually joined. She herself wore their customary tunic next to her flesh for some years before her death (*Vita Juettae*, Praefatio in vitam, par. 2 [146]). For the pronounced female influence on the Cistercian order in the thirteenth century in Belgium, see Simone Roisin, "L'efflorescence cistercienne et le courant féminin de piété au XIIIe siècle," *Revue d'histoire ecclésiastique* 39 (1943), 342–78.

80. *Vita Juettae*, chap. 14, par. 42 (153). Orval was a foundation of canons regular until the count of Chiny asked Bernard of Clairvaux to send some of his monks to replace them (de Moreau, *Histoire de l'église en Bel-*

gique, 3:399–400). Juette's son, Henry de Satenay, was abbot of Orval from 1225 until his resignation in 1228 (*Gallia christiana,* 13: col. 628; *Monasticon Belge,* 5:200).

81. ". . . quasi exoneratam se sentiens a cunctis vitae sollicitudinibus praesentis, sub districtioris adhuc voti proposito mulier devota Domino servire disposuit; omissoque ministerio Marthae, in partem Mariae, quae optima est, totam se contulit atque in cellula, quam patri secus ecclesiam: construxerat. . . . se fecit includi" (*Vita Juettae,* chap. 14, par. 42 [153]). The fact that Juette was enclosed by the abbot of Orval, her elder son's monastery, suggests her continued connection with that son. The enclosure took place in 1192, and the abbot who presided over it was Remy de Longuyon. He appears as abbot between 1192 and 1197 (*Gallia christiana,* 13: cols. 627–28; *Monasticon Belge,* 5:196–97).

82. *Vita Juettae,* chap. 19, par. 53 (156).

83. Ibid. Some insight into the behavior of this wayward son comes from the writings of Guibert of Nogent (Guibert de Nogent, *Autobiographie,* ed. and trans. Edmond-René Labande [Paris, 1981]; English translation, *Self and Society in Medieval France: The Memoirs of Abbot Guibert of Nogent (1064?–c. 1125),* ed. John F. Benton, trans. C. C. Swinton Bland, rev. by Benton [New York, 1970]), who had a similar experience of parental deprivation. Guibert, who was very attached to his mother, felt abandoned by her when she left to enter the religious life, though he (later) understood that this was for the good of her soul. Guibert also notes that his mother's decision was publicly criticized and her motherliness brought into question. After his mother's departure Guibert's newly found liberty and perhaps his resentment against his mother and the church were expressed in rebellious behavior, which included keeping company with other youths of similar disposition. Guibert's mother, like Juette, was grieved at the reports she heard of his behavior and persuaded the abbot of Saint-Germer to accept Guibert into his community, so that he could be restored to the company of his former tutor (*Autobiographie,* 101–11; *Self and Society,* 74–77).

84. *Vita Juettae,* chap. 19, par. 53 (156).

85. ". . . quem mater vellet ante mortuum aut se numquam genuisse, quam vitam nuntiari sibi de eo hujusmodi. Instat tamen orationibus, rigatur lacrymis, affligit corpus, humiliat animam, tundit pectus, vellit caput, torquetur intus et extra pro filio obnoxio mater innoxia, duo offerens, unum optat e duobus, aut mortem sibi, aut filio vitam" (*Vita Juettae,* chap. 19, par. 54 [156]).

86. *Vita Juettae,* chap. 19, par. 55 (156).

87. ". . . causas malorum adscribit partim adolescentiae, partim sociis criminum, tamquam qui ipsum ultro allicerent ad vitia . . . eo quod bona

ei de se nuntiari posse non dubaret in proximo: et sic in corde et corde cuncta locutus, egressus est a facie Domini infelix Cain" (*Vita Juettae,* chap. 19, par. 55 [156]).

88. ". . . redeunt ad genas lacrymae, necdum prioribus plene detersis, rursus planctus, rursum clamores, rursum suspiria" (*Vita Juettae,* chap. 19, par. 56 [156]).

89. *Vita Juettae,* chap. 19, par. 56 (156).

90. *Vita Juettae,* chap. 20, par. 57 (156–57).

91. *Vita Juettae,* chap. 20, par. 58 (157).

92. ". . . gratias tibi, bone Pater, quoniam exaudisti vocem ancillae tuae, nec fraudare me voluisti a desiderio cordis mei antequam morerer. Ecce jam laeta moriar converso filio uteri mei ad te Deum meum, et superstite relicto eo in gratia tua" (*Vita Juettae,* chap. 20, par. 58 [157]). The prayer echoes the first verses of the Magnificat (Luke 1:46–48), and the portrayal of Simeon and his Song (Luke 2:26, 29–32). Juette's tears and faithful prayers poured out for the sake of her unrepentant son echo the tears and prayers of Monica, Augustine's mother. Monica is western literature's clearest model of a mother steadfastly desiring and working toward her son's conversion. Juette's joy at her son's conversion may be compared to that of Monica, when she too was informed by her son of the conversion which she had long desired. A passage from the *Confessions* 9.10.26, in which Augustine remembers his mother's words, is especially close in sentiment to the words of Juette. Monica does not understand why she is still alive, now that her hope in this world has been fulfilled: "Unum erat propter quod in hac vita aliquantum immorari cupiebam, ut te christianum catholicum viderem priusquam morerer. Cumulatius hoc mihi deus meus praestitit, ut te etiam contempta felicitate terrena servum eius videam" ("The one reason why I wanted to stay longer in this life was my desire to see you a Catholic Christian before I die. My God has granted this in a way more than I had hoped. For I see you despising this world's success to become his servant" [Saint Augustine, *Confessions,* trans. Henry Chadwick (Oxford, 1991), 172]). See also *Confessions,* 5.8.15 and 3.11.19–20 (for Monica's tearful grief over her son's unrepentant state) and 8.12.30 (for her joy at Augustine's conversion). On the changing understanding of Monica in Christian thought, see Clarissa W. Atkinson, "'Your Servant, My Mother': The Figure of Saint Monica in the Ideology of Christian Motherhood," in *Immaculate and Powerful: The Female in Sacred Image and Social Reality,* ed. Clarissa W. Atkinson, Constance H. Buchanan, and Margaret R. Miles (Boston, 1985), 139–72.

93. *Vita Juettae,* chap. 20, par. 59 (157). Trois-Fontaines is in the diocese of Châlons in the archdiocese of Rheims. Juette's younger son is noted as a person of holy life in a small number of Cistercian martyrologies

of the seventeenth century. The son's relationship to his holy mother, his misspent youth, his conversion and entry into the monastery of Trois-Fontaines are recorded. All this information may have been derived from the *Vita Juettae,* yet the additional detail given of the younger son's name Eustache, is not found in the *vita* ("Praetermissi, et in alios dies rejecti," *Acta Sanctorum,* Mar., 2 [Mar. 13], 253).

94. See Atkinson's sensitive discussion of the theme of holy mothers suffering for their children in *Oldest Profession,* 144–93.

95. We know that the practice of transferring one's merits, usually accrued through penitential suffering or illness, was current in Juette's area, as it is a notable feature of the *vitae* of the *mulieres religiosae,* especially those of Christina Mirabilis, Lutgard of Awyières, Alice of Schaerbeek, and Ida of Nivelles.

96. Atkinson, *Oldest Profession,* 192.

97. ". . . ut ei de bonis Domini et de salute anime sue colloqueretur" (*Vita Abundi,* chap. 4 [15]). For Abundus of Huy (*BHL* 18c), see Roisin, *Hagiographie cistercienne,* 34–38, and Albert D'Haenens, "Abbondio di Villers-en-Brabant," *Bibliotheca Sanctorum,* 1: cols. 33–34. The *Vita Abundi* was written by a confrere of Abundus at the monastery of Villers, probably Gosuinus de Bossut, during Abundus's lifetime.

98. "Fili mi, inquit, si monachus esse desideras, ecce duo tibi propono monasteria, primum Trium Fontium, alterum Auree Vallis; elige unum e duobus ac ego promitto tibi in caritate non ficta, quia negotium tuum apud abbatem Trium Fontium faciam certissime prosperari, precipue cum de abbatis erga me presumam benivolentia et filii mei unus in monasterio Trium Fontium, alter in monasterio Auree Vallis monachi facti sua tibi mecum prestare debeant obsequia" (*Vita Abundi,* chap. 4 [15]). Abundus, however, already had his heart set on the Cistercian monastery of Villers, and so did not take her advice. Father Martinus Cawley has pointed out to me that Juette makes particular mention of the abbot of Trois-Fontaines, and mentions Trois-Fontaines before Orval, even though it is her younger son who is at the former, because Trois-Fontaines was monastically senior to Orval, as its founder. Presumably the abbot of Trois-Fontaines, who would have served as visitor to Orval, would have had considerable influence over who entered the novitiate at Orval.

Finally, something of the attraction of the Cistercian order at this time can be appreciated from the history of Abundus's brothers and sisters: two of his brothers, James and John, entered the Cistercian house of Val-St. Lambert, outside of Liège, while his two sisters, Gela and Mary, entered the Cistercian communities of Val-Notre-Dame, just north of Huy, and La Ramée, respectively (*Vita Abundi,* chap. 1 [13]).

99. "Filio quoque suo seniori, qui erat tunc temporis Abbas Aureae-

vallis, ut praediximus, mandari per nuntium fecit ut ad se veniret, volens ipsum inducere ad hoc ante obitum suum ut administrationis suae resignare officium vellet, eo quod molesta ei dudum extitisset et gravis admodum ipsius filii praelatio, cum tamen nullus sciret molestiae causam" (*Vita Juettae,* chap. 47, par. 117 [167]).

100. *Vita Juettae,* chap. 56, par. 126 (168). This indicates some measure of the public estimation of the devotion or at least duty felt by the son toward his mother.

101. *Vita Juettae,* chap. 47, par. 117 (167). The superior was the abbot of Orval's mother community. The evidence of the *vita* is supported by other sources: Juette's son last appears as abbot of Orval in the year of her death and appears again as a simple monk in 1230 (*Gallia christiana,* 13: col. 628; *Monasticon Belge,* 5:200).

102. ". . . coepit anxiari et esse magis sollicita de filiabus suis, quas Christo lucrifecerat, quasque usque in tempus istud in disciplina Domini benignissime enutrierat" (*Vita Juettae,* chap. 45, par. 114 [166]).

103. "Fuit sane inter alias virgines, quas ipsa Christo educabat, virgo quaedam juvencula, quam prae ceteris unice diligebat, instruebat, et exhortabatur, eo quod in specialem filiam ab annis eam infantiae jam dudum adoptaverat" (*Vita Juettae,* chap. 24. par. 72 [159]).

104. Gosuinus de Bossut, *De B. Arnulfo Monacho,* in *Acta Sanctorum,* Jun., 7 (Jun. 30), chap. 4, pars. 33–34 (572). This *vita* was probably written before 1236 (Roisin, *Hagiographie cistercienne,* 32–34).

105. "Frater quidam Ordinis Praemonstratensis adolescens, qui specialiter Sanctae huic ab infantia commendatus fuerat in filium spiritualem" (*Vita Juettae,* chap. 30, par. 88 [161]).

106. "Quod ipsa intelligens, ut sapientissima materfamilias vino asperae correctionis oleum benignae consolationis admiscuit, dulcibusque sermonum propositionibus juvenem ad virtutis amorem, et contemptum vitiorum instruebat" (*Vita Juettae,* chap. 30, par. 89 [162]).

107. *Vita Juettae,* chap. 35, par. 98 (163).

108. *Vita Juettae,* chap. 45, par. 114 (166) (this passage is translated in the text at n. 102). "And every one that hath left house or brethren or sisters or father or mother or wife or children or lands, for my name's sake, shall receive an hundredfold and shall possess life everlasting" (Matt. 19:29; Douay-Rheims translation).

Gracia Mendes:
Power, Influence and Intrigue

Libby Garshowitz

HE 1391 OUTBREAKS OF VIOLENCE against Jews in the Iberian Peninsula and Majorca wrought havoc in Jewish communities. Many Jews were killed, many were willingly or forcibly converted to Christianity, and many more escaped to other lands. Many converted women (*conversas*), as well as those who remained professing Jews, were forced to cope with broken engagements, broken marriages, divorces, and problems with succession and inheritance rights. How could deserted *conversas,* left without a valid Jewish divorce, remarry according to Jewish law if they were not legally free to do so? If they did remarry without valid divorces, how could the children of their new marriages avoid the stigma of being *mamzerim,* children of an adulterous union? How could women collect the provisions stipulated in their marriage contracts if their husbands were converts, or professing Jews, or had fled to other countries, never to return?[1]

The leading rabbis of the time, Isaac ben Sheshet (1327–1408) and Simon ben Ṣemaḥ Duran (1361–1444), and the latter's descendants addressed the many legal difficulties these *conversas* faced.[2] Immediately after the 1391 mass conversions, these rabbis were inclined to treat *conversas'* marriage and divorce problems with great leniency; in time, however, they began to debate the actual "Jewishness" of all *conversos:* were they still forced converts, as they had been initially, or had some of them become willing apostates? The *conversos'* sincerity in maintaining their Jewish practices was a controversial issue among rabbinic authorities and professing Jews as the *conversos* continued to increase in number and began to flee to Christian or Muslim countries where they could either resume their Judaism or remain assimilated as "new Christians."[3]

A study of the *responsa* literature, which records the opinions of noted rabbis on important or difficult legal cases, shows that the rabbis for the most part displayed considerable flexibility in their decisions concerning *conversos* in matters of marriage and divorce.[4] They facilitated *conversas'* reentry into Jewish life by handing down legal decisions which allowed *conversas* who had been married under civil law to remarry according to Jewish law. The rabbis ruled that civil marriages were invalid, and defined the previous marital status of a *conversa* to be similar to that of a mistress. Since civil marriages were invalid, no *get,* or divorce, was required to end them, nor did the end of a civil marriage entail the obligation of an "unshoeing" ceremony on the part of invalid or disqualified *levir* brothers-in-law before a woman could marry again. A further consequence of the rabbis' determination that *conversas* who had previously married under civil law were free to marry again was that the children of a *conversa*'s new marriage would not be considered *mamzerim.*

In addition to their rulings concerning the marital status of *conversos,* the rabbis were also required to decide on the nature of the legal obligations which resulted from marriage contracts and wills made by *conversos* under civil law. The variety of local legal systems under which civil contracts and wills could be formed often made these cases complex, and capable of various interpretations. These difficulties, and the enormous practical and financial significance of such legal decisions, made the rabbis' task crucial for the community.

In this study, we will consider the legal position of the *conversa* married under civil law, and the nature of the rabbis' response to her situation on reentering the Jewish community by focusing on the fascinating life of a sixteenth-century *conversa,* Doña Gracia Mendes, a woman of immense wealth, power, prestige, and, as her name indicates, grace.[5] We will examine the social and legal context, and the finanical consequences, of Gracia's marriage contract, and the wills of her husband and brother-in-law, which were all executed under civil law in Catholic-controlled countries. The details of these documents, together with the rabbis' opinions on their legal status, are recorded in the *responsa* of a number of well-known rabbis in Ottoman Turkey, where Gracia finally settled and was able to live openly as a Jew.[6]

Our examination of Gracia's family and business life, as depicted in both Jewish and non-Jewish sources, will also shed light on the difficulties of the life of the crypto-Jew and demonstrate the extent to which crypto-Jews tried to integrate their secret Jewish lives with their outwardly successful financial lives as Christians as they moved about in Christian and Muslim societies.

Gracia Mendes Nasi was born in 1510, the daughter of a wealthy *converso* family which had probably fled from Spain to Portugal after 1492 only to face forced conversion in their new homeland. In about 1528, in Portugal, she married the son of another prominent *converso* family, Francisco Benveniste-Mendes, most probably in a grand public Catholic wedding ceremony suitable to their wealthy status. This very public ceremony may have been preceded by a private Jewish one as was the custom of crypto-Jews.[7]

The new couple's written marriage contract stated that should Francisco die during his wife's lifetime his assets were to be divided among his survivors, one half for his widow and one half for his children. This provision was customary in Portuguese law even if not stated in a marriage contract.[8] There is no indication in any of the pertinent rabbinic *responsa* that a formal Jewish marriage contract was ever written specifying the dowry, property, or gifts brought to the marriage by either Gracia or Francisco Mendes. However, if Francisco had signed a *ketubbah* as Jewish husbands were wont to do, he would have guaranteed the return of her dowry and the fulfillment of any other clauses stipulated by them in case of divorce or death.[9]

Some years after her marriage Gracia gave birth to a daughter, Reyna, who was to be her only child. Gracia's husband, Francisco, died shortly after, in about 1536, the year the Inquisition was established in Portugal. His young widow Gracia became executrix of his estate as authorized by her late husband's will and the Portuguese authorities.[10] She then became actively involved in expanding its business interests as was often the practice of Jewish and Christian widows who assumed control of their family's financial enterprises.[11]

Francisco had a younger brother, Diogo, who administered Francisco's, as well as his own, considerable business interests in Flanders.[12] Before his death Francisco had made the following will in Spanish:

> I declare that in all my estate my brother Diogo *has* one-half and I the other, a share equal to his. Even though mine *may* be more, he

helped acquire it; this was always my intention. I ask him only as an act of mercy that should he die childless he make my daughter [Reyna] heiress [should she marry][13] in accordance with his wishes. . . . Moreover, I say that with respect to his [*sic*] estate one-half belongs to his wife Gracia and two-thirds of the remaining half to his heiress, his daughter Reyna, and from the remaining third whatever disbursements are necessary to implement the terms of his will and whatever remains from the said third shall go to his wife Gracia [emphasis added].[14]

There is no mention in the will of Francisco's or Gracia's earlier marriage contract.

One can only speculate as to why the terms of the will are different from those in the marriage contract and why Francisco appeared to be directing his family away from Portugal to the care of his brother in Antwerp.[15]

When he married, Francisco was naturally concerned with the welfare of his future family upon his eventual death and wished to ensure their physical and financial well-being. With the rapid deterioration in the position of crypto-Jews in Portugal, he may have concluded that it would be in the family's best interests to leave Portugal for safer shores. Furthermore, he may have been ill and facing imminent death, and in that case he seems to have wanted his wife and young daughter to have the protection of his younger brother in a country more receptive to crypto-Jews. He therefore entrusted his family to Diogo's care knowing that Diogo, wealthy, powerful, benevolent to the poor, and, like himself and his family, a crypto-Jew, would look after the spiritual, as well as financial, interests of Gracia and Reyna.[16]

An examination of Francisco's business records sometime after his death showed that he indeed had been far wealthier than his brother Diogo. Both brothers had maintained independent and meticulous records of all their business transactions, Francisco in Portugal and Diogo in Flanders; yet it is reasonable to assume that Diogo managed most of Francisco's business assets abroad because the activities of the Inquisition in Portugal threatened the business activities of the *conversos*. After Francisco's death the total assets of both brothers were combined under Diogo's control.[17]

Soon after her husband's death, Gracia left Portugal with her young daughter Reyna, her younger sister Brianda, her nephews, João Miguez and Samuel, and perhaps some other family members, to join her brother-in-law in the Portuguese colony of Antwerp, which, in addition to being a comparatively safe haven for crypto-Jews, offered many economic opportunities: a booming trade in spices, a lucrative market in precious stones, and a prosperous money exchange, much of it in the hands of new Christians.[18]

With the transfer of her late husband's wealth from Portugal to Antwerp, Gracia soon became engaged in all aspects of these commercial enterprises with Diogo and helped to expand what Baron calls the "House of Mendes [which] became one of the great merchandising firms of Europe."[19] She continued to demonstrate the same entrepreneurial spirit, resourcefulness, and adaptability in living as a crypto-Jew in a new Christian society as she had demonstrated in her Portuguese homeland.

Gracia forged important business and social alliances with the leading banking families of Europe as well as its royal circles; nevertheless, she adroitly resisted all efforts by Charles V, emperor of the Holy Roman Empire, and his sister, Marie of Hungary, queen regent of the Netherlands, to form an alliance through marriage with one of these prominent families by refusing all proposals to betroth her daughter Reyna to a Christian suitor.[20]

Gracia's links to her husband's family were strengthened when her sister Brianda married Diogo Mendes and in June, 1540, gave birth to a daughter, Gracia (henceforth Gracia Junior, corresponding to the name by which she was known, *La Chica*).[21] Now that Diogo too had an heiress, Gracia took steps to ensure that both her financial interests and those of her young daughter were protected by asking Diogo for a signed document stating that he controlled the assets of her late husband's estate. Diogo agreed; he also confirmed in writing, on the back of his brother's will, that he, Gracia, and his niece Reyna were equal beneficiaries of Francisco's estate as stipulated in his late brother's will and that he was engaged in business activities on all their behalves.[22]

Since Gracia's ultimate goal seems to have been to return to Judaism as quickly as possible,[23] she attempted to persuade Diogo to leave the Low Countries for the Germanic lands[24] or some other suitable location; should he refuse to accompany her, she requested that he transfer to her control the assets of her late husband according to the division stipulated in his will.

Diogo gave Gracia a sworn undertaking to go with her within the year; if not, he would distribute the estate according to the terms of his brother's will. Diogo, unfortunately, died shortly thereafter, about 1542–43.[25]

In his own deathbed will (written in Spanish as his brother's had been), Diogo confirmed the terms of Francisco's last will and testament. He also stated that his wife Brianda should be paid only her dowry and any other assets established at the time of their own marriage from *his* half of the total estate. The remainder of his own half Diogo bequeathed to his minor daughter, Gracia Junior, who was his heiress since he had no sons.[26]

In his will Diogo appointed his sister-in-law Gracia as his daughter's guardian until she was of marriageable age and able to administer her own affairs and her considerable estate[27] and he also chose Gracia as executrix of the vast, diverse Mendes empire. She was responsible, along with two advisers, Abraham and Joseph, in all matters pertaining to the empire's administration.[28]

Diogo also indicated that he had thus far been satisfied with Gracia's, Abraham's, and Joseph's capable management of his business interests as long as Gracia was in charge: "In her absence [death], God forbid, Augustin Enriquez would step in." He added that no accountability was necessary.[29]

Gracia's business acumen and accomplishments during the short period in which she had been in Antwerp must have been sufficiently impressive for Diogo to have had full confidence and trust in her honesty and capabilities; nevertheless, he must have thought that the extensive Mendes empire required considerable management and therefore appointed financial advisers to guide Gracia in her control of all its aspects. He may also have surmised that the precarious status of crypto-Jewry would require the shrewd advice and financial talents of several people well-placed in royal and ecclesiastical circles.

The next episode in the Mendes family's saga demonstrated their vulnerability as crypto-Jews, constantly threatened by charges of heresy and judaizing, despite their power, social integration, and good connections. After Diogo Mendes's death, Charles V ordered the confiscation of the Mendes family's records and assets for his treasury on the charge that Diogo, though a baptized Christian, had "acted like a Jew, contrary to Christian law,"[30] the penalty for which was seizure of assets. In order to prevent this, Gracia used her considerable resources to bribe the emperor with the loan of a substantial sum of money, repayable in two years.[31] When Charles repaid this loan on time and accepted substantial additional bribes, Gracia left Antwerp and eventually made her way to Venice with her daughter, sister, niece, and other members of her household, leaving her nephew Joseph to complete any further negotiations with the authorities.

Gracia may have relied on Joseph's guidance and financial and social contacts to help her fulfil the requirements of Diogo's will but she was also deeply committed to the responsibilities which she had undertaken. She may also have sworn an oath, as widows sometimes were accustomed to do, which stipulated that she would faithfully carry out her duties as executrix of the estate.[32] Also, if there was any possibility that Gracia's life as a crypto-Jew jeopardized her ability to engage in international commercial enterprises, she may of necessity have been forced to display some compliance with the authorities.

The dismantling of the Mendes empire in Antwerp and the rapid departure of the Mendes entourage infuriated Charles V. When he learned of their hasty exit, he issued instructions that any property belonging to the Mendes women discovered in his empire should be confiscated for his treasury because all four women were "Jewesses," a more serious charge than that issued against Diogo, that of having "acted like a Jew."[33]

Through Joseph's intervention Gracia was again able to pay substantial bribes to the authorities, since Joseph, by now a very influential young man in his twenties, finally was able to persuade Marie of Hungary and her brother Charles V that the Mendes sisters were indeed "good Christians."[34]

Shortly after the Mendes sisters' departure, Joseph too left Antwerp for good without having recovered all of the Mendes family property. In July 1549 Charles V retracted all the privileges that he had previously granted to new Christians; soon the most recent *converso* arrivals from Portugal were once again in flight.[35] By 1546, the Mendes family were safely ensconced in the important mercantile city of Venice and there Gracia again encountered difficulties, this time from a perhaps unexpected source.[36] Her apparently ungrateful sister Brianda[37] denounced both Gracia and young Reyna to the authorities for wanting to leave Venice for Constantinople, where the benevolent policy of Sultan Suleiman the Magnificent toward repentant *conversos* would allow them to embrace Judaism openly. Brianda and her daughter, Gracia Junior, however, wished to remain in Venice as Christians. Therefore, Brianda requested that she replace her elder sister Gracia as guardian and executrix of Gracia Junior's assets.[38]

Both sisters were brought to trial before a special court which had jurisdiction over the affairs of foreigners. Gracia was asked to deposit "half of the fortune she was administering" in the public courts until Gracia Junior reached the age of eighteen, in about two years;[39] this the senior Gracia refused to do, stating that her brother-in-law Diogo had specifically appointed her, and not Brianda his wife, to perform these duties as long as she was capable of doing so. But the authorities upheld Brianda's claim, perhaps on the strength of their interpretation of Diogo Mendes's will, which bequeathed his share of the estate to his daughter Gracia Junior, and their desire to ensure that the young Gracia would receive what was legally hers. It is also quite likely that the Venetian authorities were reluctant to lose the considerable Mendes fortune to the Ottoman Empire should the family relocate there.

As the sisters' drawn-out quarrel continued, Brianda persevered in her attempts to dislodge Gracia from her responsibilities, while the latter deployed her agents in France in order to reverse the measures pursued in Venice.[40] Brianda instructed her agent in France, a non-Jew, described as "an absolutely wicked person in everyone's opinion and a well-known informer against the Jews,"[41] to expropriate a substantial sum of money from the general capital of the estate for Gracia Junior, claiming that it was rightfully part of her daughter's inheritance. The agent, dissatisfied with his remuneration for his role in this controversy, returned to France and denounced both sisters and their daughters to the authorities as Jews.

Once again, through the mediation of powerful Venetian and Turkish authorities, Gracia paid considerable bribes, this time to Henry II of France, in order to release her assets in that country and to win her freedom in Venice, for she had been detained by the authorities there as a result of her sister's civil suit against her.[42] After her release, Gracia and her daughter Reyna went to Ferrara and in 1552 they arrived with great pomp and ceremony in Constantinople. There they were finally able to practice Judaism openly and soon came into contact with other influential Jewish women who served both the Jewish and Turkish communities. In 1554 Reyna married her cousin Joseph Nasi, most likely in a public Jewish wedding ceremony.[43]

The end of Gracia's and Reyna's lengthy journey as crypto-Jews introduced the next phase of their lives: their entrance into the large Jewish community of Constantinople as proud, enormously wealthy Jewish women who became as actively involved in their new community's affairs as they had been in their previous countries of residence.[44]

Gracia's assumption of a powerful leadership role in the Jewish community involved her ongoing efforts to rescue *conversos,* the running of what Roth has termed "an underground railway,"[45] her part in the controversial boycott of Ancona, the funding and support of synagogues and various academies of learning, and many other philanthropic acts. But Gracia also served the Ottoman rulers, extending her sphere of influence to their courts; they were quite happy to benefit from the formidable Mendes wealth.[46] Gracia, with Joseph's aid, continued to expand the business empire in money, spices, and the shipping of goods; she also became very active in the textile trade.[47]

Notwithstanding her many financial and social successes in her new homeland, Gracia's recurring disputes with Brianda concerning the Mendes estate needed to be settled. Gracia again sought advice, this time from the rabbis.[48]

The key task which confronted the rabbinic authorities in their decisions concerning the Mendes estate was the resolution of the conflicting provisions of the Mendes nuptial agreement and later will, both written in the civil courts in Portugal. The conflict was now to be adjudicated by Jewish law which had its own specific requirements for the maintenance of widows from their dowries, from the provisions of their nuptial agreements, and from their husbands' wills and testaments, as well as safeguards for widows who engaged in business.

As previously mentioned, Francisco, at the time of his marriage, had made a written commitment to his wife Gracia that in the event of his death she would share equally with their children in his estate. However, in his will, written some years later, he divided his estate equally between his wife and his brother.[49]

In her petition to the rabbinic authorities, Gracia stated that Francisco did not have the legal right to change the terms stipulated in their marriage agreement, which benefited her and her daughter, to those in his will which would ultimately benefit his brother Diogo's estate.

Before they could address the specific issues of the Mendes estate, the rabbis had to determine the validity of Gracia's and Francisco's civil marriage agreement. This was particularly important now that Gracia was a widow, and could not avail herself of the opportunity open to *converso* couples who wished to rejoin Judaism to redress their earlier civil contracts.

To be recognized as legally binding, a Jewish marriage traditionally required a written marriage contract (*ketubbah*) designating dowry, gifts, and other property settlements agreed upon by bride and groom, a symbolic transfer of goods, the traditional marriage formula customarily pronounced by the groom before qualified witnesses, and his gift of a ring to his bride.[50]

After 1391, when the new phenomenon of a rapidly increasing crypto-Jewry challenged rabbinical authorities to reintegrate true *conversos* into Jewish society, we have already noted that most rabbis proved quite flexible in aiding crypto-Jews in matters of marriage and divorce. Now, more than a century later, the rabbinic authorities in the Ottoman empire were called upon to render decisions based on the reconciliation of Jewish law and civil practices enacted in a Catholic country. They made the following observations.

First, in a Catholic wedding ceremony, entered into by many *conversos* in the presence of reliable *converso* witnesses, the rabbis noted that the officiating priest might have blessed the couple and given them the customary ring and followed all the proper procedures for a valid marriage ceremony. Second, since the *converso* couple married in a Catholic ceremony they could neither separate nor divorce, because in the eyes of the Catholic church marriage was indissoluble and should the *conversa* attempt to remarry she might be liable to censure as an adulteress.[51] Third, a *conversa* who left her husband voluntarily could not remarry since she was considered to be a married woman. Therefore, in all these circumstances the rabbis regarded as valid the *converso* marriage, contracted in good faith between the consenting parties according to proper civil or ecclesiastical procedures.

However, a Catholic marriage did not fulfill the requirements of a legally binding Jewish wedding and was, in the rabbis' opinion, invalid, thus supporting their predecessors' decisions that a *conversa* wife was an unmarried woman according to Jewish law; she would then be free to remarry according to Jewish observance and would not require a *get*.

When *conversos* (re)turned to Judaism, the rabbis would write them a new marriage contract according to Jewish law. Even if they remarried according to Jewish law without a new contract, their civil marriage became invalid. However, their original marriage contract remained valid, since marriage and business agreements contracted in civil courts were treated equally according to the principles that "the [secular] law of the land is legal and binding" and "custom supersedes law."[52]

Since a *ketubbah* was regarded as a legal business contract between man and wife similar to business contracts drawn up in civil courts, a document contracted in civil courts was considered valid. This included the *ṣadāq,* a marriage document drawn up under Muslim law which did not recognize the Jewish *ketubbah.*[53]

The rabbis' confirmation that business contracts transacted by Jews and *conversos,* wherever they lived, were valid strengthened Gracia's claim that according to the nuptial agreement she and Francisco had made in Portugal, she was entitled to half of Francisco's considerable estate and this is the decision Moses de Trani made.

But de Trani also stated that this was not as clear-cut a decision as it seemed, since all the assets had been combined after Francisco's death and the financial empire had been considerably enlarged since then. Therefore, de Trani ruled that, all things considered, Gracia was entitled to half the combined estate as her husband had stipulated in his will,[54] and not the entire estate, for the following reasons.

When Francisco and Gracia had married, their nuptial agreement stipulated that Francisco's assets were to be divided equally between his wife and their children should his death precede hers. It did not concern the future division of the entire estate between his widow and his brother as stipulated in his will. In de Trani's opinion, Francisco had made this particular provision not to empower Gracia or to disown his surviving children but to provide all of them with an equal share in what remained of his estate after the necessary disbursements and charitable donations had been made.[55]

According to de Trani, Francisco could freely distribute from his own assets gifts to relatives or charities as was the prevailing custom. Neither his children nor his wife could prevent him from making bequests to whomever he wanted during his lifetime nor after his death from "what God had entrusted to him."[56]

Despite Gracia's claim that according to Portuguese civil law a testator could not will his property to others if he had surviving sons and daughters, in this case a sole surviving daughter, Reyna,[57] de Trani ruled that half the estate was rightfully Diogo's according to the terms of Francisco's will and that Francisco's bequest to his brother stood in spite of the civil custom to divide the estate between widow and heirs. Just as marriage contracts enacted in civil courts were to be honored, so were wills.

De Trani also did not regard Francisco's bequest to his brother Diogo of half his estate as the gift of a mortally ill person in anticipation of imminent death,[58] but an admission, freely stated, that his younger brother had helped acquire their wealth and therefore Francisco had always intended to reward his brother for being an active and faithful partner in expanding the family's estate and assets.[59] Perhaps there had even been a silent partnership agreement between them and when Francisco wrote his will he "put into words what he had always felt in his heart."[60]

De Trani noted that it was highly unlikely that a testator would divert what rightfully belonged to his heirs to others without a legitimate reason. To ensure the younger Diogo's continued business integrity and to protect his young—and perhaps inexperienced—wife and daughter from fraud, Francisco had intentionally planned to make the independently wealthy Diogo beneficiary to half his estate since there was no one more qualified or experienced than Diogo. Francisco's request that Diogo make his daughter Reyna his own beneficiary should Diogo die without issue was further proof that he had always intended his brother to benefit equally with his wife and daughter.

De Trani commended Francisco's actions as particularly astute since Diogo's honesty in the administration of the Mendes empire would be hard to prove since he could always claim that the loss of precious cargo or some other business mishap had exhausted much of the estate's assets.

De Trani also concurred with Gracia's claim that she had not known the extent of Francisco's or Diogo's estates until after their deaths and agreed with Gracia's assessment of the situation regarding Gracia Junior, that the young heiress was still a minor and incapable of handling responsibilities for the administration of Diogo's share of the estate.

Gracia Junior charged that her aunt Gracia should have protested and prevented her uncle Francisco's changes to their nuptial agreement when he wrote his will in Portugal many years earlier and that her failure to do so, along with her long silence (about twelve years), could be construed as tacit approval of Francisco's change of mind as well as his departure from the requirements of civil law. Gracia replied that she had not known the details of her late husband's will; she claimed that he had withheld them from her, giving her a sealed document which she had deposited for safekeeping. She had complied with her husband's desire for secrecy and had not known the contents of his will until after his death.

De Trani, however, faulted Gracia for not having reviewed the terms of Francisco's will with him; since she had not and the custom for those who married with or without nuptial agreements was not firmly fixed, Francisco could legally bequeath half his estate to his brother. De Trani may have been guided in this aspect of his decision because Diogo's own will, most likely executed in Antwerp, a Portuguese possession, had stipulated that his widow, Brianda, was to be paid only her dowry, not half his estate, which was consistent with Jewish law.[61]

Regarding Reyna's share of the assets which were under Diogo's administration, de Trani ruled that Gracia had not asked Diogo to transfer them to her when she requested that he leave Antwerp with her, implying that she had no right to claim Reyna's inheritance from Diogo or his own daughter Gracia Junior.

In his decision, de Trani also noted that Francisco did not use the proper legal terminology, "gives" (*noten*) or "leaves" (*manniaḥ*), in willing his assets to his widow; rather, he stated "that his brother has (*tiene*) half his estate," a share equal to his own, "even though mine *may* be more," and that his widow and his brother were to share the estate equally.[62]

Regarding Gracia's concerns about the considerable expenses which she had incurred to save the family's assets in the Netherlands, de Trani ruled that Charles V's initial order to sequester the assets of the Mendes estate applied only to Diogo's assets and not those of his wife Brianda or his sister-in-law Gracia, since it was Diogo who had been denounced as "acting like a Jew." Therefore, the expenses incurred to save Diogo's property were to be deducted solely from his daughter Gracia Junior's share of the estate. However, since eventually all four women were denounced as "Jewesses" and had fled the country to take refuge elsewhere, then everyone was to share the expenses accumulated to recover the entire estate since all were beneficiaries.

De Trani praised Gracia's exemplary generosity for having chosen to protect the entire estate under her control rather than just her and her daughter's share, which could have been done with a minimum outlay of money.[63]

Regarding the considerable expenses because of Brianda's denunciations of Gracia on several occasions, de Trani ruled that Brianda was liable for these costs. To have granted Brianda's requests would have been contrary to Diogo's express wishes regarding the administration of the estate and the guardianship of his daughter.

Joseph ibn Lev, chief teacher at the academy founded by Gracia in Constantinople and the recipient of much of Gracia's benevolence, was the first to be consulted in the dispute over Francisco Mendes's will. He concurred with Moses de Trani's decision to award Gracia half the estate, as did Samuel de Medina. Both concluded that a marriage contracted legally according to civil law was valid with respect to dowry, *ketubbah,* and property rights.[64]

Ibn Lev went further than his colleagues stating that even if the assets were controlled by the heirs apparent, presumably Reyna and her spouse Joseph Nasi and Gracia Junior and her spouse Samuel Nasi,[65] the estate should be taken from them and awarded to Gracia.

Despite the rabbis' adamant and universal condemnation of the actions Brianda had taken against her sister in non-Jewish courts, they ruled that Brianda was not liable for the actions of her French agent because he had acted solely on his own initiative. Wherever they held Brianda financially responsible for expenses, the rabbis decided that if her dowry was insufficient to meet these costs, the funds were to be deducted from Gracia Junior's estate and she in turn could claim them from her mother under more favorable circumstances.[66]

The rabbis unanimously praised Gracia's success in preventing Diogo's funds from falling into the hands of the church or the various rulers with whom she had had financial transactions. Had Gracia not been able to protect the estate, Gracia Junior, in the rabbis' opinion, would have been forced to live as a Christian in a Christian environment, a situation that was to be avoided at all costs since the thrust of Francisco's and Diogo's wills, as well as the flight of the Mendes family to different countries, had been to safeguard their lives as crypto-Jews until they could resume their Jewish identities and practices openly, away from the eyes of the Inquisition and the Catholic church into which they had been baptized. The rabbis compared Gracia's success in avoiding intermarriage with "old Christian" families to having saved a life.[67]

The rabbinic authorities' flexibility in facilitating the reentry and integration of the Mendes family, as well as thousands of other *conversos,* into Jewish communities as Jews demonstrates the realistic grasp they had of the lives of true crypto-Jews; had they not been responsive to the unprecedented number of crypto-Jews enduring the consequences of the Inquisition's legitimate charges of heresy against them, many would have been lost to Judaism forever, as were many of their brethren who, for whatever reason, continued to live as *conversos* or who eventually chose to become fully integrated into Christian society. Indeed, many of Gracia's and Joseph's own agents and associates continued to live as new Christians.[68]

If, however, it appears that the rabbis deliberately chose to ignore the fact that the Mendes family, ostensibly devout Christians, had not abided by the decisions of earlier rabbinic authorities who had stated that converts must leave the Christian countries which had coerced them to abandon Judaism and not remain there because of financial considerations,[69] it must be remembered that the Mendes family, and Gracia especially, were devoted to their Jewish heritage. That heritage of which Gracia had been openly deprived for so many decades imbued her with the necessary strength and devotion to use her affluence and power to help disadvantaged *conversos*.

No less an authority than Joshua Soncino, Gracia's erstwhile opponent in the matter of the Ancona boycott, referred to her as: "the crowned gentlewoman, the glorious diadem of Israel's multitudes, stately vine, crowning glory, beautiful garland and royal mitre, the wisest of women built Israel's house in pure holiness; with her strength and treasures she extended a hand to the poor in order to rescue them and make them content, in this world and the next."[70]

But not all of the rabbinic authorities agreed with the decision to award half of the total Mendes estate to Gracia Senior. The one notable exception was Joseph Karo, who especially singled out Moses de Trani as having erred in his deliberations. Karo ruled that both Francisco's and Gracia's nuptial agreement and Francisco's will were invalid and that Reyna, her daughter, was the heiress to the entire Mendes estate.[71]

According to Karo, when *conversos* (re)turned to Judaism their civil marriage was invalid because marriage and business contracts in civil law were not analogous with Jewish law. The legal requirements of acquisition through *meshikhah* or *'aggav*, however symbolic these practices might be, had not been fulfilled.[72] Furthermore, in Karo's opinion, agreements contracted in civil courts were invalid in Jewish law since civil law was applicable only in civil matters, such as taxes, which benefited the king, not in business transactions between private citizens.[73]

Karo also considered the status of Francisco's assets at the time of his marriage to Gracia. At that time, Karo stated, Francisco and Gracia had not yet accumulated any real wealth and therefore Karo followed the *halakhic* principle that Francisco could not legally give what he did not yet have.[74] It was up to the donee, Gracia, to prove that any assets which the testator wished to bequeath her were in his possession at the time he had made his last will and testament and that he had acquired them according to the Jewish law of acquisitions.

Moreover, because Francisco's will had not been certified in the presence of qualified *Jewish* witnesses but *conversos,* whose loyalty to and knowledge of Judaism some decades after their conversion were questionable, Karo ruled that it was invalid. Furthermore, the will could not have been made in the civil courts because both Gracia and Gracia Junior had stated that it had been "a secret will"; had it been made in a civil court, it could not have been kept secret.

In Karo's view, then, the entire estate should be awarded to Reyna, Gracia's and the late Francisco's daughter, in accordance with Jewish law, which did not recognize a widow as her husband's heir and granted his estate to their daughter, if there are no male heirs. Unlike the other rabbis, Karo would not allow that arrangements made under civil law could be used to circumvent Jewish law on this matter by creating the means by which widows might indeed inherit from their husbands. Karo did, however, agree with his colleagues that Gracia, still in control of the estate, was entitled to her maintenance rights as a widow in accordance with Jewish law.[75]

Karo's decision, in contrast to those of his contemporaries, may have been merely academic since Gracia, not her daughter or son-in-law, controlled and administered the estate successfully. Karo knew that after 1492 in Spain and 1497 in Portugal there were no qualified rabbis left to deal with the problems of *conversos* since most, including Karo's family, had fled in 1492. Therefore, all contracts enacted among *conversos* after 1492 in civil law were void according to Jewish law. Amongst the rabbis judging Gracia's case, Karo is notable for the strength of his insistence that it is Jewish law by which Jews must live as far as possible, and that it takes precedence over other kinds of law in deciding the private affairs of the Jewish community.

Most historians have focused on the monumental achievements of Joseph Nasi, duke of Naxos, who, as long as his aunt was alive, was at her side in expanding the Mendes' business interests. However, after her death, Joseph became increasingly involved in political intrigue, cutting a dashing figure in Turkish and European courts. Through bad investments, and perhaps lacking proper direction and the entrepreneurial skills of his aunt, he lost most of the estate's assets, and it is said that after his death Joseph's assets were insufficient to pay his widow, Reyna, the 90,000 ducats that she had provided in her dowry.[76]

Reyna, Gracia's daughter, continued to maintain some of her mother's charitable and academic interests as long as she was financially able to do so, making her late husband's very fine library available to Jewish scholars and providing printing presses for the publication of Hebrew books.[77] With her death, and that of her cousin, the saga of the illustrious Mendes family seems to have come to an end.

In summarizing Gracia Mendes's life and achievements, we find that in medieval Jewry's most perilous age she demonstrated exemplary courage and strength in the face of adversity. Her clever outmaneuvering of political and ecclesiastical authorities as she and her family moved their wealth from country to country attests to her determination to have them survive and to survive as Jews.

Although she was aided by agents, financial advisers, and inherited wealth, it was Gracia's initiative that parlayed that wealth into an even greater fortune which empowered her to serve rulers and potentates while preserving her independence of spirit.

Her affluence and the power deriving from it may have facilitated Gracia's and her family's entrée into the Christian, Muslim, and Jewish societies in which they lived and greater maneuverability in royal and rabbinic circles but it was Gracia's resourcefulness and resilience, her determination and commitment to her religion, to her family, and to her people that earned her the unstinting admiration of the rabbis with whom she came into contact.

Many years after Gracia Mendes had begun her travels through Christian Europe as a crypto-Jew and had ended them as a professing one upon her arrival in Ottoman Turkey, Moses de Trani wrote at the conclusion of his legal judgment: "Many women have been extremely successful but Gracia has surpassed them all. I have not graced Gracia nor have I bested Brianda but I have judged Gracia [Junior] judiciously with heaven's help and writers' works."[78]

Notes

1. On the riots and mass conversions from 1391 to 1492, see Yitzhak Baer, *A History of the Jews in Christian Spain,* 2 vols. (Philadelphia, 1966),

2:95–169, 244–99, and 433–43; B. Netanyahu, *The Marranos of Spain from the Late XIVth to the Early XVIth Century* (New York, 1966), 6–22 and passim; Heim Beinart, "Mass Apostasy: The Problem and Fate of the Conversos in the Fifteenth Century" [Hebrew], in *Moreshet Sepharad: The Sephardi Legacy,* ed. Haim Beinart (Jerusalem, 1992), 280–308. On discussions as to what constituted valid divorce proceedings in Jewish law see Ze'ev W. Falk, *Jewish Matrimonial Law in the Middle Ages* (Oxford, 1966), 113–43; Reuven Yaron, *Gifts in Contemplation of Death in Jewish and Roman Law* (Oxford, 1960), 95–97. On divorce under Christianity see Roderick Phillips, *Putting Asunder: A History of Divorce in Western Society* (Cambridge, 1988), 1–39. For discussions on the legal consequences of adultery and *mamzerut* see Louis M. Epstein, *Marriage Laws in the Bible and the Talmud* (Cambridge, Mass., 1942), 195–97.

2. On the life of Isaac ben Sheshet, Spanish rabbi, talmudist, halakhist, *dayyan,* and community leader, who served in different Spanish communities and then fled to Algeria following the 1391 outbreaks, see Abraham M. Hershman, *Rabbi Isaac ben Sheshet and His Times* (New York, 1943). For the *responsa* of Rabbi Isaac ben Sheshet (Ribash) used in this study, see *She'elot u-Teshuvot Bar Sheshet* (Vilna, 1878) (henceforth cited as Ribash, *Responsa*); Netanyahu, *Marranos of Spain,* 22–32; H. J. Zimmels, "The Contributions of the Sephardim to the *Responsa* Literature till the Beginning of the 16th Century," in *The Sephardi Heritage,* ed. R. D. Barnett and W. M. Schwab, 2 vols. (vol. 1: London, 1971; vol. 2: Grendon, Northants, 1989), 1:367–401. Isaac ben Sheshet was one of the first rabbis to deal with the *halakhic* status of *conversos* following 1391 and these *responsa* have provided rich historical details for the period. Rabbi Simon ben Ṣemaḥ Duran (born in Majorca, died in Algiers) also had fled Spain after the 1391 conversions. See Netanyahu, *Marranos of Spain,* 32–76; Isidore Epstein, *Studies in the Communal Life of the Jews of Spain: The Responsa of Rabbi Simon b. Ẓemaḥ Duran as a Source of the History of the Jews in North Africa* (New York, 1968), 3–9, 30–32. There were virtually no rabbis with sufficient *halakhic* authority in Spain after 1391 to advise these *conversos* and therefore they had to rely on the help of their brethren who still remained professing Jews.

3. Netanyahu's main thesis in *Marranos of Spain* is that the Marranos (his term) were forced to become a united group because of the ecclesiastical authorities' determination to root them out as heretics. On more favorable rabbinic attitudes to crypto-Jews and the attempts to integrate them into Jewish society see Simha Assaf, "Anusei Sefarad u-Portugal be-Sifrut ha-Teshuvot," in *Be'Oholei Ya'akov* (Jerusalem, 1943), 172–74. On the phenomenon of crypto-Judaism see also Humberto Baquero Moreno, "Movimentos sociais anti-judaicos em Portugal no século XV," in *Jews and*

Conversos: Studies in Society and the Inquisition, ed. Yosef Kaplan (Jerusalem, 1985), 62–73; Baer, *History of the Jews,* 2:244–99; Renée Levine Melammed, "The Ultimate Challenge: Safeguarding the Crypto-Judaic Heritage," *Proceedings of the American Academy for Jewish Research* 53 (1986), 91–109; Leah Bornstein-Makovetsky, "Structure, Organisation and Spiritual Life of the Sephardi Communities in the Ottoman Empire from the Sixteenth to Eighteenth Centuries," in *Sephardi Heritage,* 2:314–15; Joseph Nehama, *Histoire des Israélites de Salonique,* 7 vols. (Paris and Salonika, 1935–78), 3:17–20. The term *converso* will be used throughout this paper to denote the Hebrew term *'anus,* forced convert, used in the *responsa* discussed here.

4. On the *responsa,* a vast body of rabbinic literature containing responses to legal questions which were asked by individuals and communities throughout the Jewish world, see Solomon B. Freehof, *The Responsa Literature,* published with *A Treasury of Responsa* (New York, 1973), 21–41 and esp. 210–23, dealing with the marrano experience, especially regarding the validity of marriage, divorce, the absence or conversion of *levir* brothers for remarriage purposes, and questions of inheritance. On the *responsa* which deal with the plight of *conversos* see Ribash, who based his decisions on talmudic and earlier rabbinic authorities (*Responsa,* nos. 1, 6, and 11). In one of his *responsa* (no. 99), Ribash had stated that a concubine who lives with her lover is like a woman living with her husband. See also Louis Epstein, *Marriage Laws,* 104–30, 139–42. For the most part, the rabbis were guided by the talmudic principle expressed in *Babylonian Talmud* (*BT*) Sanhedrin 44a: "A Jew, even if he has sinned, is still a Jew." See Salo Wittmayer Baron, *A Social and Religious History of the Jews* (*SRHJ*), 2d ed., 18 vols. (New York, 1952–83) 13:143–55. For a discussion of sexual mores during this period see Yom Tov Assis, "Sexual Behaviour in Mediaeval Hispano-Jewish Society" in *Jewish History: Essays in Honour of Chimen Abramsky,* ed. Ada Rapoport-Albert and Steven J. Zipperstein (London, 1988), 25–59. On the laws of concubinage see Louis Epstein, *Marriage Laws,* 34–76, esp. 62–76. On the laws of levirate marriage see Judith Romney Wegner, *Chattel or Person? The Status of Women in the Mishnah* (New York, 1988), 97–113. On the rights of Jewish widows in Spain, see Abraham A. Neuman, *The Jews in Spain: Their Social, Political and Cultural Life during the Middle Ages,* 2 vols. (Philadelphia, 1942), 2:62–63.

5. The early pioneering work on the Mendes-Benveniste families was done by Cecil Roth, *The House of Nasi: Doña Gracia* (Philadelphia, 1947), and *The House of Nasi: Duke of Naxos* (Philadelphia, 1948). To these must be added the more recent works of Benjamin Ravid, "Money, Love and Power Politics in Sixteenth Century Venice: The Perpetual Banishment and Subsequent Pardon of Joseph Nasi," *Italia Judaica: Atti de I Con-*

vegno internazionale, Bari 18–22 Maggio 1981 (Rome, 1983), 159–81; Constance H. Rose, "New Information on the Life of Joseph Nasi Duke of Naxos: The Venetian Phase," *Jewish Quarterly Review* n.s. 60 (1969–70), 330–44; P. Grunebaum-Ballin, *Joseph Naci, duc de Naxos* (Paris, 1968); Alice Fernand-Halphen, "Une grande dame juive de la renaissance," *La revue de Paris* 5 (1929), 148–65; Mark A. Epstein, "The Leadership of the Ottoman Jews in the Fifteenth and Sixteenth Centuries: The Functioning of a Plural Society" in *Christians and Jews in the Ottoman Empire,* 2 vols., ed. Benjamin Braude and Bernard Lewis (New York, 1982), 1:111–12; Avigdor Levi, *The Sephardim in the Ottoman Empire* (Princeton, 1992), 32–34, 38–39; Morris S. Goodblatt, *Jewish Life in Turkey in the XVIth Century as Reflected in the Legal Writings of Samuel de Medina* (New York, 1952), 113, 115–17; Jane S. Gerber, *The Jews of Spain: A History of the Sephardic Experience* (New York, 1992), 166–69; and especially Maria Giuseppina Muzzarelli, "Beatrice de Luna, Vedova Mendes, Alias Donna Gracia Nasi: Un'Ebrea Influente (1510–1569 CA)," in *Rinascimento al Femminile: a cura di Ottavia Niccoli,* ed. E. S. Cohen, C. Evangelisti, M. Firpo, M. L. King, S. Mantini, M. G. Muzzarelli, and G. Zarri (Rome, 1991), 83–116; and Abraham David, "New Hebrew Sources for the Mendes-Nasi Household in Italy and Constantinople," [Hebrew], *Kiryat Sefer,* 64 (1992–93), 1105–10. I am indebted to Professor Abraham David of the Hebrew University for drawing these last two articles to my attention after this essay was completed and for permitting me the use of the manuscript of his article.

6. The main source for the present study is the *responsum* of Rabbi Moses de Trani (b. 1500 in Salonika, d. 1580 in Safed) found in *'Avqat Rokhel,* a collection of *responsa* by Joseph Karo (b. 1488 in Toledo, d. 1575 in Safed), ed. Yeruham Fischel (Leipzig, 1859), no. 80, 69a–73a, with supplementary information from the *responsa* of Samuel de Medina (b. 1506, d. 1589), *She'elot u-Teshuvot me-ha-Rashdam* (Lemberg, 1862), nos. 327–32, 47b–49b (henceforth cited as Rashdam, *Responsa*); Joseph ibn Lev (b. 1505 in Monstir, Macedonia, d. ca. 1579 in Constantinople), *She'elot u-teshuvot,* 2 vols. (reprint, Jerusalem, 1958), 2, no. 23:72–74 (henceforth cited as ibn Lev, *Responsa*); Joshua Soncino (b. in Italy, d. 1569 in Istanbul), *Naḥalah li-yehoshu'a* (Constantinople, 1731) no. 12, 12b–17b; and Joseph Karo, *'Avqat Rokhel,* no. 81, 73a–75a. In his discussion of Joseph ibn Lev's *responsum,* Freehof states that Francisco, Gracia's husband, had died childless (*Treasury of Responsa,* 152); this was not the case since ibn Lev states that both brothers died "in that kingdom" (i.e., under Portuguese rule) and "the widow [presumably Gracia] and heirs [presumably Brianda, Reyna, and Gracia Junior] came to Turkey" (*Responsa,* 2, no. 23:72). Rashdam makes a similar statement but uses the term "orphans" instead of "heirs" (*Responsa,*

no. 327, 47b). In the *responsum* just cited Rashdam referred to Gracia as "one of the *conversas* of Portugal who married a rabbi, an '*anus*,*"* possibly a *converso* rabbi.

In the *responsa* literature actual names were not used. Men were usually designated as Shimon and Reuven, women as Sarah and Rivkah. In Moses de Trani's *responsum,* Reuven is the name for Francisco Mendes and Shimon denotes the younger brother, Diogo Mendes. Gracia is referred to as Hannah, her sister Brianda is Rivkah, Gracia's daughter Reyna is Sarah, and Brianda's daughter, Gracia's niece, is Dinah. In this paper the actual names of the family members will replace the names used in the *responsa* in order to avoid confusion.

7. Jews were forcibly converted in Portugal in 1497. See Haim Beinart, "The Converso Community in 16th and 17th Century Spain" in *Sephardi Heritage,* 1:457–78; I. S. Révah, "Les Marranes Portugais et L'Inquisition au XVIe siècle," also in *Sephardi Heritage,* 1:479–526; Baron, *SRHJ,* 13:44–47, 82–83; Maria José Pimenta Ferro Tavares, *Judaísmo e Inquisição: Estudos* (Lisbon, 1987), 17–54, 149–67. For some of the difficulties faced by *conversas* arriving in Turkey after the 1492 expulsion see Joseph Nehama, *Histoire des Israélites,* 3:28–31. On the practice of crypto-Jews having both a Catholic and a Jewish wedding ceremony see Freehof, *Responsa Literature,* 215, who cites *responsa* by Rabbi Simon ben Ṣemaḥ Duran's grandsons.

8. Francisco and Gracia Mendes followed Portuguese custom rather than the biblical laws of succession found in Num. 27:8–11, which specify the disposition of the testator's property to the daughter when there is no son and to his brother if there is no daughter. Maimonides, *Mishneh Torah (MT), Hilkhot Naḥalot* 1:1 gives the following order of inheritance: "When a man dies, his children shall inherit him; they precede everyone else and males precede females." See also Yaron, *Gifts,* 141–46. On the protection of widows' rights in medieval Europe see Margaret Wade Labarge, *Women in Medieval Life* (London, 1986), 30–32. On Portuguese marriage, dowry, and succession laws see *Ordenações Filipinas, Livros IV e V, in Colecção chronologica de leis extravagantas* (Lisbon, 1870), ordinances 60–66, 856–71. For a comprehensive discussion on the transition from bride-price to dowry and its implications for widows and unmarried daughters see Diane Owen Hughes, "From Brideprice to Dowry in Mediterranean Europe," in *The Marriage Bargain: Women and Dowries in European History,* ed. Marion A. Kaplan (New York, 1985), 13–58. Both ibn Lev (*Responsa,* 2:23 [72]) and Rashdam (*Responsa,* no. 327, 47b) state that according to ancient royal Portuguese custom the widow is entitled to half the deceased husband's estate whether her dowry is large or small. For a comparison of Christian and Jewish marriage customs see Falk, *Jewish*

Matrimonial Law, 35–85. For betrothal, dowry, and marriage customs in Spain see Marilyn Stone, *Marriage and Friendship in Medieval Spain: Social Relations according to the Fourth Partida of Alfonso X* (New York, 1990), and Heath Dillard, *Daughters of the Reconquest: Women in Castilian Town Society 1100–1300* (Cambridge, 1984), 101–4. This discussion is based on Moses de Trani, *'Avqat Rokhel,* no. 80, 69a–b; Rashdam, *Responsa,* no. 327, 47b–48a; ibn Lev, *Responsa,* 2, no. 23:72.

9. See Maria José Pimenta Ferro Tavares, *Os Judeus em Portugal no Século XV,* 2 vols. (Lisbon, 1982), 1:239.

10. "Ha-shofeṭim meha-medinah" (Rashdam, *Responsa,* no. 327, 47b).

11. On the legal autonomy of Jewish widows especially as compared to minor or married women see Wegner, *Chattel or Person,* 73–74, 87–91, 138–44. On the social and financial status of Jewish women particularly, see Neuman, *Jews in Spain,* 2:61–63, and Cheryl Tallan, "Medieval Jewish Widows: Their Control of Resources," *Jewish History* 5 (1991), 63–74. On the legal and economic autonomy of well-to-do medieval women, especially widows, see Labarge, *Women in Medieval Life,* 25–29, 164–68; Eleanor S. Riemer, "Women, Dowries, and Capital Investment in Thirteenth-Century Siena," in *Marriage Bargain,* 59–79. On Jewish widows being granted the right to engage in business and have access to the royal courts, see Ferro Tavares, *Os Judeus em Portugal no Século XV,* 1:220, 227.

12. A large group of Portuguese *conversos* had fled to Flanders where, at first, the business acumen of the "new Christians" was warmly welcomed. Diogo Mendes had opened a branch of the Mendes business in about 1512 and was considered to be one of the richest merchants in Antwerp with important connections to many Christian banking families as well as to the emperor Charles V. On Diogo's vast business interests see J. M. Lopes, *Les Portugais à Anvers au XVIème siècle* (Antwerp, 1895), 39–40; Roth, *Doña Gracia,* 21–49; Baron, *SRHJ,* 13:122–29; I. S. Révah, "Pour l'histoire des Marranes à Anvers: Recensements de la 'nation portugaise' de 1571 à 1666," *Revue des études juives* 122 (1963), 123–47; and Grunebaum-Ballin, *Joseph Naci,* 27–43.

13. Restored from Rashdam, *Responsa,* no. 328, 48b: "casando." On the maintenance of minor daughters from a husband's estate see Yaron, *Gifts,* 181; Wegner, *Chattel or Person,* 72–73.

14. De Trani, *'Avqat Rokhel,* no. 80, 69b, "Declaro que en toda mi hacienda tiene mi hermano Shimon la mitad y yo otro tanto en lo que el tiene por sí y aunque la mía sea más él lo ayudo a ganar y mi intención fue asi siempre solamente lo fizo por merced que muriendo el sin hijos hago heredera a mi hija Sarah cuando ella a su voluntad. . . . Y digo más que en su fazienda tiene la mitad su mujer Hannah . . . y por heredera en los tercios de la otra mitad su hija Sarah y que del último tercio tomen lo que

fuere necesario por las despechas que en su testamento mandara hacer y lo que quedare del tercio dicho deja para su mujer Hannah." H. J. Zimmels, in *Die Marranen in der Rabbinischen Literatur: Forschungen und Quellen zur Geschichte und Kulturgeschichte der Anussim* (Berlin, 1932), points out the peculiar shift from the first person, Francisco presumably, ["declaro," "fizo"], to the third person, ["su mujer"], even though from the context of the declaration the reference must be to the testator Francisco (108, n. 3). This document, found also with minor variations in Rashdam (*Responsa,* no. 328, 48b), does not correspond precisely with the version translated into Hebrew by Moses de Trani in *'Avqat Rokhel,* no. 80, 72a. I wish to thank Professor Jill Ross, Notre Dame University, and Rabbi Amram Assayag of Congregation Petah Tikvah Anshe Castilla, Toronto, for graciously transliterating and translating the Hebrew-Spanish document.

15. According to Rashdam (*Responsa,* no. 327, 48a), it was Francisco's intention to go to "Togarmah" (Turkey) with his wife after their marriage so that they could return to Judaism openly.

16. A new ordinance would be issued on Sept. 30, 1537, which would allow "les nouveaux-chrétiens du Portugal à venir s'établir aux Pays-Bas avec leurs femmes, enfants, serviteurs et bien meubles pour y jouir de tous les droits, libertés et franchises reconnus aux marchands étrangers" (Grunebaum-Ballin, *Joseph Naci,* 30). On Diogo's brief arrest in Antwerp for being a crypto-Jew see Lopes, *Les Portugais,* 39–40; Baron, *SRHJ,* 13:123–28; Fernand-Halphen, "Une grande dame juive," 153–55; Roth, *Doña Gracia,* 32–37. However, the safety of crypto-Jews in Antwerp was not always assured, since in 1538 Emperor Charles V's sister, Marie, ruled that Antwerp was no longer to be a way station for these Jews on their way to Salonica, where they could adopt Judaism openly.

17. De Trani, *'Avqat Rokhel,* no. 80, 69b. The *responsa* do not mention the extent of the individual or combined Mendes estates. Presumably Gracia and Diogo, as Francisco's heirs, as well as the authorities for tax purposes, would have access to all business documents pertaining to the estate. All the major sources used in this essay document the considerable amounts of monies in various currencies which the family had at their disposal and spent during their stay in various countries.

18. Baron, *SRHJ,* 13:119–25. João Miguez (1520–79) became the later Joseph, duke of Naxos; his brother Samuel was also known by his Christian name, Bernardo Miguez. They were likely the sons of Gracia's and Brianda's brother, Dr. Migues, royal physician in Portugal. See Roth, *Doña Gracia,* 12. The other family members who left along with the Mendes sisters may have included Augustin Enriquez, who was to be named as a trustee of the Mendes estate in the event of Gracia's death.

19. Baron, *SRHJ*, 13:122.

20. Charles V (1519–58), who also reigned as Charles I of Spain (1516–56), played a major role in the lives of the Mendes family. See Nehama, *Histoire des Israélites*, 3:11, 17–18, 33, 59; Roth, *Doña Gracia*, 42–45; Baron, *SRHJ*, 13:122–23, 274–79; Lopes, *Les Portugais*, 20; Grunebaum-Ballin, *Joseph Naci*, 29–43, 63.

21. Grunebaum-Ballin, *Joseph Naci*, 32 and n. 2.

22. See de Trani, *'Avqat Rokhel*, no. 80, 69b. Cf. *BT Giṭṭin* 71a; Maimonides, *MT, Hilkhot Naḥalot*, 4:1.

23. See Rashdam, *Responsa*, no. 327, 48a; Roth, *Doña Gracia*, 28–30, 39; Grunebaum-Ballin, *Joseph Naci*, 29, 33, 47.

24. "Allemagnia" in de Trani, *'Avqat Rokhel*, no. 80, 69b.

25. Different dates have been given for his death, sometime between 1542–47. Grunebaum-Ballin states that Diogo died in 1543 (*Joseph Naci*, 34). According to Goodblatt, his death occurred in 1547 (*Jewish Life*, 116); and according to Roth, Diogo died at the end of 1542 or the beginning of 1543 (*Doña Gracia*, 39). No matter when Diogo died, Gracia was a relatively young widow in charge of a large fortune whose maintenance required expert management and advice.

26. On the payment of the wife's dowry upon her husband's death, see Maimonides, *MT, Hilkhot 'Ishut*, 16:1, 23:11. On dowries and marriage in Jewish law in general see Isidore Epstein, *The "Responsa" of Rabbi Solomon ben Adreth of Barcelona as a Source of the History of Spain (1235–1310)* (London, 1925), 80–88. An estate could consist of additional sums of money as well as jewelery and other assets the husband bestowed upon his bride at the time of their marriage or during his lifetime. Since the Mendes family engaged mainly in commodities because of their frequent moves, it is unlikely that their assets included real estate. For a partial account of Diogo's will, see Lopes, *Les Portugais*, 40. For additional details about Diogo's will and Brianda's dowry, see Grunebaum-Ballin, *Joseph Naci*, 34 and 51 respectively. We do not know the extent of Brianda's dowry or whether she had given her husband Diogo a nuptial gift in accordance with Jewish custom; if she had, had her sister Gracia helped supply it since Brianda had no parents to dower her? Had Brianda's husband Diogo given her gifts, and if so, how extensive were they, since she too was able to employ agents and engage in business? In Jewish marriage and succession laws the wife is not a legal heir to her husband's estate (*M. Baba Batra* 8:1, 2). Rashdam was also asked whether the widow's claim to half the estate could be rejected by the heirs and limited only to her dowry (*Responsa*, no. 327, 47b). On the "labyrinth" of ecclesiastical, royal, and secular courts' involvement in lawsuits regarding dowries and succession rights see Richard L. Kagan, *Lawsuits and Litigants in Castile, 1500–1700* (Chapel Hill, N.C., 1981), 34, 43, 85.

27. De Trani, *'Avqat Rokhel,* no. 80, 69b–70a, "Y declaro que y por bien que la dicha Hannah mi cuñada sea tutera de la dicha Dina mi hija y administratura y su hacienda hasta de la dicha Dina mi hija sea edad de casar y de la poder regir y administrar." On the legal responsibilties of a guardian see, for example, Maimonides, *MT, Hilkhot Naḥalot,* 10:6, in which he states that a court-appointed guardian should be male, trustworthy, strong, and capable of transacting the minor's business. However, a testator had the legal right to appoint a woman as guardian. On the medieval French widow being left "the guardianship of the children and the usufruct and administration of the family goods, often without having to give inventory or accounting," see Labarge, *Women in Medieval Life,* 167–68.

28. Following the tradition of the *responsa* the two male advisers' names are not stated explicitly. Grunebaum-Ballin identifies Abraham as Abraham Benveniste, known as Augustin Enriquez, Diogo's cousin, and Joseph as Gracia's nephew, João Miguez, who by this time would have been old enough and sufficiently familiar with his aunt's business dealings to have been her adviser (*Joseph Naci,* 34). If this were so, then Gracia's advisers would have included representatives from both Diogo's family and her own. Roth, in *Duke of Naxos,* 5–7 and passim, in *Doña Gracia,* 18, 115–16, 178–81, and in his article, "'Salusque Lusitano': (An Essay in Disentanglement)" (*Jewish Quarterly Review* n.s. 34 [1943–44], 65–85), also makes this identification. Pier Cesare Ioly Zorattini identifies "Abraham Benvenisti" with Anrriquez Nunez, an itinerant "new Christian" whose travels and dates coincide with those of the Mendes entourage. Involved in royal and social circles, he too faced charges of judaizing which resulted in his facing the Venetian Inquisition. Since he was born in 1531 in Portugal to Nuno Anrriquez, alias Senior Benvenisti, and left Portugal in 1536 to go to Antwerp with his mother and aunt, it seems improbable to assume that Diogo Mendes would have named him as Gracia Junior's guardian, while he was still a teenager, in the event of Gracia's death. Perhaps his father was meant. See Pier Cesare Ioly Zorattini, "Anrriquez Nunez alias Abraham Alias Righetto: A Marrano Caught between the S. Uffizio of Venice and the Inquisition of Lisbon," in *The Mediterranean and the Jews: Banking, Finance and International Trade (XVI–XVIII Centuries),* ed. Ariel Toaff and Simon Schwarzfuchs (Ramat Gan, 1989), 291–307, esp. 301–5. See also Rose, "New Information," 338. Further implications of the selection of these two male advisers may be that in the absence of direct male beneficiaries other close male relatives would have been present to oversee the assets and in this way they would also be included in the "lineage of the heiress-wife" and daughters. See Hughes, "From Brideprice to Dowry," 44.

29. According to Maimonides, if a court-appointed guardian is found to be untrustworthy he may be removed and another appointed in his place

(MT, Hilkhot Naḥalot, 10:7). Diogo's assessment of Augustin Enriquez's honesty and financial capabilities was to prove erroneous because many years later Joshua Soncino described the extensive litigation which Gracia instituted against Augustin for his misappropriation of funds she had entrusted to him and detailed the spirited letter which Gracia had sent to Augustin Enriquez concerning this matter while he was still in Ferrara and she in Constantinople *(Naḥalah li-yehoshuʿa,* no. 20, 28a–29a).

30. De Trani, *'Avqat Rokhel,* no. 80, 70a; Grunebaum-Ballin, *Joseph Naci,* 35.

31. Grunebaum-Ballin quotes the sum of "quarante mille ducats" *(Joseph Naci,* 35); Roth gives the sum of "100,000 ducats, free of interest, for two years" *(Doña Gracia,* 42). Charles V had long been aware that the goal of crypto-Jews was to reach Turkey so that they could lead Jewish lives.

32. On the swearing of oaths see Wegner, *Chattel or Person,* 141–44. On the possibility of Gracia's having sworn an oath see de Trani, *'Avqat Rokhel,* no. 80, 72b.

33. On these accusations against the four Mendes women and Diogo, see de Trani, *'Avqat Rokhel,* no. 80, 70a, 72b.

34. On the difficult and protracted negotiations see Grunebaum-Ballin, *Joseph Naci,* 35–43; Rose, "New Information," 334.

35. Grunebaum-Ballin, *Joseph Naci,* 42–43.

36. On their stay in this city, which offered shelter to *conversos* until their expulsion in 1550, and the various intrigues which brought them into conflict with the Venetian authorities, see Grunebaum-Ballin, *Joseph Naci,* 45–65; Roth, *Doña Gracia,* 50–64; Rose, "New Information," 343–44 and n. 39; Brian Pullan, *The Jews of Europe and the Inquisition of Venice, 1550–1670* (Oxford, 1983), 168–98; Ravid, "Money, Love and Power Politics," 162–76.

37. Rashdam later described her actions, as well as Brianda herself, as "cruel" *(Responsa,* no. 331, 49b).

38. The details of Gracia's and Brianda's trial in Venice, as well as Gracia Junior's attempts to enter a convent, are found in Grunebaum-Ballin, *Joseph Naci,* 47–65. Ottoman Turkey at this time was ruled by Suleiman (1520–66), who had amicable relations with the Venetian rulers. His successor, Selim III (1566–74), continued the former's favorable policy toward *conversos,* being on especially friendly terms with Gracia's nephew, Joseph Nasi. In addition to the details in *'Avqat Rokhel,* see also Rashdam, *Responsa,* no. 331, 43a, 49b; Soncino, *Naḥalah li-yehoshuʿa,* no. 12, 17b; Nehama, *Histoire des Israélites,* 3:32–33, 40 and passim; Gerber, *Jews of Spain,* 150–61; and Baron, *SRHJ,* 18:46–121.

39. Grunebaum-Ballin, *Joseph Naci,* 47–48.

40. Grunebaum-Ballin *(Joseph Naci,* 47–48), Ravid ("Money, Love and

Power Politics," 162–81), and Muzzarelli ("Beatrice de Luna," 91–94) describe Joseph Nasi's extensive negotiations with the authorities to free Gracia's assets.

41. De Trani, *'Avqat Rokhel,* no. 80, 70a.

42. On the attempts to expropriate Gracia's holdings in France see *'Avqat Rokhel,* no. 80, 70a; Rashdam, *Responsa,* no. 332, 49b; Roth, *Doña Gracia,* 55–56; Grunebaum-Ballin, *Joseph Naci,* 48. In August 1550, Henry II too had permitted "new Christians" to settle in his kingdom (Baron, *SRHJ* 13:117–18).

43. On the safe conduct given to Gracia, the dates of her and Reyna's stay in Ferrara, and their taking up residence in Constantinople see the discussions in Grunebaum-Ballin, *Joseph Naci,* 67–71; Roth, *Doña Gracia,* 66, 69–70, 83–87; Aron di Leone Leoni, "Documenti e notizie sulle famiglie Benvenisti e Nassi a Ferrara," *La rassegna mensile di Israel* 58 (1992), 111–36. For the controversy surrounding the marriage of Reyna and Joseph and the putative earlier marriage between Gracia Junior and Joseph see Ravid, "Money, Love, and Power Politics," 164–81. On other influential Jewish women in the Turkish courts, and the tragic end one of them suffered, see Roth, *Doña Gracia,* 105–8; and Baron, *SRHJ,* 18:83, 131–34.

44. The famous Ferrara Bible, a Hebrew edition with a Spanish translation, was dedicated to Gracia Mendes, its benefactress, as was Samuel Usque's Portuguese book, *Consolation for Israel's Tribulations,* a book still read in the schools of Portugal (Grunbaum-Ballin, *Joseph Naci,* 49, n. 1).

45. Roth, *Doña Gracia,* 31. On the help both Diogo and Gracia had given to *conversos* escaping from Portugal to Turkey see Grunebaum-Ballin, *Joseph Naci,* 34. See also Soncino, *Naḥlah li-yehoshuʻa,* no. 12, 12b.

46. Gracia organized the Jewish boycott of the port of Ancona when twenty-four former *conversos,* who had been assured of protection before reverting to Judaism, were burned at the stake in 1558. On the repercussions of this major boycott, "the first time since their scattering over the world, that the Jews attempted to use concerted, united action in self-defense" (Freehof, *Responsa Literature,* 150–58, esp. 152), see Roth, *Doña Gracia,* 134–75; Nehama, *Histoire des Israélites,* 4:96–121; Zimmels, *Die Marranen,* 115–29; Fernand-Halphen, "Une grande dame juive," 160–63; Grunebaum-Ballin, *Joseph Naci,* 76–78; and Marc Saperstein, "Martyrs, Merchants and Rabbis: Jewish Communal Conflict as Reflected in the *Responsa* on the Boycott of Ancona," *Jewish Social Studies* 43 (1981), 215–28, esp. 222–26. Joshua Soncino, the Italian-born rabbi of one of the congregations in Constantinople, in his *Nahalah li-yehoshuʻa,* no. 20, 27a–29b, states that he opposed the boycott because it would also have affected the livelihood of Ancona's "professing Jews," not only that of the *conversos.* Another of his *responsa,* no. 39, 44b–45b, deals with Gracia's attempt to

divert the Jewish trade from Ancona to Pesaro. Gracia's role as patron of the arts and benefactor to many charities and her help to her nephew Joseph in the rebuilding of Tiberias—a project which eventually failed—and its resettlement with crypto-Jews with the sultan's approval, are described by Soncino, *Naḥalah li-yehoshuʿa*, no. 12, 11b; Roth, *Doña Gracia*, 122–31; Grunebaum-Ballin, *Joseph Naci*, 67–83; and Baron, *SRHJ*, 18:77–83, 109–18.

47. Baron, *SRHJ*, 18:77–83; Roth, *Doña Gracia*, 111–16.

48. Brianda and Gracia Junior arrived in Constantinople in about 1558, having declared that in their hearts and souls they were Jewish and wished to remain so. See Roth, who states that "Don Samuel and his wife [Gracia Junior] rejoined their kinsfolk in Constantinople, and the family circle was re-united" (*Doña Gracia*, 179), and Grunebaum-Ballin, who describes Brianda's own substantial loans to Venetian and French noblemen in order to obtain safe conduct passes to Constantinople (*Joseph Naci*, 62–65). According to documents cited by Abraham David, "New Hebrew Sources," Brianda died in 1564. The discussion concerning the Mendes estate and succession rights is based on de Trani, *'Avqat Rokhel*, no. 80, 70a–73a; Joseph Karo, ibid., no. 81, 73b–75a; Rashdam, *Responsa*, nos. 327–32, 47b–49b; and ibn Lev, *Responsa*, 2, no. 23:72–74.

49. Portuguese civil law required that in the final disposition of one's estate a mortally ill testator (*shekhiv me-ra'*) could stipulate orally or in writing that one-third of the children's half of the estate (or one-sixth of the entire estate) be awarded to whomever the testator designated as long as the surviving children received two-thirds; the half that was willed to his wife was hers. Whether Francisco indeed faced imminent death when he made his will is one of the key issues discussed by the rabbis whom the Mendes sisters consulted. On the definition of a mortally ill testator and the wife's inheritance rights, see Yaron, *Gifts*, 29–31, 153–60, and passim; and Riemer, "Women, Dowries, and Capital Investment," 69, for similar cases.

50. On the requirements for a marriage consecrated according to Jewish law see, for example, Maimonides, *MT, Hilkhot 'Ishut*, 3:1–3. See also Falk, *Jewish Matrimonial Law*, 35–36, 68; Wegner, *Chattel or Person*, 71–74; and Baron, *SRHJ*, 13:151–55. Stone describes some of the requirements for Christian betrothal, marriage, and inheritance in Castile (*Marriage and Friendship*, 35–38, 41, 46, 48–49). On *ketubbah* rights and Jewish marriage customs in fifteenth-century Portugal, see Ferro Tavares, *Os Judeus em Portugal no século XV*, 1:239–47. The *ketubbah*, a business contract between two families, provided for a wife's maintenance in case of divorce or widowhood and also for sons' and daughters' inheritance rights. See also Yaron, *Gifts*, 175–81.

51. See also Isidore Epstein, *Responsa of Rabbi Simon Duran,* 79–80, regarding marriages contracted under civil law. In *Jewish Matrimonial Law,* Falk describes the evolution of Jewish and Christian marriage practices (56–59, 68–85 passim). On pages 70–71 Falk states "why various customs which had pertained to engagement—such as the bestowing of the ring . . . were transferred to the wedding." It was possible to dissolve a marriage in Catholic law if one of the partners "was not a Christian," which was not true in the Mendes marriage since both had been baptized. See Phillips, *Putting Asunder,* 2–3, 17–18, 34; and the discussion of de Trani, *'Avqat Rokhel,* no. 80, 71a.

52. On the principle that "the law of the land is legal and binding" (*dina de-malkhuta dina*) and that "custom supersedes law" (*ha-minhag mevattel halakhah*) see *BT, Baba Qamma,* 113b, and Maimonides, *MT, Hilkhot Mekhirah,* 7:6 respectively. De Trani, in *'Avqat Rokhel,* no. 80, 71a–71b, reviews legal precedents and relies mostly on the decisions of Moses Maimonides. Most respondents from the Franco-German and Spanish schools agree that civil contracts are valid. On the fact that Spanish rabbinic authorities tended to agree with the principle that "the law of the land is legal and binding" in civil cases among Jews, as long as it was equally applied to all citizens, see Yom Tov Assis, "Jewish Attitudes to Christian Power in Medieval Spain," *Sefarad* 52 (1992), 291–304, esp. 300–301. Yom Tov Assis states that the application of Jews to non-Jewish courts was originally intended to apply only to monetary matters ("The Jews of Spain in Gentile Courts [13th and 14th Centuries]," in *Culture and Society in Medieval Jewry* [Hebrew], ed. Menahem Ben-Sasson, Robert Bonfil, and Joseph Hacker [Jerusalem, 1989], 399–430); eventually an elite within Jewish society turned more and more to secular courts in all matters, including marriage, divorce, and succession rights, because they knew they could rely on the support of these courts.

53. According to the *ṣadāq,* half the marriage settlement had to be deposited by the groom with the bride on their wedding day, "and the other half at leisure, or on divorce or death" (Isidore Epstein, *Responsa of Rabbi Simon Duran,* 79–80 and 82–84, n. 3). As Joseph Karo pointed out in *'Avqat Rokhel,* no. 81, 74a, the *ṣadāq,* as the Arabic term indicates, was observed in Muslim countries such as North Africa, not among the Christians, as Moses de Trani had stated in his *responsum,* no. 80, 71b. See also Renée Levine Melammed, "Sephardi Women in the Medieval and Early Modern Periods," in *Jewish Women in Historical Perspective,* ed. Judith R. Baskin (Detroit, 1991), 121–26.

54. De Trani, *'Avqat Rokhel,* no. 80, 71b, "Y declaro mas qui en su hacienda tiene la mitad su mujer Hannah [Gracia]." ("I declare that in all his estate his wife Hannah [Gracia] has one half.") See also Roth, *Doña Gracia,* 14–15.

55. De Trani, *'Avqat Rokhel,* no. 80, 72a.

56. Ibid.

57. This was true also of Jewish law. See Maimonides, *MT, Hilkhot Naḥalot,* 1:1–3. *M. Baba Batra* 8:1 states that a woman is not entitled to her husband's estate but does receive her *ketubbah* obligations, dower rights, and her own property brought into marriage. On Jewish law see also Wegner, *Chattel or Person,* 138–41, and for Spanish law Fernando de Arvizu y Galarraga, *La disposicion "mortis causa" en el derecho español de la alta edad media* (Pamplona, 1977), 53–101, and Antoni M. Udina i Abello, *La successió testada a la Catalunya altomedieval* (Barcelona, 1984), 58–61. It can be assumed that Portuguese succession laws were similar and also not firmly fixed.

58. The Hebrew term used by de Trani in *'Avqat Rokhel,* no. 80, 72a, is *hoda'ah,* which is found with variant spellings in the *responsa.* The legal implications of the last will and testament of a mortally ill testator as well as what constitutes "gifts," the transfer of assets or property without payment, are lengthy and complicated and beyond the scope of this paper. On some of the details see Maimonides, *MT, Hilkhot To'en ve-niṭ'an,* 7:1, 4, and Yaron, *Gifts,* passim.

59. This information, and the rest of de Trani's judgment, is based on his *responsum* in *'Avqat Rokhel,* no. 80, 71b–72b.

60. De Trani, *'Avqat Rokhel,* no. 80, 72a.

61. The rabbis whom Gracia consulted were not in complete agreement on this point. De Trani stated that even though Diogo's will was made in Antwerp, Diogo and Gracia were governed by the same laws that were in effect in Portugal. Joseph ibn Lev stated that the custom to bequeath half the estate to the widow was probably firm (*minhag qavua' beineihem 'al ha-setam*) (*Responsa,* 2, no. 23:72). Rashdam ruled that since Francisco had designated Gracia as beneficiary to half the estate and had made her guardian of any children they might have, Gracia was entitled to her half as well as to the profits which she had accumulated because of her financial acuity (*Responsa,* no. 327, 48b).

62. The terms "gives" and "leaves" are necessary for the legal transfer of title. See de Trani, *'Avqat Rokhel,* no. 80, 71b; Karo, ibid., no. 81, 74b; Yaron cites the talmudic authorities (*Gifts,* 124–29).

63. De Trani, *'Avqat Rokhel,* no. 80, 72b.

64. Ibn Lev, *Responsa,* 2, no. 23:72–74; Rashdam, *Responsa,* no. 327, 48b. Ibn Lev had been asked whether "the widows are entitled to half the estate or just the dowries they had brought their husbands," which would be in agreement with Jewish law. See also Freehof, *Treasury of Responsa,* 152–56. In *Hilkhot 'Ishut,* 23:12, Maimonides states that when a woman collects her dowry, she collects the sum stipulated in the *ketubbah,* accord-

ing to the custom of the country, no matter whether she brought more or less than the amount stated. Ribash, *Responsa,* no. 345, concurs, as did earlier rabbinic authorities. Ibn Lev's main concern, as was Joseph Karo's as we shall see, was the disposition of property that was not yet in existence and may not yet have been legally acquired according to established practices of acquisition.

65. Joseph Nasi died Aug. 2, 1579, and Reyna, his widow, in about 1599. Samuel Nasi, Gracia Junior's husband and Joseph's brother, died in the fall of 1569, shortly after Gracia's death that spring. It is not known whether the infant daughter cited in documents, who died before 1569, was Joseph and Reyna's or Samuel and Gracia Junior's. In any event, it appears that neither couple had an heir. According to documents cited by David, "New Hebrew Sources," Brianda had died in 1564. See also Roth, *Joseph Nasi,* 216–21.

66. De Trani, *'Avqat Rokhel,* no. 80, 73a. Karo, *'Avqat Rokhel,* no. 81, 75a, concurred with de Trani's assessment of payment for the damages caused by Brianda.

67. Both cousins had fulfilled their father's wishes to make suitable marriages, Reyna by marrying her cousin, Joseph Nasi, and Gracia Junior by also marrying her cousin, Samuel Nasi, Joseph's brother. The phrase used by Karo in *'Avqat Rokhel,* no. 81, 75a, to describe Gracia Junior's situation, *she-țițame' bein ha-goyim* 'contaminated among non-Jews', is found in Maimonides, *MT, Hilkhot 'Avadim,* 1:4, and Rashdam, *Responsa,* no. 331, 49b, as *nitma'* 'to be assimilated' among non-Jews. On the possibility that Brianda had considered betrothing her young daughter to a Christian family see Grunebaum-Ballin, *Joseph Naci,* 52. On the strict laws and penalties governing the denouncement of a fellow Jew (*malshinut*) to civil authorities see Maimonides, MT, *Hilkhot Hovel u-mazziq,* 8:9.

68. The most notable example was Francisco Coronello, descendant of the last chief rabbi of Castile, Abraham Señor, a court Jew and a 1492 convert. See Baron, *SRHJ,* 18:98.

69. Ribash, *Responsa,* no. 4, and Soncino restated the Maimonidean position that forced converts must leave their domicile and go to other countries where they could return to Judaism (*Nahalah li-yehoshu'a,* no. 12, 12a).

70. *Nahalah li-yehoshu'a,* no. 12, 12b: "ha-gevirah ha-ma'atirah, 'ateret șevi'șeva'ot yisra'el, gefen 'aderet, golat ha-koteret, 'ateret tif'eret u-șenif melukhah, hokhmat nashim banetah beit yisra'el bi-qedushah u-ve-țaharah; be-heila, ve-'oșeroteha heheziqah yad 'ani ve-'evyon le-hoshi'am, le-hargi'am ba-'olam ha-zeh u-ve-'olam ha-ba'." Soncino made similar, but not as lavish, comments about Joseph and Samuel Nasi. Roth describes the profuse praises scholars and rabbis heaped upon Gracia's many accomplishments (*Doña Gracia,* 122–33).

71. Karo, *'Avqat Rokhel*, no. 81, 73a–74b. During their legal careers, Karo and de Trani, the latter Karo's successor to the rabbinate in Safed, differed on more than one occasion in their decisions.

72. Yaron cites the various methods of acquisition (*qinyan*) described by talmudic authorities (*Gifts*, 34–36, 90–94), as does Maimonides, *MT, Hilkhot Zekhiyyah u-mattanah*, 8:12, 13 and *Hilkhot Mekhirah*, 5:5. The term *'aggav* usually refers to the symbolic legal acquisition of land, *meshikhah* is the term which refers to the purchase of any goods.

73. See also Assis, "Jews of Spain in Gentile Courts," 402–3.

74. On the principle that "a vendor cannot sell what is not in his possession" see Maimonides, *MT, Hilkhot Mekhirah*, 22:1, 5, 6, 8, 10, 11; and *Hilkhot Sheluhin ve-shutafim*, 4:2. Ibn Lev, following his authorities, states that a husband can legally give his wife an undertaking regarding future acquisitions (*BT Baba Mesi'a* 49a) but a vendor can only buy and sell what he has (*Responsa*, 2, no. 23:73). See also Yaron, *Gifts*, 55.

75. Karo, *'Avqat Rokhel*, no. 81, 75a, and *Shulkhan 'Arukh, 'Even ha-Ezer* (reprint, New York, 1966), 94:1–5; Rashdam, *Responsa*, no. 327, 48a. See also Yaron, who cites the relevant rabbinic sources (*Gifts*, 174–76); and Wegner, *Chattel or Person*, 139–41. Roth, in summarizing the details of the controversy surrounding the Mendes estate, states that there was no clear-cut resolution of the problem (*Doña Gracia*, 108–11). See also Baron, *SRHJ*, 13:154–55, who describes the various difficulties encountered by the rabbis with respect to the problems of crypto-Jews.

76. See Baron, *SRHJ*, 18:104, who repeats the findings of earlier historians.

77. Ibid.

78. De Trani, *'Avqat Rokhel*, no. 80, 73a, "Ve-rabbot banot 'asu hayil ve-hannah 'altah 'al kullanah. Lo hananti le-hannah ve-lo sararti le-sarah ki'im ke-din danti 'et Dinah ke-fi mah shehere'uni min ha-shamayim mi-pi soferim u-mi-pi sefarim."

Intercession and the High-Medieval Queen: The Esther Topos

Lois L. Huneycutt

LTHOUGH THE MEDIEVAL QUEEN seldom ruled in her own right, she could and did exercise considerable political power throughout the Middle Ages. The sources show that women ruled as regents during military campaigns or during the minority of a son, that they controlled factions of both lay and ecclesiastical magnates, and most of all, that their very proximity to the king and the sources of political decision-making made them valuable allies whose timely intercession could be useful to anyone who had business at court. Scholars, led by Pauline Stafford and Suzanne Wemple, have recognized the power of the medieval queen, particularly during the earlier Middle Ages, when political power was so clearly a matter of personalities and when the palace was both the private residence of the king and queen and the arena where public decisions were made and executed.[1] Indeed, several treatises from as early as the ninth century survive to demonstrate that medieval political theorists recognized the importance of the queen's role within the palace and, thus, the kingdom at large. Sedulius Scotus's idealized formula for running a proper palace portrays the queen as a woman of wisdom, a benevolent maternal figure whose advice will be sought and whose words will carry weight, while Hincmar of Rheims assumes that the queen will be responsible for the day-to-day running of the palace, including control over the treasury and thereby the all-important distribution of gifts and patronage.[2] The sources also tell us of wicked queens, women whose evil influence and bad advice brought doom to the kingdom in question.

It is perhaps not surprising, then, that influential churchmen of the medieval period used biblical imagery in an effort to direct individual queens to use their power wisely and effectively. Janet L. Nelson has shown that the early medieval chronicler's use of the epithet "Jezebel" could profoundly affect the way contemporaries and historians alike have perceived the actions of individual queens, and John Parsons has demonstrated how identification of the earthly queen with the Virgin Mary, the queen of Heaven, was used and manipulated by various groups in thirteenth-century England.[3] In this essay, I propose to explore writings urging female intercession in the period between the ninth and twelfth centuries and particularly the manipulation of the story of Queen Esther, who served as a role model for medieval queens. I will speculate on the importance of intercessory imagery to one medieval woman, Matilda, queen to Henry I of England between 1100 and 1118. In Matilda I believe we have an example of a medieval queen who fully realized the power and influence she could wield if her subjects perceived her to be successful in interceding with her royal husband. To some extent, she adopted Esther as a model for her own behavior. The relative plethora of sources for Matilda's reign illustrate the importance of the queen's role at the opening of the twelfth century and show that many of Matilda's contemporaries realized the power of the intercessory model and tried to influence her behavior through manipulation of that model.

Before discussing the manipulation of the Esther story, it is necessary to set forth the elements of the narrative. The Old Testament book of Esther tells the story of the Hebrew girl who became queen of the Persians because of her great beauty but who, at the advice of her uncle, Mordecai, concealed her Jewish identity until the time when the king's evil counselor, Haman, decided to eliminate the entire Hebrew race because Mordecai had insulted him. In a desperate attempt to save her people, Esther entered the king's chamber unbidden, an act that could have cost her her life. But the king was lenient and allowed Esther to persuade him to attend a series of banquets. Intrigued, and knowing that his queen would not have risked her life for the sake of a few dinner parties, the king promised to do whatever Esther requested of him, even, he said, if it involved alienating half his kingdom. At the crucial moment, Esther unmasked Haman's plot and the evil counselor was eventually hanged on the gallows he had built for the Hebrews.

The story as it appears in the Vulgate reflects two separate narrative traditions. The Hebrew version (found in modern-day Protestant Bibles) is a rather straightforward account that stresses God's providence rather than Esther's actions. A Greek version of the story, incorporated into the Vulgate along with the Hebrew version, forms a much more dramatic narrative, stressing Esther's personal danger in approaching the king unbidden, elaborating on her inner struggle to determine the proper course of action, and emphasizing the feminine wiles employed by the beautiful queen. For example, the Hebrew author tells us, in the first verse of the fifth chapter of his account, that Esther fasted for three days before approaching the king and that she put on her royal robes so that her appearance might find favor with the king, but the Greek version elaborates on her distress: "Then Queen Esther, trembling because of the imminent danger, took refuge in the Lord. When she had stripped off her royal attire, she dressed in clothes suitable for tears and mourning. Instead of varied perfumes she strewed ashes and dung over her head. She abased her body by fasting and all the places where she had previously been accustomed to rejoice she filled with the tearings of her hair. And she prayed to the Lord God of Israel."[4] Esther reminded the Lord that she despised the royal headdress that she was forced to wear, considering it as loathsome as menstrual cloth ("pannum menstruatae"). On the third day, though, having accepted her position, "she put aside her mourning garments and put on her glorious apparel."[5] The narrative emphasizes the weakness that eventually became the source of her power:

> When she was shining in her royal robes and had invoked God, the ruler and savior of all, she took two maids; on the one she leaned for support, as if because of luxury and excessive softness she could not support her own body, while the other maid followed her mistress, bearing her train which trailed upon the ground. With her face flushed with a rosy color and with gracious and shining eyes she concealed her heart that was sad and constricted by very great fear. She passed through all the doors in order and stood opposite the king where he sat on the throne of his kingdom, dressed in royal vestments and shining with gold and precious stones; and his appearance was terrifying. When he looked up, his burning eyes revealing the anger in his heart, the queen sank down, and turning pale, bent her weak head upon her maid. Then God changed the spirit of the king to gentleness, and in haste and fear he leapt from the throne and took her in his arms until she came to herself.[6]

The king then assured the queen that the law that he not be approached by anyone who had not been specifically summoned to his presence applied only to his subjects and not to his queen. Esther, after claiming to have been awed into silence by the sight of the king in majesty, invited him to her banquets, where she eventually revealed Haman's plot against the Hebrew people.

The dramatic episodes of the Greek narrative provided much of the imagery employed by medieval commentators on the book of Esther. These commentators developed allegorical interpretations of the story, in which Esther stood for the church and the Hebrew people represented the world, or where the tale illustrated Christ's promise that those persecuted for the sake of the faith would ultimately triumph.[7] In at least one instance, the commentary was dedicated to an earthly queen. Hrabanus Maurus's ninth-century commentaries on the books of Esther and Judith were dedicated to the empress Judith, second wife of Louis the Pious. In his prologue, he urges the empress to take the biblical women as her models, models which were especially appropriate, given that she was equal to the one in rank and to the other in name.[8] He commended Esther to her in these words: "Likewise, always place Esther, a queen like you, before the eyes of your heart, as someone to be imitated in every act of piety and sanctity."[9] Hrabanus later rededicated the works to Ermengard, wife of Louis's rival, Lothar I.[10] Other writers of the period used the Esther image as a way of inspiring women whom they addressed. For instance, Pope John VIII, writing to the wife of Charles the Bald, implored her to act as an advocate on behalf of the imperial church in the same manner that Esther had for the people of Israel.[11]

The *ordines* for the coronation of a medieval queen often invoked Esther as a role model, sometimes just in a list with other Old Testament females worthy of imitation but in other cases with a reference to a specific episode from Esther's story. The earliest of the surviving *ordines,* composed by Hincmar for the coronation of Charles the Bald's daughter (also named Judith) in 876, contains prayers invoking the precedents of several Old Testament queens, including Esther, who was so favored by God as an intercessor: "That you [God], by means of her prayers, inclined the savage heart of the king toward mercy and salvation for those believing in you."[12]

The example of Queen Esther provided several lessons in the didactic literature of the Middle Ages.[13] First, it provided a justification for the lavish lifestyle of royalty and the aristocracy in that it sanctioned worldly splendor as long as it was used in the proper manner. The author of the life of St. Margaret of Scotland, most likely writing in the first decade of the twelfth century, recalled the scene where the Old Testament queen abased herself and carefully pointed out that Queen Margaret (reigned c. 1070–93) also "[t]rampled all her ornaments in her mind like another Esther, and underneath the gems and gold considered herself nothing but dust and ashes."[14] In the same vein, a thirteenth-century manual for preachers lists Esther's prayer as an appropriate text for sermons addressed to noblewomen.[15] Durand of Champagne, in a treatise for the consort of Philip the Fair of France, remarked that Esther's beauty of form was overshadowed by the beauty of her virtues. Durand also praised Esther's humility because, despite the loftiness of her rank, she was willing to abase herself before the Lord.[16]

The example of Esther also allowed medieval writers to explore the theme of wifely obedience. To Christine de Pisan, Esther provided an example of a good and obedient wife who gained and held the trust of her husband and who was suitably rewarded for her proper behavior.[17] Conversely, other writers praised Esther's courage in disobeying the order of the king and her decision to risk her life in service of her people. Marbod of Rennes, writing near the year 1100, listed Esther as one of the "seven stars" among Old Testament wives who should serve as examples to contemporary matrons. He praised Esther for her courage and concern for the welfare of the Hebrews.[18] Sedulius Scotus saw Esther as an example of "piety, prudence, and sacred authority," qualities he deemed suitable to adorn his ideal queen.[19] Esther was often used as an example of one who could mollify the king or bring about a peaceful solution to the kingdom's problems. Chroniclers writing within a century of the death of Matilda of Scotland, who had carried the bloodline of the old kings of Wessex, referred to her as "a second Esther for us in our times" who ended the bitterness between the conquering Normans and the conquered English, and, as an added benefit, ensured peace between England and Scotland.[20] Two centuries later, the French queen, Jeanne of Champagne-Navarre, consort of Philip the Fair, was hailed as a "second Esther" by critics of the inquisition in Languedoc who were hoping to gain the queen's sympathy.[21]

In much the same vein, Esther imagery was used to encourage the queen in her duty as intercessor. Churchmen had long recognized the power of a wife to influence her husband's course of action, and, as

Sharon Farmer has shown, some literature of the medieval period displays a conscious effort to offer role models for medieval wives. These good wives of the medieval period were to use their "persuasive voices" to further the goals of the church, whether it be in patronizing a certain monastic house or, in Matilda's period, pursuing the goals of the reform papacy.[22]

The familiar topos of the queen as intercessor gained new importance during the Gregorian reform era for a variety of reasons. Chief among them was that the rise of administrative kingship, coupled with changes in the structure of the noble family, began to close down traditional means through which females had sometimes directly exercised public power.[23] As the possibility for direct exercise of power became more remote, writers began to stress the queen's duty to use the less direct, but no less potent, means of persuasion and intercession.[24] Historical analysis of these changes has not addressed the question of whether medieval women realized and reacted to the loss of their public power, but I believe that we can demonstrate that some noblewomen actively encouraged intercessory imagery as a new definition of their political authority. Further, as Caroline Bynum has shown, a sense of belonging to a group and the use of role models to create a corporate identity were among the defining aspects of the development of twelfth-century individuality.[25] We are limited by the paucity of sources that reveal the self-image of any medieval female, so it is difficult to determine whether the women who functioned as medieval queens ever believed themselves to belong to a group with a role that we might call "queenship." I have argued elsewhere, however, that the saints' lives, letters, coronation *ordines,* and laudatory poetry written between about 1070 and 1150 show an increasing awareness of an abstract ideal of queenly behavior taking shape during that period. Writers who helped shape this ideal often referred to biblical and historical women whose behavior deserved praise and urged their patrons to follow the example and fill the roles defined by these models.[26] And, while we keep Bynum's arguments in mind, a careful look at the sources for the life of Matilda of Scotland shows not only that Matilda believed herself to be filling a role but also that she consciously adapted her behavior toward the pattern presented to her in the didactic literature she read.

Matilda is an ideal candidate for this type of analysis, for she seems to have had a flair for the dramatic gesture, and one of the more puzzling episodes in her life may have been her way of patterning herself after the literary image of her mother, Queen Margaret of Scotland, who was already being referred to as a saint. During the 1105 Easter court gathering, Matilda performed an uncharacteristic act of *imitatio Christi* by inviting a group of lepers into her chambers where she washed their feet as Christ had washed the feet of his disciples. She called her younger brother David to her room to witness her act, but David objected that should her husband, King Henry, discover that she was kissing the lepers, Henry would never again put his lips to hers. Matilda pronounced the lips of the heavenly king to be preferable to those of any earthly king and urged David to follow her example. David declined, and as he told the chronicler, "to my blame, I returned to my friends, laughing."[27]

Although Matilda did patronize leper hospitals, this kind of personal piety seems foreign to her nature, and there is no record of any similar occurrence at any time during her life.[28] I believe this action was in direct response to the *vita's* description of Margaret's Lenten austerities, which included washing the feet of six paupers every morning of Lent.[29] Matilda's identification with Margaret is a theme in much of the literature addressed to her, and Matilda also commemorated her mother in charitable donations.[30] But although Margaret's *vita* remained a powerful influence on Matilda throughout her life, it was not the only voice that influenced her behavior. Matilda's ability to intercede with her royal husband was appreciated by those who sought access to King Henry; and some of these suppliants stressed the queen's intercessory role in letters, poems, and other works addressed to her. Matilda's own letters and actions show that she accepted the role defined for her and also that she herself was capable of shaping and manipulating the intercessory topos.

Throughout the twelfth century, a queen with a strong personality and a desire to exert influence over the public sphere of her kingdom continued to find the means to do so. From the beginning of her reign, Matilda showed herself to be one of those strong-willed women. She is first depicted in the sources in 1093, as a runaway nun, when Anselm, the newly appointed archbishop of Canterbury, wrote to his suffragan bishop in Salisbury to request that he compel her to return to the monastery at Wilton.[31] She appears never to have done so and later explained that her parents had sent her to the monastery only to be educated, having always intended that she would eventually marry. But, because she had been seen wearing a habit, some objected in 1100 when Henry wanted to make her his queen. Anselm called an episcopal council to settle the matter, and Matilda insisted upon addressing the assembled bishops directly.[32] She explained that as a child she had sometimes worn the habit when the abbess, her maternal aunt, had compelled her to do so, but that she had never willingly dressed as a nun: "That garment I did indeed wear in her presence, sighing and trembling, but as soon as I could get myself out of her sight, I would pull it off and throw it on the ground and trample it underfoot, and thus in that manner, I used to rage very foolishly with the hatred against it that boiled up in me."[33] After obtaining corroboration of her story, the council declared her free to marry.[34]

As soon as she was married and consecrated as queen, Matilda began to take an active part in political affairs, witnessing many of Henry's charters, serving as his vice-regent when he traveled in Normandy, participating in meetings of the *curia regis,* and sitting in justice on several occasions. She also commanded vast dower lands and a large household of her own, and she exercised sufficient patronage that several of her household officials were promoted to episcopal positions.[35] Matilda was also perceived to have a great deal of unofficial influence over Henry, and much of the literature that she commissioned or that was directed to her contains references to that influence and her duty to exert it in the proper direction. This literature consists of her mother's biography, which presents the pattern of the "perfect princess," poetic offerings from her many correspondents, and letters of instruction, exhortation, and rebuke from the leading churchmen of her day. The authors of these works attempted to control Matilda's intercessory powers, either by blatant invocation of biblical images, including the Esther topos, or by more subtle means.

It must be conceded that at least a passing reference to Esther became nearly formulaic in the literature addressed to medieval queens. A striking example of this occurs in a letter written to Matilda by Herbert Losinga, first bishop of Norwich, referring to Esther as "the eastern queen who took more delight in piety than royal pomp," but as Herbert extended the simile between Matilda and Esther, he showed that he was unfamiliar with the biblical narrative and confused Esther with the queen of Sheba at Solomon's court.[36] However, the Esther topos, in its more conventional form, was one with which Matilda was familiar. There is evidence that Matilda was able to read both French and Latin, and she commissioned numerous literary works in addition to the biography of her mother where the Esther topos is clearly invoked.[37]

The biography, possibly the most influential of the works available to Matilda, was composed at her request, most likely between 1104 and 1107, early in Matilda's tenure as England's queen. Margaret, who was already attracting the cult that would lead to her canonization in the following century, is presented as the ideal wife and mother as well as a politically active woman who took responsibility for maintaining the royal dignity, ordering the palace, influencing legislation and enforcing law, furthering commerce, maintaining peace, and above all promoting Christian charity and church reform. Part of Margaret's effectiveness lay in the example that she set for the king and kingdom. Indeed, she influenced Malcolm to the degree that "he dreaded to displease that queen of such a venerable life in any way, because he perceived Christ truly to live in her heart."[38] The author of the *vita* even shows Margaret presiding over a church council. Modern authors have been reluctant to accept a woman in a such a role, and Robert L. Ritchie has rejected the description as "well-intended hyperbole" describing such actions as "unprecedented in Christendom."[39] We can never be sure of the true extent of the queen's activities in Scotland, but Ritchie's comments reflect his modern bias. Certainly the author of Margaret's *vita* betrays no surprise or disapproval of her acting as head of the council.[40] Nor would the role of the active queen have been foreign to Matilda, since on at least one occasion she acted in a capacity similar to that described for her mother. In 1116, she chaired a meeting of English bishops, abbots, and lay nobles who were called together to respond to papal complaints about the treatment of legates and the transfer of sees without papal approval.[41]

The author of Margaret's *vita* intended the document not as a straightforward biography but rather as a didactic text for Matilda, and it is certainly possible that he exaggerated Margaret's role in order to provide a suitable example for her daughter. The author stresses his didactic intent in the dedicatory prologue, when he commends Matilda for wanting to know more of her mother's exemplary behavior and manner of living so that she might have "a more complete knowledge of her virtues" constantly before her.[42] Later he reports Margaret's deathbed wish that he serve as a teacher to her children, particularly to those who might reach the "summit of earthly dignity."[43] Margaret's biography includes a comparison of her virtues with those of her Old Testament predecessor. Like Esther, the Scottish queen thought nothing of her queenly splendor, "for although she went abroad dressed in precious clothing as was suitable for a queen, like a second Esther, she trampled upon all her ornaments in her mind."[44] It is not known whether the author of the biography had been present during Matilda's appearance before the council in 1100, but it is certainly suggestive that he chose to refer to Margaret's attitude toward her queenly apparel in almost the same words that the chronicler reports Matilda used in reference to her monastic dress, and that the author of the biography invoked the legitimizing precedent of the Esther narrative when he did so.

The messages in the *vita* legitimizing the queen's positive actions were echoed and reinforced in other literature directed toward Queen Matilda. The duty to influence legislation appears in an anonymous poem that praises Matilda for persuading Henry to pass better laws in England, referring to Henry as the "Caesar" who listened to the prayers and pleading of his queen.[45] Hildebert of Lavardin, bishop of LeMans, wrote to praise her for her observance and support of the law, and the monk Benedeit, author of the Anglo-Norman *Voyage of St. Brendan,* lauded Matilda as the queen who furthered divine law and helped ensure peace within the kingdom.[46] Hildebert also remarked that because Matilda had helped maintain a peaceful kingdom, England's natural prosperity had been allowed to flourish.[47] The language of some of Henry's donation charters indicates that certain of his gifts were given at the queen's instigation.[48] It is also clear that Matilda's contemporaries recognized that she could influence Henry's actions, as evidenced in a letter from the German emperor Henry V, who addressed her as his "helper" and included a plea for her continued goodwill and assistance at court.[49]

But important as prosperity or beneficial legislation might have been, the real focus of many of the writings addressed to Matilda was the proper functioning of the Anglo-Norman church, particularly during the period before the compromise of 1106, when Henry, Pope Pascal II, and Archbishop Anselm came to terms over investiture. Matilda had a special fondness for Anselm, which she rather pointedly displayed in 1103, on the eve of his exile, by witnessing one of Henry's charters with the "sign of Matilda, the queen and the daughter of Archbishop Anselm."[50] During his exile, Matilda corresponded with Anselm and Pope Paschal, both of whose letters continually urged her to use her influence in the right direction. One of Paschal's letters asks Matilda to "turn the heart of the king away from the bad advice" of his "evil counselors" (consiliarios perditionis). He stressed Matilda's duty, urging her to "censure, entreat, and chide" Henry until he capitulated, reminding her of the New Testament precept that "an unbelieving husband will be saved by a believing wife."[51] Anselm reinforced the papal urgings, adding his request that Matilda counsel Henry in the ways of righteousness: "Reflect upon these things, make them known to our lord the king in private and public and repeat them often and carefully go over them as much as may pertain to you."[52]

Matilda clearly accepted the role that was assigned to her, and advised Anselm about appropriate times for certain actions, once assuring him that "[the king's] heart is better disposed toward you than many men estimate, and with God assenting and me suggesting however I can, it will become more obliging and agreeable toward you."[53] Having persuaded Henry to restore some of the confiscated Canterbury revenues, she wrote confidently that "Truly, what he now permits you to receive from your revenues, he will allow the same and better and more fully in the future, when according to time and circumstance you shall ask it."[54] In one of her own charters, Matilda let it be known that all the enumerated gifts (to the abbey of Abingdon) were given by Henry, to her and the abbot, "by my own intervention."[55]

But, however often churchmen attempted to manipulate topoi to influence Matilda's actions, she was never the innocent tool of her ecclesiastical allies. Sally N. Vaughn and Sir Richard Southern have both drawn attention to her political acumen and the careful manipulation of language in her own letters. For example, she may have agreed with the reformers on the investiture issue, but she was noncommittal on the issue of Canterbury's primacy over the other archbishoprics of Britain, neglecting to mention Scotland or York in a letter addressed to Anselm as "Archbishop of the first see of England and primate over Ireland and all the northern islands which are called the Orkneys."[56] In another letter, Matilda showed herself to be capable of manipulating intercessory imagery, detailing her efforts and asking that Anselm not become bitter and turn his back on her or the kingdom, reminding the archbishop of his own duty to intercede with God on their behalf.[57] Anselm rather testily replied that he could make no promises about his future prayers, but reassured her that God did not punish wives for the sins of their husbands and urged her to persevere in her efforts to bring Henry to terms: "For when, through desire for my return, you strive to soften the heart of my lord the king toward me, you do what is fitting to you and what I think to be useful to him."[58] In another of her letters, Matilda invoked the language of either the passage in her mother's biography or the passage in the book of Esther itself when she wrote, begging that the archbishop return and threatening to seek out Anselm personally unless he hastened to his orphaned flock: "Moreover, if neither my tears nor my public prayers will induce you, having cast aside my royal dignity and abandoned my insignia, I shall lay down my office, despise my crown, trample my purple and linen, and come to you worn out with sorrow."[59]

The last incident to be discussed here occurred during a royal procession in 1105. Eadmer writes that Matilda was approached by a group of about two hundred ragged, barefoot parish priests who claimed that they had been ruined, first by Anselm's decrees that they put aside their wives and then by Henry's harsh fines against offenders. They begged Matilda to intercede for them, because they were poor and could not survive without their wives. According to Eadmer, the queen dissolved in tears because, although she sympathized with their plight, "constrained by fear she was prevented from intervening."[60] As we have seen, Matilda was not normally a shrinking violet, and this incident demands explanation and integration with what we already know of her personality and her conception of her duty as queen. Could she have been sincere, in that she did sympathize with the plight of the parish priests? It has been suggested that Matilda objected to the hypocrisy of denying wives to parish priests while some of the wealthy Anglo-Norman bishops maintained wives and concubines, but this interpretation cannot be supported from the sources, and in view of her alliances with the reformers, it is unlikely that Matilda approved of clerical marriage. Eadmer's rendering of the scene implies that the priests needed their wives for economic support more than anything else, and Matilda had been well schooled in the need to intercede with the king on behalf of the poor and oppressed. The priests probably staged the pitiful spectacle in hopes that their poverty would provoke her sympathy and that she might persuade the king to issue a kind of "tax rebate." However, the sources speak of 1105 and 1106 as years of extremely harsh taxation throughout the kingdom, and Matilda may have witnessed many such scenes. She may have already known that Henry, who was gathering funds for their daughter's dowry as well as for his planned invasion of Normandy, could not be persuaded to give up any source of revenue. It is conceivable that she had approached the king on other occasions and been rebuffed, even that she had provoked his legendary wrath on a previous occasion.

It is no wonder that the priests' plight drew such an emotional re-action from the queen. With the political changes that were afoot in the England of Henry I, Matilda was gradually losing her ability to exercise direct power to a rising class of professional bureaucrats. This loss had been mitigated by the newer, more powerful intercessory role, the "Esther topos" of which we have spoken. Everything that Matilda had read, all that she had been taught, had focused on her ability to influence her husband for the good of the kingdom. Matilda had ac-cepted that role, and even manipulated its language herself. If she now felt herself to be impotent in softening the heart of the king on behalf of his oppressed subjects, she would have seen herself as a failure in this important queenly function.

Although this was just one episode in the life of one queen, and one who was later perceived as extremely successful, even hailed as a "sec-ond Esther," Matilda's fears were real. The power of a medieval queen rested on a perception of influence rather than any institutional base, and the loss of that perceived influence could spell disaster. The queen who had no income of her own and no influence over her husband could have no allies at court and thus little control over her own fate.[61] The Esther image and the intercessory role provided one means by which a medieval queen could exert influence, but it often proved to be a perilous role on which to rely. The danger of relying on wielding power indirectly was, of course, not unique to medieval queens. For, as the ancient historian Tacitus wrote of the downfall of Agrippina the Younger: "Of all things human, the most precarious and transitory is a reputation of power which has no strong support of its own."[62]

Notes

I would like to thank Dr. John C. Parsons of the Centre for Reformation and Renaissance Studies, Victoria University, for organizing the conference session where this paper was first presented and for continued encourage-ment in pursuing questions of medieval queenship in my graduate work. Professor Jeffrey B. Russell of the University of California, Santa Barbara, kindly read an earlier draft. Members of Professor Russell's 1989–90 grad-uate research seminar, particularly Lauren Helm Jared, also were helpful in talking through some of the ideas presented here.

1. Pauline Stafford, *Queens, Concubines and Dowagers: The King's Wife in the Early Middle Ages* (Athens, Ga., 1983), and Suzanne Fonay Wemple, *Women in Frankish Society: Marriage and the Cloister, 500 to 900* (Philadelphia, 1981). See also Wemple and Jo Ann McNamara, "The Power of Women through the Family in Medieval Europe," originally published in 1981, reprinted in Mary Erler and Maryanne Kowaleski, eds., *Women and Power in the Middle Ages* (Athens, Ga., 1988), 83–102; and Janet L. Nelson, *Politics and Ritual in Early Medieval Europe* (London, 1986).

2. Sedulius Scotus, "Liber de rectoribus Christianis," in J.-P. Migne, ed., *Patrologia cursus completus, series latina,* 221 vols. (Paris, 1844–64), 103:299–302 (hereafter cited as PL); and Hincmar of Rheims, "De ordine palatii," ed. Alfredus Boretius and Victor Krause, *Monumenta Germaniae Historica,* Legum Sectio II, Capitularia Regum Francorum, vol. 2 (Hannover, 1897), 517–30 (hereafter cited as MGH).

3. Nelson, *Politics and Ritual,* 1–48; John C. Parsons, "Earthly Queen, Heavenly Queen: Intercession and Appeal in Thirteenth-Century England," presented at the Twenty-fourth International Congress on Medieval Studies, Kalamazoo, Mich., May 1989. Both Esther and the Virgin lend themselves to use in intercessory imagery. In the period before the twelfth century, Esther was more likely to be invoked than the Virgin, while afterward, the Virgin came to dominate. In later medieval writings, Esther is more likely to be drawn upon as a symbol of honor, virtue, or courage than as an intercessor.

4. "Esther quoque regina confugit ad Dominum, pavens periculum, quod imminebat. Cumque deposuisset vestes regias, fletibus et luctui apta indumenta suscepit, et pro unguentis variis, cinere et stercore implevit caput, et corpus suum humiliavit jejuniis omniaque loca, in quibus antea laetari consueverat, crinium laceratione complevit. Et deprecabatur Dominum Deum Israel" (Esther 14:1–3).

5. ". . . deposuit vestimenta ornatus sui, et circumdata est gloria sua" (Esther 15:4).

6. "Cumque regio fulgeret habitu, et invocasset omnium rectorem et salvatorem Deum, assumsit duas famulas, et super unam quidem innitebatur, quasi prae deliciis et nimia teneritudine corpus suum ferre non sustinens; altera autem famularum sequebatur dominam, defluentia in humum indumenta sustentans. Ipsa autem roseo colore vultum perfusa, et gratis ac nintentibus oculis tristem celabat animum, et nimio timore contractum. Ingressa igitur cuncta per ordinem ostia, stetit contra regem, ubi ille residebat super solium regni sui, indutus vestibus regiis, auroque fulgens, et pretiosis lapidibus; eratque terribilis aspectu. Cumque elevasset faciem, et ardentibus oculis furorem pectoris indicasset, regina corruit, et

in pallorem calore mutato, lassum super ancillulam reclinavit caput. Convertique Deus spiritum regis in mansuetudinem, et festinus ac metuens exsilivit de solio et sustentans eam ulnis suis, donec rediret ad se" (Esther 15:5–11).

7. As a rule, learned authors favored the first interpretation. See Hrabanus Maurus, "Expositio in librum Esther," PL 109:635–70; Walafrid Strabo, "Glossa ordinaria, Liber Esther," PL 113:739–48; and Hugh of St. Victor, "Allegoriae in vetus testamentum, liber nonus," PL 175:733–37.

8. Hrabanus Maurus, "Expositio in librum Judith," PL 109:539–40.

9. "Esther quoque similiter reginam regina, in omni pietatis et sanctitatis actione imitabilem, vobis ante oculos cordis semper ponite" (ibid., 541).

10. Stafford, *Queens, Concubines and Dowagers*, 20.

11. Ibid., 26. The letter is printed in Pope John VIII, "Epistolae et decreta," PL 126:698, where the relevant passage reads "et eritis pro Ecclesia Christi apud pium conjugem more sanctae illius Esther pro Israelitica plebe apud maritum."

12. "Ut efferatum cor regis ad misericordiam et salvationem in te credentium ipsius precibus inclinares" (Hincmar of Rheims, "Coronatio Iudithae Karoli II. filiae," ed. Alfredus Boretius and Victor Krause, MGH, Legum Sectio II, Capitularia Regum Francorum, vol. 2 (Hannover, 1897), 425–27, quotation from 426.

13. The allegorical interpretation of Esther as "church" was also of concern to the medieval churchman but is not explored within this essay. Nor do I tackle Aelfric's Anglo-Saxon translation of the book. For an intriguing beginning, see Laurence Marcellus Larson, *The King's Household in England before the Norman Conquest* (Madison, Wis., 1904; reprint, New York, 1969), 117–18.

14. "Omnia ornamenta velut altera Esther mente calcavit; seque sub gemmis et auro nihil aliud quam pulverem et cinerem consideravit" (*Vita Margaritae*, chap. 2, par. 12 [326]). All citations of the *vita* are to the Bollandist edition in *Acta sanctorum quotquot toto orbe coluntur. . .* , 70 vols., 3d ed. (Paris, 1863–1940), June, 2 (June 10), 324a–31a. The author of the *vita* is unknown but presumed to be Margaret's chaplain Turgot, later a monk of Durham and bishop of St. Andrew's. Two versions of the *vita* are extant, a short version appearing only in one fourteenth-century manuscript and the longer version, also extant in only one manuscript that appears to date from the second half of the twelfth century. The manuscript used by the Bollandists for their edition of the *vita* is now lost, but a comparison between the Bollandist redaction and the British Library manuscript reveals no significant differences. The longer version includes a prologue that states the life was written at the behest of Margaret's daugh-

ter, Queen Matilda. For speculation on the relationship between the two versions of the *vita,* see Derek Baker, "'A Nursery of Saints': St. Margaret of Scotland Reconsidered," in Baker, ed., *Medieval Women* (Oxford, 1978), 119–41; and my "The Image of a Perfect Princess: *The Life of St. Margaret* in the Reign of Matilda II," *Anglo-Norman Studies* 12 (1991), 81–97.

15. See Carla Casagrande, ed., *Prediche alle donne del secolo XIII: Testi di Umberto da Romans, Gilberto da Tournai, Stefano di Borbone* (Milan, 1978), 46. I am indebted to Professor Sharon A. Farmer for this reference.

16. Durand of Champagne, *Speculum dominarum,* Paris, Bibliothéque Nationale MS. Latins 6784, fol. 23r.

17. In these instances, Esther is often compared to the king's first wife, who lost favor by refusing to appear at a royal banquet when summoned. See Christine de Pisan, *The Treasure of the City of Ladies, or The Book of the Three Virtues,* trans. Sarah Lawson (Harmondsworth, Middlesex, 1985), referring to the incident "in the first chapter of the book of Esther" (63). Stephen Langton used the story of Vashti, the disobedient wife, to stand for the faithful soul led astray by temptation, only to be replaced by Esther, the virgin bride of the King of Kings. See Phyllis B. Roberts, "Stephen Langton's *Sermo de Virginibus,*" in Julius Kirshner and Suzanne F. Wemple, eds., *Women of the Medieval World: Essays in Honor of John H. Mundy* (Oxford, 1985), 103–18. Toward the end of the Middle Ages, the authors of the *Malleus maleficarum* cite Esther among their half-dozen or so examples of virtuous women throughout history. See *The Malleus malificarum of Heinrich Kramer and James Sprenger,* trans. Montague Summers, 2d ed. (London, 1948; reprint, New York, 1971), 43.

18. "Sara, Rebecca, Rachel, Esther, Judith, Anna, Noem, / Sidera ceu septem quas saecula prisca tulerunt" (Marbod of Rennes, "Liber decem capitulorum," PL 171:1701). Marbod of Rennes listed Esther with other Old Testament women of whom "it is written [lit.: "they are read"] that they equaled or exceeded men" ("aequiparasse viros, aut exsuperasse leguntur"), commenting that "eternal fame commends Queen Esther, who, married to a cruel tyrant like a lamb to a wolf, did not fear to cross the threshold at the risk of her life" ("Esther reginam commendat fama perennis / Quae velut agna lupo crudeli nupta tyranno / Non timuit, capitis discrimine, limen inire"). Christine de Pisan compared Joan of Arc to the biblical heroines Esther, Judith, and Deborah "Qui furent dames de grant pris, / Par lesqueles Dieu restora / Son pueple, qui fort estoit pris." See Christine de Pisan, *Ditié de Jehanne d'Arc,* ed. Angus J. Kennedy and Kenneth Varty (Oxford, 1977), 33. A treatise often attributed to Jean Gerson, *De quadam puella,* written in the spring of 1429, makes the same comparisons. See Dorothy G. Wayman, "The Chancellor and Jeanne d'Arc, February–July A.D. 1429," *Franciscan Studies* 17 (1957), 273–305, esp. 299. See also

Georges Peyronnet, "Gerson, Charles VII, et Jeanne d'Arc: La propagande au service de la guerre," *Revue d'histoire ecclésiastique* 84 (1989), 334–70, esp. 339–43. An English translation of the treatise is appended to Anne Llewellyn Barstow, *Joan of Arc: Heretic, Mystic, Shaman* (New York, 1986), 135–41. See also Henry Richards Luard, ed., *Flores Historiarum,* 3 vols., Rolls Series 95 (London, 1890), 1:48. (Rolls Series volumes will hereafter be cited as RS).

19. "Quam decoret pietas, prudentia, sacra potestas, / Esther ut alma floruit" (Sedulius Scotus, "Liber de rectoribus christianis," 302).

20. ". . . alteram nobis Esther nostris temporibus" (Aelred, "Genealogia regum anglorum," PL 195:736). For Matilda as peacemaker see *Flores historiarum,* 2: 36.

21. See Joseph R. Strayer, *The Reign of Philip the Fair* (Princeton, 1980), 17–18.

22. See Sharon Farmer, "Persuasive Voices: Clerical Images of Medieval Wives," *Speculum* 61 (1986), 517–43.

23. McNamara and Wemple, "Power of Women through the Family," may go too far in their contention that female power through the family was lost by c. 1100, but it is true that new and more indirect means of female action had to be created in response to changing political factors. See my "Medieval Queenship," *History Today* 39 (June, 1989), 16–22.

24. Diane Bornstein's survey of explicitly didactic literary works shows a three-century gap between the ninth and the twelfth century, when *Specula dominarum* again survive. The revival of the old literary form may have been in response to the need for new rules for the new roles royal and aristocratic women began to play in the twelfth century and beyond. Bornstein was solely concerned with courtesy literature, but here I extend the definition of "didactic literature" to include any works of any genre written to instruct the reader. See Bornstein, *The Lady in the Tower: Medieval Courtesy Literature for Women* (Hamden, Conn., 1983).

25. Bynum, "Did the Twelfth Century Discover the Individual?" in *Jesus as Mother: Studies in the Spirituality of the High Middle Ages* (Berkeley, 1982), 82–109.

26. Huneycutt, "Images of Queenship in the High Middle Ages," *Haskins Society Journal: Studies in Medieval History* 1 (1989), 61–71. Another example of a writer consciously drawing on females of the past in order to inspire a contemporary woman occurs with Hugh of Fleury's *Historia Ecclesiastica,* written for Matilda's sister-in-law, Countess Adela of Blois. Kimberly LoPrete of the history department of Temple University is preparing a study on the *Historia,* portions of which are printed in PL 163:821–54. See also Janet Nelson, "Perceptions du pouvoir chez les historiennes du haut Moyen Age," in Michel Rouche and Jean Heuclin, eds., *La femme*

au Moyen Age (Maubeuge, 1990), esp. 76–77, for a speculation concerning women's self-perceptions over this period.

27. ". . . ego mea culpa ridens ad socios remeavi" (the story, which Aelred narrates in David's voice, appears in "Genealogia regum Anglorum," PL 195:736). Subsequently, it was repeated by nearly every chronicler who wrote about twelfth-century England, and was appended to John of Tynemouth's manuscript containing the short version of the life of St. Margaret. See the redaction of Tynemouth's version in John Pinkerton, ed., *Vitae antiquae sanctorum qui habitaverunt in ea parte Britannia nunc vocata Scotia vel in ejus insulis* (London, 1789), 373–83, with the passage in question on 383.

28. For Matilda's patronage of the leprosaria, see Edward J. Kealey, *Medieval Medicus: A Social History of Anglo-Norman Medicine* (Baltimore, 1981), 89–91, and M. B. Honeybourne, "The Leper Hospitals of the London Area," *Proceedings of the Middlesex Archaeological Society* (1962), 4–61.

29. *Vita Margaritae,* chap. 3, par. 21 (328).

30. There are only two surviving originals among the many notices of charters recording Matilda's gifts to religious houses. Only eight of the notices are complete enough to contain the clauses naming the souls who are to benefit from the queen's gifts. Of these eight, two list the souls of Matilda's parents. The two surviving originals have more elaborate beneficiary clauses, naming Matilda's parents as well as her siblings, husband, and offspring. The longer lists in the originals suggest that some clauses may have been abbreviated or deleted in cartularies by copyists who did not share Matilda's devotion to her natal family members. The two surviving originals are housed in the Library of the Dean and Chapter of Durham Cathedral, charters 1.3.Ebor.13 and 1.2.Spec.23*.

31. Francis S. Schmitt, ed., *S. Anselmi Cantuariensis archiepiscopi opera omnia,* 6 vols. (Seckau, 1938–61), 4: 60–61 (letter 177). See also Walter Frölich, "The Letters Omitted from Anselm's Collection of Letters," *Anglo-Norman Studies 6* (1983), 58–71.

32. There are two surviving twelfth-century accounts of the council. The earliest and most reliable of these is in Eadmer, *Historia novorum in Anglia,* ed. Martin Rule, RS 81 (London, 1884), 121–25. Hermann of Tournai's chronicle includes a later account colored by the then-recent death of Henry and Matilda's only son; see "De restauratione monasterii S. Martini Tornacensis," MGH, Scriptorum 14 (Hannover, 1883; reprint, 1956), 281–82.

33. "Quem pannum in ipsius quidem praesentia gemens ac tremebunda ferebam, sed mox ut me conspectui ejus subtrahere poteram arreptum in humum jacere, pedibus proterere, et ita quo in eum odio fervebam quamvis insipienter consueveram desaevire" (Eadmer, *Historia novorum in Anglia,* 122).

34. Ibid., 123.

35. Two of Matilda's chancelors, Reinhelm and Bernard, were promoted to bishoprics during Henry's reign. One chaplain became a dean of Waltham, and a clerk in her court later joined the household of her brother, David, earl of Huntingdon (later king of Scotland). Matilda also appointed an abbot to Malmesbury Abbey. See chap. 3 of my dissertation, "Another Esther in Our Times: Matilda II and the Creation of A Queenly Ideal in Anglo-Norman England" (Ph.D. diss., University of California, Santa Barbara, 1992).

36. "Ester quae potius pietate quam regni fastidio delectabatur, illa orientalis regina" (Robert Anstruther, ed., *Epistolae Herberti de Losinga primi episcopi norwicensis . . .* [London, 1869; reprint, New York, 1964], 48). The letter was written to Matilda during a period when Henry was in Normandy and she was acting as regent. The letter requests clarification of Herbert's exempt status in regard to some new tax about to be collected, and it is possible that it was written in 1105, when feudal aids for the marriage of the king's daughter were being levied.

37. Other works attributed to Matilda's patronage include William of Malmesbury's *De gestis regum Anglorum* and the Anglo-Norman poetic version of the life of St. Brendan. For William of Malmesbury, see Rodney M. Thompson, "William of Malmesbury as Historian and Man of Letters," *Journal of Ecclesiastical History* 29 (1978), 387–413; and Ewald Könsgen, "Zwei unbekannte Briefe zu den Gesta Regum Anglorum des Wilhelm von Malmesbury," *Deutsches Archiv für Erforshung des Mittelalters* 31 (1975), 204–14. The date and patronage of the St. Brendan poem are still matters of speculation. See E. G. R. Waters, ed., *The Anglo-Norman Voyage of St Brendan* (Oxford, 1928), for the best statement of the textual problems, although Waters (without being dogmatic) ultimately settles on a later date than would be consistent with Matilda's patronage (xxii–xxvi). For compelling arguments in favor of the earlier date, see R. L. G. Ritchie, "The Date of the *Voyage of St Brendan*," *Medium Aevum* 19 (1950), 64–66; and M. Dominica Legge, "Letre in Old French," *Modern Language Review* 56 (1961), 333–34, and continued in her *Anglo-Norman Literature and Its Background* (Oxford, 1963), 8–18.

38. "Ipsam tam venerabilis vitae Reginam quoniam in ejus corde Christum veraciter habitare perspexerat, ille quoquomodo offendere formidabat" *(Vita Margaritae,* chap. 3, par. 11 [326]).

39. R. L. Graeme Ritchie, *The Normans in Scotland* (Edinburgh, 1954), 397, n. 5.

40. *Vita Margaritae,* chap. 2, par. 13–16 (326–27).

41. Eadmer, *Historia novorum in Anglia,* 239. See also *Chronica Magistri Rogeri de Houedene,* ed. William Stubbs, 4 vols., RS 51 (London, 1868–

71), 1:171; and Simeon of Durham, "Historia regum," in Simeon of Durham, *Opera omnia,* ed. Thomas Arnold, 2 vols., RS 75 (London, 1882–85; reprint, 1965), 2:250.

42. ". . . impressam [vitam matris] desideratis jugiter inspicere; ut quae faciem matris parum noveratis, virtutum ejus notitiam plenius habeatis" (*Vita Margaritae,* Prologue, par. 1 [324]).

43. ". . . et cum in culmen terrenae dignitatis quem libet ex eis exaltari videris, illius maxime pater simul et magister accedas" (ibid., chap. 4, par. 27 [330]).

44. "Nam cum pretioso reginam decebat cultu induta procederet, omnia ornamenta velut altera Esther mente calcavit" (ibid., chap. 2, par. 12 [326]).

45. André Boutemy, "Notice sur le recueil poétique du manuscrit Cotton Vitellius A xii du British Museum," *Latomus* 1 (1937), 278–313, see 305. For an excellent review of the poetic sources of the Anglo-Norman period, see Elisabeth M. C. van Houts, "Latin Poetry and the Anglo-Norman Court, 1066–1135: The *Carmen de Hastingae Proelio,*" *Journal of Medieval History* 15 (1989), 39–62.

46. Hildebert of LeMans, "Epistolae," PL 171:290; and Waters, *Anglo-Norman Voyage of St Brendan,* 3. This emphasis on the queen and the law seems more than formulaic, however nothing is known of the queen's role in legislation or legal practice. The compiler of the *Leges Henrici primi* worked during Matilda's lifetime as is made clear from his dedicatory preface. See L. J. Downer, ed. and trans., *Leges Henrici primi* (Oxford, 1972).

47. A. Brian Scott, ed., *Hildeberti Cenomannensis episcopi carmina minora* (Leipzig, 1969), 24.

48. See H. W. C. Davis, Charles Johnson, H. A. Cronne, and R. H. C. Davis, eds., *Regesta regum Anglo-Normannorum 1066–1154,* 4 vols. (Oxford, 1913–69), 2:18, entries 568 and 569.

49. See "Udalrici Babenbergensis Codex," *Monumenta Bambergensia,* Bibliotheca rerum Germanicarum 5 (Berlin, 1869; reprint, 1964), entry 142, 259.

50. "Signum Matilldis reginae et filiae Anselmi archiepiscopi" (Thomas Hearne, ed., *Textus Roffensis* [Oxford, 1720], 225–27). See R. W. Southern, *Saint Anselm and His Biographer: A Study in Monastic Life and Thought 1059–c.1130* (Cambridge, 1963), 191–93.

51. "Te ergo, filia carissima, rogamus . . . cor illius a consiliis pravis avertere. . . . Memento quod dicit apostolus: 'salvabitur vir infidelis per mulierem fidelem [1 Cor. 7:14].'Argue, obsecra, increpa [2 Tim. 4:2]'" (*S. Anselmi opera omnia,* 5:292 [letter 352]).

52. "Haec consulite, haec secrete et publice intimate domino nostro regi et saepe repetite, et quantum ad vos pertinet, studiose rectractate" (ibid., 4:217 [letter 296]).

53. "Est . . . illi erga vos animus compositior quam plerique homines aestiment, qui deo annuente et me qua potero suggerente vobis fiet commodior atque concordio[r]" (ibid., 5:249 [letter 320]).

54. "Quod vero vobis in praesenti de redditibus vestris fieri permittit, idem et melius ampliusque in futurum, cum ex re et tempore postulaveritis, fieri permittet" (ibid.).

55. ". . . hoc totum dominus meus, rex Henricus, mihi praedictoque abbati, me ipsa interveniente, concessit" (Joseph Stevenson, ed., *Chronicon monasterii de Abingdon*, 2 vols., RS 2 [London, 1858; reprint, 1966], 2:52).

56. "Anglorum primae sedis archiepiscopo Hibernorum omniumque septentrionalum insularum, quae Orcades dicuntur primati" (*S. Anselmi opera omnia*, 4:150 [letter 242]). See also Southern, *Saint Anselm and His Biographer*, 191; and Sally N. Vaughn, *Anselm of Bec and Robert of Meulan: The Innocence of the Dove and the Wisdom of the Serpent* (Berkeley, 1987), 276–79.

57. "Ubi quamvis amplius quam aequum iudicem sibi teneat: oro tamen vestrae pietatis affluentiam, ut excluso amaritudinis humanae rancore, qui vobis inesse non assolet, dilectionis vestrae dulcedinem ab illo non avertatis; immo vero apud deum pro ipso et me et communi sobole et regni nostri statu pium vos intercessorem exhibeatis" (*S. Anselmi opera omnia*, 5:249 [letter 320]).

58. "Quod desiderio reditus mei nitimini cor domini mei regis erga me mitigare, facitis quod vos decet et quod illi expedire intelligo" (ibid., 5:250 [letter 321]).

59. "Si autem nec te fletus mei nec publica vota sollicitant: postposita regia dignitate, relictis insignibus, deponam fasces, diadema contemnam, purpuram byssumque calcabo et vadam ad te maerore confecta" (ibid., 5:245 [letter 317]).

60. "Illa, ut fertur, pietate mota in lacrimas solvitur, sed timore constricta ab interventione arcetur" (Eadmer, *Historia novorum in Anglia*, 173).

61. See the case of Adelaide of Sicily in my "Medieval Queenship," 21–22.

62. "Nihil rerum mortalium tam instabile ac fluxum est quam fama potentiae non sua vi nixae" (Tacitus, *Annals*, 13.19.1; translation from *The Annals of Tacitus*, ed. Henry Furneaux, 3 vols., 2d ed., rev. H. F. Pelham and C. D. Fisher [Oxford, 1896–1907, 1930], 2:176).

The Queen's Intercession in Thirteenth-Century England

John Carmi Parsons

O AN ARDENTLY PATRIARCHAL SOCIETY suspicious of wom-
en's power, medieval queens were a disturbing anomaly. Though as wife and mother a queen filled conventional female roles that subjected her to male control,
her marriage linked her intimately to a hereditary, char-
ismatic ruler who embodied and protected a male-defined social order
to which women were anomalous, their power inimical. A king's wife
had greater resources and more opportunities than other women to
exercise and increase her power, and most queens actively sought those
ends, but medieval society was generally unwilling that a queen should
acquire any share in her husband's authority.[1] Her influence was instead
directed to areas in which her role complemented the king's: as a
foundress of monasteries and churches, for example, she appeared as
the nurturing mother of the church the king was sworn to protect.[2] The
queen's idealization as a virtuous maternal figure complementing the
king as ruler and lawgiver reflects the prevalence in medieval male
writings of constructs that identify the male with culture and the female with nature—that patriarchal equation among whose oldest
daughters is the cliché that "if the king is law, the queen is mercy."[3]
Cliché it may be; but it underlay a complementary role for which the
queen's life experiences in the unofficial sphere well prepared her by
accustoming her to deal with others independently of institutions or
offices, responding to requests and appealing to authority: her intercession with the king, to soften his heart toward his subjects and improve his rule.[4]

Coronation of the Virgin, detail of thirteenth-century ivory dip-
tych, French. The Metropolitan Museum of Art, The Cloisters
Collection, 1970. (1970.324.7ab)

As Lois Huneycutt has shown, the decline of the English queen's role in government from the early twelfth century made her intercession an important means to create and sustain the impressions of power and influence upon which her position increasingly depended. In this process, the biblical Esther provided a model for churchmen who urged intercessory behavior on the queen; queens could adopt her as a model to be emulated, or manipulated to legitimize their actions.[5] The present essay examines English queens' intercession in the thirteenth century, by which time their official role in the kingdom had become further limited by growth in royal administration. Ironically, it was this same administrative development that generated the record evidence that sets the intercessory process in a broader context for the thirteenth century than is afforded by twelfth-century correspondence between bishops and queens. By their nature those letters can convey little about petitioners' viewpoints, but the thirteenth-century chancery and exchequer records reveal a profile among petitioners—who they were, how often the queens were approached, and in what circumstances. Petitioners' letters also survive, and reveal something of their thinking as they sought out the king's wife. Since the petitioners' understanding of the process was the element most vital to the formation of perceptions of the queen's power, this essay will concentrate on them, though other related questions are implied and will be treated as well: within thirteenth-century social and administrative contexts, actors may have redefined attitudes toward intercession, and fresh models for the queen's behavior may have appeared to encourage, construct, and legitimize her role as intercessor.

To define those new contexts, the evolution of the queen's official role from the twelfth century provides a necessary background. Eleventh- and early twelfth-century English queens were prominent women who often acted as regents for absent husbands, and they drew independent wealth from dower estates held during their marriages. From Henry II's accession in 1154, however, strict control of queens' resources limited their independence: they ceased to hold dower lands during their husbands' lives, and for the bulk of their income depended on corrodies paid by the kings' clerks as authorized by his writ. At the same period the queens' coronation rite was superficially elaborated, but while added prayers enhanced her office, they also inscribed limitations on her relationship with her husband. The queens' official role in government was further diminished as Eleanor of Aquitaine ceased to witness royal charters from 1155, or to issue writs in her own name after 1163.[6] Eleanor's disgrace in 1173 ended the queens' regencies, further reducing their public role, and the matrimonial careers of Richard I and John increased the queens' declining prominence. The widowhoods of Berengaria of Navarre and Isabella of Angoulême, moreover, reveal the slim foundations upon which a queen's position rested. Childless and unknown in England, Berengaria struggled for decades to secure her dower; Isabella, relegated by John to obscurity and financial dependence, never established a viable power base in England, and as a widow chose to preside over her Poitevin inheritance rather than lead a dowager's life in England.[7]

After decades of near abeyance, the queenship underwent fresh changes following Henry III's marriage in 1236. Eleanor of Provence did not enter her dower lands upon marriage but was provided with an independent income from a succession of wardships, and in order to manage these she soon came to preside over a powerful administration; that her efforts to increase her prerogative income were the object of complaints at the Oxford parliament in 1258 shows that her expanded sphere of activity was causing controversy.[8] The full implications became clear as Edward I's wife, Eleanor of Castile, aggressively exploited her resources to acquire extensive new lands, an endeavor which drew direct and repeated criticism.[9] At the same period, the growing importance of ceremony and ritual to royal government associated queens prominently with the public life of a powerful monarchy. One consequence of the renewed eminence of the thirteenth-century queens was that despite their exclusion from the center of magisterial authority, both Eleanors, vigorous and determined women, were suspected of undue political influence on their husbands.[10]

It is in the context of this newly reemergent English queenship that the queens' intercessory role surfaces in thirteenth-century record evidence as a conspicuous area of their endeavors.[11] The sheer bulk of this evidence after 1236 far outweighs the four surviving thirteenth-century papal and episcopal letters that urge English queens to intercede with their husbands. All four address particular moments of crisis between king and church; only two relate the queen to the kingdom at large, and Esther appears but once, as though at a time of growing tension between royal and papal power it was felt better to downplay the regal aspects of the situation. Churchmen now sought other scriptural and learned authorities: Isidore's etymology of "mulier" and, from wisdom literature, Ecclus. 26:1, "Blessed the man who has a good wife," or 36:27, "he who has no wife mourns his lack," were all expounded to show that it is a wife's duty as woman, more clement and merciful than man, to soften her husband's heart.[12] With one exception to be noted later, these letters do not define a certain role as proper to the queen so much as they echo the didactic literature noted by Huneycutt, which urged wives to improve their husbands' ways of life so they might win salvation.

The abundant record material, on the other hand, suggests the queens saw intercession as a means to sustain perceptions of their influence. Evidence points to an increase in such activity as widowhood neared or childbearing ended, implying that queens exploited the role with public relations in mind, or to manifest the strength of their marriages after they ceased to give the most obvious proof of intimacy with their husbands.[13] A recurrent concluding sentence in Eleanor of Castile's letters to royal clerks to whom she forwarded petitions shows she manipulated the process to construct networks of mutual obligation: "Do this for love of us, so that he shall know our prayer has been worthwhile, for which we will be especially held to thank you for him"; "Do this for love of us, so that he may know our prayer to you has been of value to him, for which we will be the more held to thank you."[14] The practical results could be invaluable; Eleanor's 1266 intervention with Henry III on behalf of William de Haustede won her two generations of service from that family.[15] Thirteenth-century evidence also supports Huneycutt's idea that the intercessory role afforded royal women the self-defining sense of belonging to a group with activities peculiar to themselves. Queens were responsible for educating their children, especially daughters, and that Edward I's daughters interceded with him implies that the experiences they shared with their mother and grandmother helped to shape the tactics by which they solicited the center of power.[16] A 1287 incident shows, moreover, that one queen could accept such intervention by another even if it crossed her own interests. The townspeople of Southampton refused to pay Eleanor of Castile a sum granted her by Edward I and appealed to his mother, who duly sent him a message that the payment would impoverish the town. When that letter reached Edward, his wife angrily commanded his lieutenant to take order with the situation—but she directed her fury at the townspeople, not at her mother-in-law, who had merely responded to a petition as was expected of her.[17]

The amount and nature of the surviving evidence considerably broadens this evolving picture of attitudes toward queenly intercession by allowing consideration from the petitioners' standpoint. There were many of them and they came from across the social spectrum. Magnates did approach the queens to obtain favors from the king, though the bulk of noble petitions involve crisis less than the paraphernalia of status: grants of land, permission to enclose a manor house, respite of knighthood, exemption from the burdens of royal administration, a pardon for the fine so the widow of a tenant-in-chief might marry whom she chose.[18] Here we have a clue to the dynamic of the queen's relations with the aristocracy. The intimate arena of a royal marriage intersected the realities of royal power, most especially the dispensing of patronage that was critical to effective royal lordship; and if the queen could channel patronage in a certain direction she might also obstruct it, a diversion of royal largess that was bound to cause resentment among those who thought themselves entitled to the king's bounty.[19] Eleanor of Castile indeed used her access to Edward I as an explicit threat in her 1287 letter ordering the earl of Cornwall to sort out the men of Southampton, and letters from the count of Bigorre in 1278 and the bishop of Worcester in 1283 show both men fearful of Eleanor's wrath when they could not obey her wishes.[20] For the upper strata of society whose members had the most to lose from her enmity, the queen's influence could be a malign force.

Perspectives on a queen's intercessory role as seen by the lower classes are found in a lucky combination of chronicle and letter touching an encounter in April 1275 between Eleanor of Castile and the townspeople of St. Albans, who disputed their obligation to full cloths in the abbot's mill. As the queen in her coach neared the town, the abbot came to meet her and saw the crowd who hoped to lay their complaints before her. He had her coach turned to another gate, but the people pursued them with loud cries; when the queen halted her coach the crowd, holding out their hands, begged for her help against the abbot, who took it all very patiently, even when Eleanor scolded him for trying to keep the crowd away from her. The encounter settled nothing—the town's spokeswoman was struck dumb in the royal presence—so the townspeople sent Eleanor a letter asking her to induce the king to order that the abbot produce the charters he was refusing to show. Given its request for her intercession, the letter's address attracts immediate attention:

A lur treschere dame par la grace de deu Reyne de Engletere les sons Burgeis de Seynt Alban saluz. Chere dame mout Vus enmercium de vos eides ke a nous souent avet fet e en ky tote nostre esperaunce

remeynt a touz iours cum a cele dame ky pleyne est de misericorde
e de pite. . . . Treschere dame a Vus merci crium si il Vus venge a
pleysir ke endevers nostre seynur li Reys ky deu gard veylet prier e
requere pur nous ke si ly plest face comaunder al Abbe de seynt Alban ke il monstre ses chartres les queus il a defi a monstre.[21]

Most striking is the phrase "en ky tote nostre esperaunce remeynt a
touz iours cum a cele dame ky pleyne est de misericorde e de pite."
Whether this be taken, as it likely should, to mean "all our hope remains in you forever, as [it does] in that Lady who is full of mercy and
pity," or whether the Anglo-Norman merely ascribes these qualities to
the queen, the evident Marian flavor is reinforced by the word "pleyne," irresistibly recalling the angelic salutation, and "tote nostre esperaunce," a phrase familiar from many hymns and poems to the Virgin,
especially the "Salve Regina."[22]

If the image of the Blessed Virgin was a more powerful popular
model than that of Esther for the interceding queen, we have a valuable tool with which to approach petitioners' perceptions of the queen
and her role. It is basic to the following discussion that appeal to the
queen's intercessory role was a popular response to the thirteenth-century English queens' renewed prominence, but not only in the sense
that they were more visible than their twelfth-century predecessors:
given the controversy and distrust surrounding these women, the intercessory role could be seen to limit the queen's relationship to authority by reducing it to the law-mercy construct—in effect isolating her
from authority by relegating her to the role of merciful intercessor. The
role of the Marian image in shaping popular expectations of the queen's
role, as mediator as well as in other areas of her activity, will be examined as a fundamental aspect of that limiting process.

It must be considered, then, how popular thinking came to assimi-
late intercession by the heavenly and earthly queens, and the Marian
image must be related to differing attitudes toward the queen shown
by the nobility and the lower classes. Michael Mullett discerns among
the lower classes in the later medieval period a conviction that the individuals at the head of secular society were benign and gracious, and
suggests the Virgin and Christ as images strong enough to nourish such
expectations; Edmund Leach has observed that recourse to intercessory figures is most common among those held furthest from the cen-
ters of power.[23] Mullett's ideas imply that only the Virgin could have

offered a positive female image strong enough to offset the contention and suspicion aroused by thirteenth-century English queens; Leach's model recalls the rapid growth in English government and administration in the twelfth and thirteenth centuries, which brought with it important developments affecting the queen. First, the increasingly complex, literate administrative world made intercessory figures attractive to many people, especially among the lower classes, whose encounters with that literate administration often found them at a disadvantage. Second, the queen became ever more isolated from government, in the process emerging as an attractive intercessor for those apprehensive of officialdom. This last point finds a parallel in contemporary quickening of Marian veneration—and in thirteenth-century England of appeal to Mary's intercessory capacity in particular—as the church developed its government and extended its presence in all aspects of Christian life; if we recall Victor Turner's evocation of Mary as "the Church in nonlegalistic form" and "a protection against law," we meet again the king:law::queen:mercy equation.[24]

Modern theory thus offers some pegs on which to hang this discussion, but the mechanics remain to be investigated. A point of departure is provided by the imagery summoned by Robert Grosseteste in a 1243 letter to Eleanor of Provence, urging her intercession with Henry III. In this last of the four episcopal letters to be considered here, Grosseteste cited Ecclus. 26:21, "Like the sun rising on the Lord's loftiest heights, so is the beauty of a good woman as she keeps her house in order," setting the queen in a protective relationship to church and realm by likening the effects of her mercy to the light of dawn that scatters the shadows of night and nourishes all living things.[25] Her intervention, like that of the prudent Esther—her one appearance in these letters—would ensure that Henry, like the king "sitting in the seat of judgment . . . [will scatter] all evil with his glance" (Prov. 20:8).[26] Grosseteste's imagery is echoed by a eulogy for Eleanor of Castile in an anonymous St. Albans chronicle written eighteen years after her death: "As the dawn when night is through scatters its shadows with her rays of light, so by the promotion of this most holy woman and queen, through all England the night of faithlessness was expelled, the . . . of wraths and discords were cast out."[27]

The use of dawn imagery by both bishop and monastic chronicler to evoke the effects of a queen's mercy echoes an association of the Virgin and the light of dawn found in the letters of St. Jerome, who put Cant. 6:9 into the mouths of angels marveling at Mary's Assumption into Paradise ("Who is this woman who comes forth like the rising dawn, fair as the moon, choice as the sun?").[28] This association was little remarked upon until the ninth century when Paschasius Radbertus amplified it in a letter long regarded as another of Jerome's works, and it achieved wider currency in the next centuries as the growth of the Virgin's cult accelerated the development of Marian imagery.[29] In the eleventh century Herbert de Losinga repeated Paschasius in a Marian sermon; Bernard's sermons on Cant. 6:9 and Apoc. 12:1 ("a woman clothed with the sun") further disseminated the image, and Marian hymns elaborated on the theme.[30] In the thirteenth century both Bonaventure and Aquinas maintained that sunlight is the most fitting Marian metaphor and described the light of dawn as the perfect expression of the effects of her mercy, echoing Bernard for whom Mary's mercy falls like the sunlight on everyone, good and bad alike. Dawn imagery also afforded a link to Esther, a Marian type introduced in sermons for the Virgin's feasts through the rising sun in Esther 11:11 ("The light and the sun rose up") and 8:16 ("To the Jews a new light seemed to rise").[31]

Just as the townspeople of St. Albans turned to the language of popular Marian devotion when seeking intercession by the king's wife, then, bishop and chronicler borrowed Marian imagery from learned exegesis and sermon tradition when they sought or described the queen's mercy. Given the medieval tendency to project the earthly hierarchy onto the heavenly, to legitimize the former by appeal to the latter, it is understandable that imagery associated with earthly queens attached to their heavenly counterpart and vice versa.[32] That scriptural passages describing queens' coronations were appropriated to the liturgy of the Virgin, for example, did not prevent chroniclers using the same texts to describe the investitures of earthly queens, as Thomas Wykes used Vulgate Ps. 44:10 "The queen stood at thy right hand," prominent in the liturgy for the feast of the Assumption, to describe the coronation of Edward I and Eleanor of Castile in 1274.[33] In the present case, however, it must be acknowledged that few townspeople would have heard those sermons and fewer could have compared them with chronicles or letters to shape parallels evident to the modern observer. A wider look for influences that shaped popular perceptions is required, and in the context of associations between earthly and heavenly queens, the search inevitably turns to one of the most pervasive medieval images of the Virgin, her coronation.

As early as the sixth century, western art depicted the Virgin with the attributes of Byzantine royalty, and tenth-century development at Winchester of the iconography of her coronation had close links to the growing reverence for secular kings and their consorts.[34] The church's observance most closely linked with Marian queenship was the feast of the Assumption, for which the liturgy, including the coronation imagery of Cant. and Ps. 44, favored the proliferation of coronation portals, paintings, and windows throughout Europe in the twelfth and thirteenth centuries. Through repeated portrayal of the Virgin as part of an identifiably royal ritual, hands joined or arms upraised in recognizable gestures of intercession, her coronation offered a widely disseminated linking of mediation by the heavenly and earthly queens, inviting observers (in Nigel Morgan's words) to identify the experience of human action with action in the holy image.[35] This association was itself enacted in royal ritual, for in what were undoubtedly carefully choreographed gestures, English queens at their coronations interceded for royal pardons. Probably only the lack of surviving evidence accounts for the few documented cases—Eleanor of Provence in January 1236 and Katherine of Valois in February 1421, though Anne of Bohemia in 1382 and Joan of Navarre in 1403 also obtained pardons at the time of marriage or coronation.[36] The queen's prescribed seating during the coronation, and at the banquet that followed as an integral part of the festivities,[37] virtually presupposed her intercession, for despite biblical precepts that the queen should sit to the king's right (Ps. 44:10; III Reg. 2:19), the English queen took a ceremonial seat at her husband's left. She was thus associated with the virge of justice and equity he held in that hand, not with the right hand in which he held the scepter symbolic of the power to command, a spatial arrangement that figured her seclusion from his magisterial authority and from functions such as justice that could be delegated but also related her to such qualities as mercy that he could not delegate, emphasizing the immediacy of her relationship to him. Within the coronation theater in Westminster Abbey, moreover, as a newly crowned couple were enthroned facing the altar, the queen would have sat to the north and the king to the south, an orientation that (as has been inferred from liturgical practice and the architecture of English convents for women) associated the couple respectively with the Old and New Testaments and with the moon and sun, relationships also evocative of that between the Virgin and Christ.[38] Perhaps these coronation intercessions were the prototypes of tableaux in later medieval entry pageantry in which queenly intercession was explicitly juxtaposed with that of the Virgin, probably fostering even closer popular association of the two. It is not implied here, however, that these ritual intercessions were what first suggested parallels between the heavenly and earthly queens; only that the association of gesture and image can hardly have been missed by the witnesses or by those who heard accounts of the ceremonies.[39] The association also obtained expression in sermons, as in a fourteenth-century Franciscan exemplum first published by Eileen Power: "We ought to imitate the man who has incurred the King's anger. What does he do? He goes secretly to the Queen and promises a present. . . . So when we have offended Christ, we should first go to the Queen of Heaven and offer her, instead of a present, prayers, fasting, vigils and alms; then, like a mother, she will come between thee and Christ, the father who wishes to beat us, and she will . . . soften the king's anger against us."[40]

Sermon, liturgy, art, and ritual can help explain popular association of intercession by the two queens; but if the Marian image is easily related to the attitude of the lower classes towards a king's wife, it is less readily assimilated to the nobility's negative view of the queen—the pervasiveness of which is evident among the records of a judicial inquiry held in 1291–92 into Eleanor of Castile's administration. Complaints brought then by Eleanor's tenants rarely if ever implicated her; instead they accused abusive manorial officials, and when Eleanor was mentioned it was as a remote and gracious figure to whom tenants appealed over the heads of stewards and bailiffs. In complaints by members of the landed class, however, the queen is an immediate and unattractive presence who fails to keep promises, orders her officials to harass neighboring landlords, and obtains new estates by sharp practice.[41] There is, moreover, a palpable relationship among the male nobility's view of powerful women as capricious and faithless, the lady of courtly literature who is angered when her suitor's ardor flags, and the miracle stories in which the Virgin withholds her favors from, or punishes, those who fail to honor her as they should—a parallel also found in sermons: "The mother of mercy grants three gifts, namely the golden belt of chastity, the gloves of charity, and the robe or hood of humility. Surely, if you were to repudiate the gifts of some great lady, it would be considered for ill. If you do not accept the gifts of the Blessed Virgin, you make her your enemy."[42]

There is nothing surprising in the notion that a patriarchal society should project identical expectations and apprehensions on the two most powerful female figures it knew. Rather closer to examination of noble attitudes, however, is Margaret Miles's work on the prevalence in fourteenth-century Italian art of scenes from the lives of the Virgin and the Magdalene.[43] Miles suggests that these paintings, ordered by the male urban patriciate, offered an image of submissive femininity that helped male rulers deal with anxieties caused by the independence of Italian townswomen. This attitude of submission was perfectly expressed in the queen's intercession: requests for her to intervene with the king acknowledged noble petitioners' inferiority to her, but implicit in the queen's request was her subjection to the king, strengthening the sense that she did not wield magisterial authority. Given that the vigorous thirteenth-century queens were distrusted by English magnates, enacting the intercessory role at the coronation—which did not otherwise define a relationship between queen and realm—could have served as both reminder and reassurance.[44]

Miles also theorizes that the artistic works she discusses implied a rejection of female biology and sexuality. From the petitioners' viewpoint, the intercessory role depended on the queen's access to her husband; but for a royal marriage, medieval society was less inclined to praise wifely charms than to condemn feminine wiles, as is clear from the suspicions of improper influence exerted by both Queens Eleanor. Simply put, the king cannot show himself susceptible to his wife's enticements. Distrust of a queen's sexual nature is reflected in English chroniclers' praise of royal wives through the masculinizing topoi associated with virginity since Jerome's time: the same eulogy that likens Eleanor of Castile's mercy to the light of dawn refers to her as "by sex a woman, but manlike in courage and virtue," while Eleanor of Provence was a "a noble and pious virago," who supported her husband "as manfully as the most puissant virago."[45] Such passages relate as well to elements of the queen's coronation other than enactment of the intercessory role. These obscured her sexual reality: she appeared at the ceremony with her hair unbound as if still virgin, and while she was blessed to share the king's bed and bear his children, she was exhorted to preserve such chastity within marriage as to merit the palm next to virginity, so that with the five prudent virgins she might be worthy of the Heavenly Bridegroom. It is in this sense that fears of the queen's influence relate to Miles's idea that depictions of the Virgin and the Magdalene imply rejection of female sexuality: if the king cannot show himself vulnerable to his wife's blandishments, she may not seek her goals through carnal subtleties.[46]

Of course no one will suggest that English queens were individually or personally identified with the Heavenly Queen; still less that any queen deliberately manipulated intercessory imagery to offer herself to the kingdom as a secular counterpart of the Queen of Heaven. In the thirteenth century, implicit popular associations of the two focused less on the woman than on her intercession. (In the later Middle Ages, such associations were more explicit in popular culture and at court—where they also emphasized the queen's dynastic motherhood—but the mechanisms involved require further study.)[47] Invested with new urgency by administrative expansion, the intercessory role allowed society to direct or limit the power of royal wives at a time when English queens enjoyed newly reemergent independence and were actively developing the resources to support it. The Marian cult, its growth closely linked to development of the church's administration, offered a universally accessible legitimizing image, unlike Esther who, as Huneycutt notes, was generally held up in the later Middle Ages as a model for noblewomen, not their less-favored sisters. Like familial models of marriage and motherhood, moreover, the Marian image both exalted and limited women and was susceptible to interpretation by different groups:[48] for church and nobility, the queen as chaste and submissive mediatrix was safely secluded from authority, and those less intimate with the court could project a loving and gracious face onto the king's wife as they sought her mercy. The chroniclers' gender-crossing topoi linked to virginity stress the multivalence of both Marian and virginal imagery—the former celebrating and confining, the latter eliciting a masculinization associated with assertiveness and tenacity. The prevalence of such symbolism in rituals of queenship could, then, idealize a benevolent wife chastely inclining her husband to justice and mercy, even as it implied (or threatened) the legitimation of new spheres of activity for a vigorous and determined queen. It seems almost superfluous to repeat Turner's characterization of Mary as "a paradigm of the Christian theme of the power of the weak."[49]

Queenly intercession indeed emphasized just that emotional, intuitive aspect of a woman's power, associated with her abject posture and with the disempowered,[50] that posed the greatest risk to male order, giving a tinge of urgency to the process by which an image as powerful as that of the Virgin was summoned to legitimize the queen's role as government expanded, and as society more sharply defined gender roles and limits between kingly authority and queenly influence. The ramifications of this reasoning, however, might imply that intercession carried less positive implications for the queen's position. Regardless of distinctions in the concerns that brought them before her, earl, townsperson, or tenant solicited the queen on the same footing; as intercessor, she thus stood not in what Victor Turner calls a particularistic or normative relationship to her petitioners—a relationship characteristic of hierarchy—but rather in that simpler, generic relationship Turner associates with the liminal state he calls "communitas."[51] The sources invite evaluation of queens' intercession in this light. Accounts of petitioners' approaches to thirteenth-century queens suggest experiences comparable to pilgrimage as they left home, traveled to a royal manor, entered the queen's chamber, submitted to her favor, and in some cases became her clients. There is no evidence for mass excursions to the queens as Chaucer might have described, but petitioners were likely gathered together in groups as they waited to enter the queen's presence, and such moments do suggest the liminal equality Turner associates with pilgrimage.[52]

For Turner, liminality implies among other things a sharpened awareness of social order that generates criticism of existing structures—a criticism perhaps already implicit in petitions the queen received.[53] Her intercessory action thus associated her with a kind of horizontal leveling, as antithetical in its way to the vertical hierarchy the king embodied as was her potential diversion of the patronage through which he supported hierarchy. The queen's association with a liminal equality perhaps heightened the tensions royal marriage so often generated among observers; her marriage's ritually enhanced immediacy might even nurture suspicions of a meddlesome consort. Just as the imagery of the Virgin of Mercy—the *mater omnium,* sheltering humanity with her cloak—was invested with tokens of hierarchy,[54] however, the queen's intercessory action did not lack implications for the preservation of social order. That she was made to act as her petitioners' messenger, or servant, marks her intercession as a site of role inversion, a liminal state common to rituals of rulership that emphasizes the necessity of preserving order by manifesting chaos as the inevitable alternative and allays distrust of power by revealing the ruler's goodness.[55] Even as the queen's intercession suspended social structures it affirmed them, and with them the king's dominance: by appropriating the qualities exemplified in her actions, the king profited as his wife's role in construct-ing relations of domination and subordination helped to secure that "difficult alchemy" of consent that bound his subjects to him. Coro-nation intercessions, which showcased queenly humility and regal magnanimity in a setting replete with meaning for the affirmation of hierarchy, thus did not merely introduce English queens as submissive wives who humanized the face of government: queenship became an instrument of order and lordship.[56]

While intercession might seem less a source of power to the queen than merely another example of gendered role complementarity, the process did offer certain advantages. Her adoption of an intercessor's humble posture conformed to ecclesiastical and social expectations based on both Marc. 9:34 and 1 Cor. 1:27,[57] allowed her to manipulate successfully behind the scenes, legitimized her crossing of boundaries between influence and authority, and perhaps permitted her to convey some criticism to her husband; she thereby projected the image of an influential wife and could forge networks of great practical benefit to her. Her revelation of the king's authority as just and merciful elicits further consideration of her ritual roles. That kings heeded their wives' counsel reveals a willingness to countenance female modification of male official behavior, analogous to what Caroline Bynum has called a male desire to temper official authority with the nurturing and emo-tional qualities associated with the maternal. Dean Miller broadens the perspectives implied here by pointing to an essentially divisive tendency in western rites of rulership, in contrast to combinatory rites of Byz-antine rulership: the eastern priest-king appropriated both masculine and feminine potencies, while the western warrior-king required a com-plementary female figure to express solicitude or mercy and to affirm male power and authority—or, in Paul Strohm's words, queens supplied a "male lack." The rumors of saintly chastity or sexual depravity that often constellated around bachelor kings in the medieval West lend weight to Miller's ideas, and imply that the queen's roles as interced-ing wife and mother of the king's heir were part and parcel of the pro-cesses by which the court mirrored the divine order and generated human order: if intercession created a sacred identity for her, it is easy to see what identity the king assumed by attending to her requests— much as later Marian allusions at royal childbearing created Christo-logical affinities for their heir, strengthening his hereditary claim to a throne that was never truly dynastic. A gendered complementarity in royal roles was, then, fundamental to western rulership, and as European courts from the thirteenth century relied increasingly on the ceremonies and rituals that standardized such roles, queens were enabled to exploit them to sustain prominence and influence.[58]

A last conundrum in conclusion: the queen was expected to soften the king's heart, but her natural methods for doing so were suspect. Of course, medieval society more readily accepted in positions of power women whose status implied chastity or celibacy, such as abbesses or widowed queens-mother. But the denial of a queen-consort's sexual nature contradicted her role as perpetuator of the royal line—she is ideally fertile, yet her sexual nature must be masked by images of masculine virtue and virginal continence. That this anomaly parallels that implied in the mystery of a Virgin Mother may be yet another factor that favored assimilation of the Heavenly and earthly consorts.[59] And perhaps, too, it suggests an even more fundamental reason for Esther's eclipse: the Scriptures never do tell us that Esther had a child.

Notes

Portions of this material were presented at a March 1990 Fordham University conference, "Gender and the Moral Order in Medieval Society," at the May 1989 Congress on Medieval Studies at Western Michigan University, and at the February 1990 Toronto Conference on the history of medieval women. I am grateful to Professor Thelma Fenster for an invitation to speak at Fordham, and to Elizabeth A. R. Brown, Sharon Farmer, Susan Reynolds, the late Rev. Michael M. Sheehan CSB, Pauline Stafford, and Brian Stock for their comments; Gordon Kipling and Paul Strohm kindly provided copies of unpublished material, and I've profited from discussion with Lois Huneycutt and Elizabeth McCartney. Their advice, and audience reactions, are gratefully acknowledged though of course all conclusions are my own.

Unless otherwise noted all manuscript material is in the Public Record Office, London (S.C. 1/=Ancient Correspondence; JUST 1/=Justices Itinerant, *olim* Assize Rolls [formerly J.I. 1/]; E 159/ = King's remembrancer, memoranda rolls); *CPR=Calendar of Patent Rolls, CClR=Cal. of Close Rolls* (both ed., P.R.O.); RS=Rolls series; MGH=Monumenta Germaniae Historica, SS=Scriptores; PL=*Patrologia cursus completus, series latina*, ed. J.-P. Migne, 221 vols. (Paris, 1844–64); Paris, *CM*= Matthew Paris, *Chronica Majora*, ed. Henry Richards Luard, 7 vols., RS 57 (London, 1872–84); Parsons, *CHEC*=J. C. Parsons, *The Court and Household of Eleanor of Castile in 1290* (Toronto, 1977); *EHR=English Historical Review; BIHR=Bulletin of the Institute of Historical Research; JMH=Journal of Medieval History;* SCH=Studies in Church History.

1. In Michelle Zimbalist Rosaldo and Louise Lamphere, eds., *Woman, Culture and Society* (Stanford, 1974), see Rosaldo, "Woman, Culture, and Society: A Theoretical Overview," 17–42, and Jane Fishburne Collier, "Woman in Politics," 89–96; J. M. Taylor, *Eva Perón: The Myths of a Woman* (Chicago, 1979), 90–92, 145–46; Pauline Stafford, *Queens, Concubines and Dowagers: The King's Wife in the Early Middle Ages* (Athens, Ga., 1983); cf. Peter of Blois's explicit warning to Eleanor of Aquitaine, c. 1173, to submit to her husband (PL 207:448–49). On women and the male social order, Georges Duby, *Les trois ordres ou l'imaginaire du féodalisme* (Paris, 1978), 122, 164–67, 180, 255–56; Caroline Walker Bynum, "Women's Stories, Women's Symbols: A Critique of Victor Turner's Theory of Liminality," in Bynum, *Fragmentation and Redemption: Essays on Gender and the Human Body in Medieval Religion* (New York, 1991), esp. 35–36.

2. Taylor, *Eva Perón,* 14–17; Ann Crawford, "The Piety of Late Medieval English Queens," in Caroline M. Barron and Christopher Harper-Bill, eds., *The Church in Pre-Reformation Society: Essays in Honour of F. R. H. Du Boulay* (Woodbridge, Suffolk, 1985), 53–57. See also John Carmi Parsons, "Ritual and Symbol in English Queenship to 1500," in Louise Olga Fradenburg, ed., *Women and Sovereignty, Cosmos 7* (1991 [Edinburgh, 1992]), 60–77, and "Piety, Power and the Reputations of Two Thirteenth-Century English Queens," in T. M. Vann, ed., *Queens, Regents and Potentates,* Women of Power, 1 (Cambridge, 1993), 107–23.

3. Edmund Leach, *Culture and Nature or La femme sauvage* (London, 1968); Sherry B. Ortner, "Is Female to Male as Nature Is to Culture?" in Rosaldo and Lamphere, *Woman, Culture and Society,* 67–87; Carol P. MacCormack, "Nature, Culture and Gender: A Critique," in MacCormack and Marilyn Strathern, eds., *Nature, Culture and Gender* (Cambridge, 1980), 1–24; Caroline Walker Bynum, *Holy Feast and Holy Fast: The Religious Significance of Food to Medieval Women* (Berkeley, 1987), 282–88; R. A. Sydie, *Natural Women, Cultured Men: A Feminist Perspective on Sociological Theory* (Toronto, 1987); on such formulations in medieval thought and their impact on the status of women, see also Susan Mosher Stuard, "The Dominion of Gender: Women's Fortunes in the High Middle Ages," in R. Bridenthal, C. Koonz, and S. M. Stuard, eds., *Becoming Visible: Women in European Society,* 2d ed. (Boston, 1987), 153–72, esp. 165–66.

4. Nancy Chodorow, "Family Structure and Feminine Personality," in Rosaldo and Lamphere, *Woman, Culture and Society,* 43–66; cf. David Herlihy, *Medieval Households* (Cambridge, Mass., 1985), 120–22. As Paul

Strohm notes, there is nothing essentially feminine about intercession, but in a patriarchal society it was "a socially constructed prescription for femininity, a guide . . . for actual as well as imagined female behavior" (Strohm, "Queens as Intercessors," in Strohm, *Hochon's Arrow: The Social Imagination of Fourteenth-Century Texts* [Princeton, 1992], 104–5, quotation on 105).

5. See Huneycutt's essay in this collection.

6. Marion F. Facinger, "A Study of Medieval Queenship: Capetian France, 987–1237," *Studies in Medieval and Renaissance History* 5 (1968), 7–8; W. L. Warren, *Henry II* (Berkeley, 1973), 118–21; Elizabeth A. R. Brown, "Eleanor of Aquitaine: Parent, Queen and Duchess," in William W. Kibler, ed., *Eleanor of Aquitaine: Patron and Politician* (Austin, Tex., 1976), 9–34. H. G. Richardson correctly states that Eleanor issued no writs after 1163, but I cannot accept all conclusions in "The Letters and Charters of Eleanor of Aquitaine," *EHR* 74 (1959), 193–213, esp. 195 and 198 n. 6 on dower; cf. *Chronica Rogeri de Hoveden,* ed. William Stubbs, 4 vols., RS 51 [London, 1868–71], 3:27, and *Chronica Johannis de Oxenedes,* ed. Henry Ellis, RS 13 [London, 1859], 73). Eleanor witnessed no royal charters after March 1155 (R. W. Eyton, *Court, Household and Itinerary of King Henry II* [London, 1878], 6–7); on corrodies, Eyton, index 321, s.v. "England, Eleanor, Queen of." The inadequacy of her income from the prerogative known as queen-gold is clear in the 1180s (Charles Johnson, ed., *Dialogus de Scaccario by Richard, Son of Nigel* [London, 1950], 123). Twelfth-century elaboration of the queen's coronation is noted below.

7. John Gillingham, "Richard I and Berengaria of Navarre," *BIHR* 53 (1980), 157–73; Sidney Painter, *The Reign of King John* (Baltimore, 1949), 227, 235–36; W. L. Warren, *King John* (London, 1961), 75, 139; Richardson, "Letters and Charters," 209–11, and introduction to *The Memoranda Roll for the First Year of the Reign of King John (1199–1200),* Pipe Roll Soc., n.s. 21 (London, 1943), xix, xxxix, xcvi. John may have had the exchequer collect queen-gold in Isabella's name while keeping it for himself (Margaret Howell, "The Resources of Eleanor of Provence as Queen-Consort," *EHR* 102 [1987], 373 n. 3).

8. Hilda Johnstone, "The Queen's Household," in T. F. Tout, *Chapters in the Administrative History of Medieval England,* 6 vols. (Manchester, 1920–33), 5:232–35, 264–70, superseded by Howell, "Resources of Eleanor of Provence," 372–93. Cf. R. F. Treharne and I. J. Sanders, eds., *Documents of the Baronial Movement of Reform and Rebellion, 1258–1267* (Oxford, 1973), 78–79.

9. John Carmi Parsons, *The Court and Household of Eleanor of Castile in 1290* (Toronto, 1977), 17–22, and "Eleanor of Castile: Legend and Reality through Seven Centuries," in David Parsons, ed., *Eleanor of Castile 1290–1990: Essays to Commemorate the 700th Anniversary of Her Death: 28*

November 1290 (Stamford, 1991), esp. 28–35; *Registrum Epistolarum Fratris Johannis Peckham Archiepiscopi Cantuariensis,* ed. Charles Trice Martin, 3 vols., RS 77 (London, 1882–86), 2:619–20; *Annales Prioratus de Dunstaplia,* ed. Henry Richards Luard, RS 36 pt. 3 (London, 1866), 362; *The Chronicle of Walter of Guisborough,* ed. Harry Rothwell, Camden Soc., 3d. ser. 89 (London, 1957), 216.

    10. R. F. Treharne, *The Baronial Plan of Reform, 1258–1263* (Manchester, 1932), 308; *Registrum Epistolarum Peckham,* 2:555.

    11. A scarcity of evidence may be all that conceals the full scope of such activities in earlier centuries, but for reason to think the intercessory role might have become more prominent in the thirteenth century, see below. For earlier sources, see Huneycutt's essay in this volume; Frantisek Graus, *Volk, Herrscher und Heiliger im Reich der Merowinger: Studien zur Hagiographie der Merowingerzeit* (Prague, 1965), 406–16; J. M. Wallace-Hadrill, *Early Germanic Kingship in England and on the Continent* (Oxford, 1971), 92–93; Geoffrey G. Koziol, *Begging Pardon and Favor: Ritual and Political Order in Early Medieval France* (Ithaca, N.Y., 1992), 71–73, 81. Rosamund McKitterick sees for Ottonian Germany an ideal of queenship linked to the role of peacemaker ("Women in the Ottonian Church: An Iconographic Perspective," in W. J. Sheils and Diana Wood, eds., *Women in the Church,* SCH 27 [Oxford, 1990], 87); cf. the tenth-century *Vita Mahthildis reginae posterior,* ed. Georg Waitz, MGH SS 4 (Hannover, 1841), 287. Matilda of England, wife of Emperor Henry V, was said to be regarded by the Germans as a mediator with her husband (M. Chibnall, "The Empress and Church Reform," *Transactions of the Royal Historical Society,* 5th ser., 38 [1988], 170); the *Gesta Stephani* emphasizes Matilda of Boulogne's resort to supplication on her husband's behalf (*Gesta Stephani,* ed. K. Potter and R. H. C. Davis, 2d ed. [Oxford, 1976], 123; cf. *The Chronicles of John and Richard of Hexham,* in J. Stevenson, trans., *The Church Historians of England. Translated from the Original Latin with Preface and Notes by Joseph Stevenson,* 5 vols. [London, 1853–58], 4:1, 19; and William of Newburgh, *Historia Novella,* with translation by K. Potter [London, 1955], 57–58).

    12. Ecclus. 26:1, "Mulieris bonae beatus vir"; and 36:27, "ubi non est mulier, ingemiscit egens." Matthew Paris cites a papal letter to Eleanor of Provence, not in Innocent IV's manuscript registers (*CM,* 4:349; cf. *Isidori Hispalensis Episcopi Etymologiarum sive Originum libri XX,* ed. W. M. Lindsay, 2 vols. [Oxford, 1911], book 11, chap. 2). The other letters are in *Roberti Grosseteste Episcopi quondam Lincolniensis Epistolae,* ed. Henry Richards Luard, RS 25 (London, 1861), 271–72, and *Registrum Epistolarum Peckham,* 2:555.

    13. Henry III's acts at his wife's request increase in his last years, perhaps through pardons solicited after the Barons' Wars; she was notably

active as an intercessor in her son's reign. Enrolled intercessions by Edward I's second wife, forty years his junior and not the mother of his heir, are more abundant for her seven years as consort than Eleanor of Castile's for eighteen years; but the latter seemingly did accelerate the tempo of her intercessions after bearing her last child (John Carmi Parsons, "Petitions to the Queen's Mercy in Thirteenth-Century England," paper delivered at the Twenty-second International Congress on Medieval Studies, Kalamazoo, May 1987). David Loades, though describing a staged incident "designed to impress," thinks Catherine of Aragon had a loftier view of her role (*The Tudor Court* [Totowa, N.J., 1987], 4–5).

14. ". . . pur lamour de nous, issi qe il pusse <sentir qe nostre priere> ly vaillie vers vous pur que nous vous seums tenue especiaument a mercier pur ly" (S.C. 1/23/48A, to the chancellor on behalf of Philip, parson of Partingham [Caernarvon, 22 July 1283 or 1284]); ". . . issi kil puisse sentire ke nostre pryere vers vous ly vaille, pur qey nous seeons le plus tenue a mercier" (S.C. 1/30/47, to the king's lieutenant on behalf of Henry le Waleys of London [Bellegarde in Gascony, 27 Nov. 1288]). Cf. ". . . pro quo vobis teneri volumus oportunis temporibus ad actiones uberes graciarum" (S.C. 1/10/56 *bis*, to Mr William de Middelton urging Robert Burnell's speedy confirmation as bishop of Bath and Wells [Faversham, 4 Feb. 1275]); ". . . por le amour de nus, issi ke il puisse sentir ke nostre priere ly vaille" (S.C. 1/23/46, to the chancellor on behalf of the queen's chandler [Long Bennington, 17 Feb. 1284]).

15. *CPR 1258–1266*, 567–68; *CClR 1264–1268*, 466–67; Parsons, *Court and Household*, 35–38.

16. Cf. Chodorow, "Family Structure and Feminine Personality," passim. On Edward's daughters, e.g., *CPR 1301–1307*, 36, 37, 38, 65, 102, 254, 313, 389; M. A. E. Green, *Lives of the Princesses of England from the Norman Conquest*, 6 vols. (London, 1859–69), 2:298–99, 300.

17. *CPR 1281–1292*, 229; the dowager's letter is S.C. 1/23/21 (Marlborough, 22 Apr. s.a.), Eleanor of Castile's S.C. 1/30/44 (Blanquefort in Gascony, 17 Jan. s.a.).

18. For Eleanor of Provence see Paris, *CM*, 4:158; *CClR 1234–1237*, 314, 317; *CPR 1232–1242*, 280; *CPR 1247–1258*, 599, 607, 613, 626; *CPR 1266–1272*, 5, 41, 104, 226, 242, 332, 342, 345, 605, 729. For Eleanor of Castile see *CPR 1258–1266*, 400; *CClR 1264–1268*, 330; *CPR 1272–1281*, 202, 335; *CClR 1272–1279*, 483, 564; *CClR 1279–1288*, 205. For Edward I's second wife see *CClR 1296–1302*, 286, 343; *CPR 1292–1301*, 414, 502, 513, 538 (cf. *CClR 1296–1302*, 368); *CPR 1301–1307*, 56 *bis*, 60, 134, 154–55, 163, 179, 291, 378, 507, 532; *CClR 1302–1307*, 288, 481–82. This selective list does not purport to be comprehensive.

19. J. S. Hamilton, *Piers Gaveston, Earl of Cornwall 1307–1312: Politics*

and Patronage in the Reign of Edward II (London, 1988), shows Gaveston's appropriation of Edward II's patronage for himself and his family aroused baronial hatred more effectively than did his personal relationship with the king (109–11).

20. S.C. 1/30/44: "Kar sachet ke nous avons dit au Rey . . . <ke> nous garnierons vous . . . de totes les choses auandites"; S.C. 1/15/66 (s.d.): "Item domine Reuerende cum reuerenda domina nostra illustrissima . . . Regina nos si placet excusetis nam nobis datum est intelligi quod ipsa nos habet odio eo quod minus in Nauarram quod vitare nequimus cum fuissimus moniti . . . ferre." For the bishop's letter, J. W. Willis Bund, ed., *Episcopal Registers, Diocese of Worcester: The Register of Bishop Godfrey Giffard, September 23rd, 1268 to January 26th, 1302*, Worcester Historical Society (Oxford, 1898), 175–76, poorly calendars Hereford and Worcester Record Office MS. 713, fols. 155v–56r.

21. "To their dearest lady, by the grace of God Queen of England, her burgesses of St Albans send greeting. Dear lady, we thank you much for the help you have often given; and in you all our hope remains forever as in that lady who is full of mercy and pity. . . . Dearest lady, we shall be thankful if it please you that you agree to pray and require of our lord the King (whom God keep) for us that if he please he shall cause order to be made to the Abbot of St Albans that he show the charters which he has refused to show" (Thomas of Walsingham, *Gesta Abbatum Monasterii Sancti Albani,* ed. Henry Thomas Riley, 3 vols., RS 28, pt. 4 [London, 1867–69], 1:411–12; the letter is S.C. 1/11/90 [s.d.]). An anonymous letter possibly touching the same incident is S.C. 1/31/132 (s.d.): "Salutem quam sibi. Precor vos quatinus negocium . . Latricis presencium quod continetur in peticione quam vobis tradidi apud Sanctum Albanum deliberetis celius quo potestis. Domina enim nostra Regina expedicionem ipsius negocii desiderat admodum et festinatis. Feliciter valeat."

22. For advice on the text I am grateful to the late Rev. Michael M. Sheehan CSB, Prof. Peter Grillo of the University of St. Michael's College, and Prof. Brian Merrilees of Victoria University. On Marian imagery, Anselm Salzer, *Die Sinnbilder und Beiworte Mariens . . .* (Linz, 1893; reprint, Darmstadt, 1967), and for thirteenth-century England in particular, the rich bibliography in Nigel Morgan, "Texts and Images of Marian Devotion in Thirteenth-Century England," in W. M. Ormrod, ed., *Thirteenth Century England,* Proceedings of the 1989 Harlaxton Symposium, Harlaxton Medieval Studies 1 (Stamford, 1991), 69–103. For "spes nostra," Henri Barré, *Prières anciennes de l'occident à la mère du Sauveur des origines à saint Anselme* (Paris, 1963), 280–84; John Wickham Legg, *The Sarum Missal Edited from Three Early Manuscripts* (Oxford, 1916), 490; Anselm of Canterbury, *Hymni et Psalterium de Sancta Virgine Maria,* PL 158:1037. Cf. the

sequence for the feast of the Assumption, "Mediatrix nostra, quae est post Deum spes sola" (Franciscus Henricus Dickinson, ed., *Missale ad usum insignis et praeclarae Ecclesiae Sarum* [Oxford, 1861–63; reprint, Farnborough, 1969], cols. 668, 869, 895), and "On God Ureisun of Ure Lefdi," in Richard Morris, ed., *Old English Homilies and Homiletic Treatises,* EETS o.s. 29 (London, 1868), 190–91 (ll. 5–6), 196–97 (l. 125). On the "Salve Regina" in popular literature, Spurgeon Baldwin and James W. Marchand, "The Virgin Mary as Advocate before the Heavenly Court," *Medievalia et Humanistica* n.s. 18 (1992), 92.

23. Michael Mullett, *Popular Culture and Popular Protest in Late Medieval and Early Modern Europe* (London, 1987), 77–82 (McKitterick sees Christ and the Virgin bestowing "some special role on the Saxon queen as well as on the king" in the eleventh century ["Women in the Ottonian Church," 87]); Edmund Leach, "Virgin Birth," in *Genesis as Myth and Other Essays* (London, 1969), 85–122; cf. above, 160 and n. 54.

24. On the complexity of petitioning the king in thirteenth-century England, G. O. Sayles, *The King's Parliament of England* (New York, 1974), 79–80. See Morgan, "Texts and Images of Marian Devotion," 89, 95–96; Victor Turner and Edith Turner, *Image and Pilgrimage in Christian Culture: Anthropological Perspectives* (Oxford, 1978), 140, 171, 198–99; and David I. Kertzer, *Ritual, Politics and Power* (New Haven, 1988), 108–9. Robert Deshman sees an analogous development as tenth-century Christ-centered monastic piety influenced a shift from Davidic-theocentric Carolingian kingship to Christ-centered Ottonian kingship (*"Benedictus Monarcha et Monachus:* Early Medieval Ruler Theology and the Anglo-Saxon Reform," *Frühmittelalterliche Studien* 22 (1988), 204–40).

25. *Roberti Grosseteste Epistolae,* 310–11 ("Sicut sol oriens mundo in altissimis domini, sic mulieris bonae species in ornamentum domus eius"). Translation from *The Complete Bible: An American Translation* (Chicago, 1939).

26. Ibid. ("In solio judicii residens . . . omne malum intuitu suo dissipet").

27. "Sicut Aurora transactae noctis tenebras radiis suae claritatis depellit, ita hujus sanctissimae mulieris et reginae promotione, per omnem Angliam nox infidelitatis expellitur, [. . .] irarum atque discordiarum propelluntur (*Opus chronicorum,* in *Johannis de Trokelowe et Henrici de Blaneforde . . . chronica et annales,* ed. Henry Thomas Riley, RS 28, pt. 3 [London, 1866], 50 [the ellipsis represents an omission noted by Riley]). Cf. Grosseteste, 1243: "Sol autem oriens mundo tenebrarum propellit horrorem, luminis inducit jocundam suavitatem, nocturnos timores et turbulentias abigit" (*Roberti Grosseteste Epistolae,* 310). On "claritas," cf. the use of "cleere" for the interceding queen in *Athelston: A Middle English Romance,* ed. A. McI. Trounce, EETS o.s. 224 (Oxford, 1951), 78, a reference I owe to Patricia Eberle.

28. "Que est ista que progreditur quasi aurora consurgens, pulchra ut luna, electa ut sol."

29. PL 22:425; cf. PL 22:30, 134; Albert Ripberger, *Der Pseudo-Hieronymus-Brief IX 'Cogitis Me': Ein Erster Marianischer Traktat des Mittelalters von Paschasius Radbert* (Freiburg, 1962), and *Paschasii Radberti Epistula Beati Hieronymi ad Paulam et Eustochium de Assumptione Sanctae Mariae Virginis,* Corpus Christianorum, Continuatio Medievalis 55C (Turnhout, 1985). The image is an ancient one (Samuel Noah Kramer, *Sumerian Mythology: A Study of Spiritual and Literary Achievement in the Third Milennium B.C.,* rev. ed. [New York, 1961], 90); Gertrud Schiller notes that symbols from pagan mythology, sun and moon among them, were little used in Christian art until Carolingian times, perhaps one reason the image failed to flourish (*Iconography of Christian Art,* trans. J. Seligman, 2 vols. [London, 1971–72], 2:107). Association of Canticles with the Virgin was clearly a twelfth-century phenomenon; e.g., Alan of Lille, *Elucidatio in Cantica Canticorum* (PL 210:94), Honorius of Autun, *Sigillum Beatae Mariae* (PL 172:512), Hugh of St. Victor, *Sermo de Assumptione B. Virginis* (PL 177:1209–22), and Peter of Blois, *Sermo XXXIV (in Assumptione Beate Virginis)* (PL 207:663–64).

30. The phrase from the Apocalypse is "Mulier amicta sole." For the Marian sermons, see Edward Meyrick Goulbourn and Henry Symonds, eds., *The Life, Letters and Sermons of Bishop Herbert de Losinga,* 2 vols. (Oxford, 1878), 2:340–41 (cf. PL 30:134); R. Morris, ed., *Old English Homilies of the Twelfth Century from the Unique Ms. B.14.52 in the Library of Trinity College, Cambridge,* EETS o.s. 53 (London, 1873), 158–67; G. R. Owst, *Literature and Pulpit in Medieval England: A Neglected Chapter in the History of English Letters and of the English People,* 2d. rev. ed. (Oxford, 1961), 19. On Bernard's sermons see PL 183:421, 429–38, and for their artistic and liturgical context, Penny Schine Gold, *The Lady and the Virgin: Image, Attitude and Experience in Twelfth-Century France* (Chicago, 1985), 51–61. For hymns and sequences see J. W. Legg, *Sarum Missal,* 490, 491; Franz Joseph Mone, *Lateinische Hymnen des Mittelalters aus Handschriften herausgegeben und erklärt,* 3 vols. (Freiburg-i-B., 1853–55; reprint, Aalen, 1964), 2:7–8, 94–95, 154–55, 322–23, 355–56, 373–75, 392–93. See also Conradus de Saxonia OFM, *Speculum seu Salutatio Beatae Mariae Virginis ac Sermones Mariani,* ed. Petrus de Alcantara Martinez OFM, (Grottaferrata, 1975), esp. 314–16, 325–51; Richard of St. Laurence, *De Laudibus Beatae Mariae Virginis,* in *D. Alberti Magni . . . Opera Omnia,* ed. Augustus Borgnet and Æmilius Borgnet, 38 vols. (Paris, 1890–99), 36:384–90.

31. Esther 11:11, "Lux et sol ortus est," and 8:16, "Iudeis autem nova lux oriri visa est." Two of Bonaventure's sermons for the Nativity of the Virgin are based on the verse Grosseteste used for his letter to Eleanor of Provence. See *Doctoris seraphici S. Bonaventurae S.R.E. Episcopi Cardina-*

lis Sermones de tempore, de sanctis, de Beata Virgine Maria et de Diversis, in *Opera omnia* . . . *tomus IX* (Quaracchi, 1901), 698, 706–8, 712; cf. *S. Thomae Aquinatis Doctoris Angelici* . . . *Opera omnia* . . . *tomus XXIV: Opuscula Alia Dubia* . . . , 3 (Parma, 1869), 231–33; cf. Bernard, *Sermo in Dominica infra Octavam Assumptionis Beate Virginis Mariae,* PL 183:430–31. For Esther, see Conradus de Saxonia, *Speculum seu Salutatio,* 193, 196, 236, 263, 356; *D. Alberti Magni Biblia Mariana,* in *D. Alberti Magni* . . . *Opera Omnia,* 36:388–89. Aspects of the relationship between the Virgin and light in thirteenth-century piety are also discussed in J. S. Neaman, "Magnification as Metaphor," in Ormrod, *Thirteenth Century England,* 105–22, esp. 118–19.

32. Taylor, *Eva Perón,* 87–89; Robert Deshman, "*Christus Rex et Magi Reges:* Kingship and Christology in Ottonian and Anglo-Saxon Art," *Frühmittelalterliche Studien* 10 (1976), 397–99; Mary Clayton, *The Cult of the Virgin Mary in Anglo-Saxon England* (Cambridge, 1990), 164–65.

33. Ps. 44:10, "Astitit regina a dextris tuis." *Chronicon Thomae Wykes,* ed. Henry Richards Luard in *Annales Monastici,* 5 vols., RS 36 (London, 1864–69), 4:260. For Ps. 44:10 in a ritual honoring the English queen, Parsons, "Ritual and Symbol," 68.

34. Stafford, *Queens, Concubines and Dowagers,* 27, 127, 133; Deshman, "*Christus Rex et Magi Reges,*" 397–99; Clayton, *Cult of the Virgin Mary,* 146, 164–65, 273; McKitterick, "Women in the Ottonian Church," 88–89. A. Heslop thinks the Virgin in English art appeared with royal attributes only from 1100 ("The Virgin Mary's Regalia and Twelfth-Century English Seals," in A. Borg and A. Martindale, eds., *The Vanishing Past: Studies in Medieval Art, Liturgy and Metrology Presented to Christopher Hohler* [Oxford, 1981], 53–62); but cf. Marion Lawrence, "Maria Regina," *Art Bulletin* 7 (1924–25), 150–61; and George Zarnecki, "The Coronation of the Virgin on a Capital from Reading Abbey," *Journal of the Warburg and Courtauld Institutes* 13 (1950), 1–12.

35. Gold, *Lady and Virgin,* 51–61 (note that Vulgate Ps. 44 is Ps. 45 in the AV); Georges Duby, *Le temps des cathédrales: L'art et la société 980–1420* (Paris, 1976), 150–52, 185–88; Morgan, "Texts and Images of Marian Devotion," 89, 94 (cf. Neaman, "Magnification as Metaphor," 119). See also Leo Scheffczyk, *Das Mariengeheimnis in Frömmigkeit und Lehre der Karolingerzeit* (Leipzig, 1959), 477–96; and Philippe Verdier, *Le couronnement de la Vièrge* (Montreal, 1980). Evolution of Marian liturgy underlay exegetical development as well as the artistic expressions discussed here (E. Ann Matter, *The Voice of My Beloved: The Song of Songs in Western Medieval Christianity* [Philadelphia, 1990], 151–59). Coronation windows were more popular in England than portals (John A. Knowles, *Essays in the History of the York School of Glass-Painting* [London, 1936], 177); cf. the later

English hymn, "As the sun that shines through glass / So Jesus in His mother was" (William Anderson, *The Rise of the Gothic* [London, 1985], 30); Margaret R. Miles, *Image as Insight: Visual Understanding in Western Christianity and Secular Culture* (Boston, 1985), 76; and the relationship between the Virgin and dawn discussed above.

36. Parsons, "Ritual and Symbol," 64–65. Koziol shows that kings' ritual coronation prostrations also carried overtones of supplication, to God (*Begging Pardon and Favor*, 100–101).

37. The banquet hall would have publicized the act more widely. Early medieval queens' ritual actions at royal feasts had sensitive implications for the legitimation of hierarchy (Michael J. Enright, "Lady with a Mead-Cup: Ritual, Group Cohesion and Hierarchy in the Germanic Warband," *Frühmittelalterliche Studien* 22 [1988], 170–203.)

38. Double coronations took place in England only in 1274, 1308, and 1483; but, however rarely observed, the prescriptions noted here do not lack meaning. For the banquet, Anne F. Sutton and P. W. Hammond, eds., *The Coronation of Richard III: The Extant Documents* (Gloucester, 1983), 279; E. Hall, *The Union of the Two Noble Families of Lancaster and York 1550* (London, 1550; reprint, 1970), Henry VIII, fol. 3v; A. H. Thomas and I. D. Thornley, eds., *The Great Chronicle of London* (London, 1938; reprint, Gloucester, 1983), 340–41. The first rubricated English coronation ordo dates from the 1380s, but the queen's lower seat was older custom (Parsons, "Ritual and Symbol," 63–64); on right- and left-hand symbolism in European sovereignty, Dean A. Miller, "Byzantine Sovereignty and Feminine Potencies," in Fradenburg, *Women and Sovereignty*, 252–53. By the thirteenth century, French queens sat to the kings' right on occasions other than the coronation; as potential regents they were thus linked to the power to command (Elizabeth McCartney, "The King's Mother and Royal Prerogative in Early Sixteenth-Century France," in John Carmi Parsons, ed., *Medieval Queenship* [New York, 1993], 127, 139–40). English queens' intercession repeatedly reenacted their seclusion from royal authority; on such customs as grounded in gender, Parsons, "Family, Sex, and Power: The Rhythms of Medieval Queenship," in Parsons, *Medieval Queenship*, 7. For the theater, L. W. Legg, ed., *English Coronation Records* (Westminster, 1901), 81; on north-south symbolism, D. Baker, "Politics, Precedence and Intention: Aspects of the Imperial Mosaics at San Vitale, Ravenna," in B. Wheeler, ed., *Representations of the Feminine in the Middle Ages*, Feminea Medievalia 1 (Cambridge, 1993), 180–81, 211; and on its Marian nuances, especially for a high-status male audience, Roberta Gilchrist, "'Blessed Art Thou among Women': The Archaeology of Female Piety," in P. J. P. Goldberg, ed., *Woman Is a Worthy Wight* (Stroud, 1992), 212–26.

39. I must thank Prof. Gordon Kipling for a draft of his forthcoming

monograph on these pageants; see also Kipling, "The London Pageants for Margaret of Anjou: A Medieval Script Restored," *Medieval English Theatre* 4 (1982), 5–27. Cf. Sydney Anglo, *Spectacle, Pageantry and Early Tudor Policy* (Oxford, 1969), 253–54; Parsons, "Ritual and Symbol," 61; E. W. Ives, *Anne Boleyn* (Oxford, 1986), 283–84. In two cases kindly pointed out to me by Margaret Howell, fourteenth- and fifteenth-century coronation windows in Sussex were later identified as royal portraits—at Bexhill (Henry III and Eleanor of Provence) and at Hooe (Edward III and Philippa of Hainaut); see Agnes Strickland, *Lives of the Queens of England from the Norman Conquest*, 2d ed., 8 vols. (London, 1851; reissued 1854), 1:378–79; and I. Nairn and N. Pevsner, *The Buildings of England: Sussex* (Harmondsworth, 1965), 415, 539.

40. Eileen Power, introduction to Johannes Herolt, *Miracles of the Blessed Virgin Mary*, trans. C. C. Swinton Bland (London, 1928), xiv (in the English translation only).

41. Johnstone, "Queen's Household," in Tout, *Chapters*, 5:270–72; M. E. Fenwick, *The Inquiry into Complaints against the Ministers of Eleanor of Castile, 1291–92*, M.A. thesis (Univ. of London, 1931); Natalie M. Fryde, "A Royal Enquiry into Abuses: Queen Eleanor's Ministers in North-East Wales, 1291–92," *Welsh History Review* 5 (1970–71), 366–76; and Parsons, "Eleanor of Castile: Legend and Reality," 30–37, 40–41. The remainder of this discussion has been greatly influenced by Robert K. Merton, "The Role-set: Problems in Sociological Theory," *British Journal of Sociology* 8 (1957), 106–20, and "On Sociological Theories of the Middle Range," in Merton, *On Theoretical Sociology: Five Essays, Old and New* (New York, 1967), 39–72, esp. 41–45, a reference for which I am indebted to Prof. Brian Stock.

42. "Mater misericordie tria donaria cuilibet presentat, videlicet zonam auream castitatis, cerothecas caritatis, peplum siue capellum humilitatis. Certe si repudiares munera alicuius matrone, pro malo haberetur. Sic si donaria Beate Uirginis non recipis, ipsam inimicam tuam constituis" (Phyllis B. Roberts, "Stephen Langton's *Sermo de Virginibus*," in Julius Kirshner and Suzanne F. Wemple, eds., *Women of the Medieval World: Essays in Honor of John H. Mundy* [Oxford, 1985], 109, 117 [giving Latin and English]; my thanks to Phyllis Roberts for drawing this article to my attention). See also Duby, *Temps des cathédrales*, 151; Rosemary Radford Ruether, *New Woman, New Earth: Sexist Ideologies and Human Liberation* (New York, 1975), 52; and Paule Bétérous, "Quelques aspects de la piété populaire au XIIIe siècle à travers les miracles mariaux," in *La piété populaire au Moyen Age: Actes du 99e congrès national des sociétés savantes (Besançon 1974)*, 1 (Paris, 1977), 283–91, esp. 287–88.

43. Miles, *Image as Insight*, 75–87. On the Magdalene as a model of

submission, penitence, and redemption for medieval women, occupying the unbridgeable gap between Eve and the Virgin, see Victor Saxer, *Le culte de Marie Madeleine en Occident des origines à la fin du Moyen Age*, 2 vols. (Auxerre, 1959).

44. The notion of queens as abject, kneeling supplicants was embedded in popular thinking through art, literature, and staged performances "meant to impress," such as coronation intercessions (see n. 13); cf. Strohm, "Queens as Intercessors," passim; Strickland, *Lives of the Queens*, 1:423–24; the miniature added to Richard II's 1389 charter for Shrewsbury obtained by Anne of Bohemia (Jonathan J. G. Alexander and Paul Binski, *Age of Chivalry: Art in Plantagenet England, 1200–1400* [London, 1987], cat. no. 716, 520); and *Athelston*, ed. Trounce, 75–76. Documentary evidence does not imply that queens regularly knelt to intercede. Eleanor of Castile's meeting with Edward I on Agnes de Sparkeford's behalf was a simple explanation of Agnes's plight (G. O. Sayles, ed., *Select Cases in the Court of King's Bench under Edward I*, 3 vols., Selden Society 55, 57–58 (London, 1936–39), 1:65–66, 2:20–23, 3:xcix n. 4; and JUST 1/542 m. 8r); Lucy de Grey's letter seeking Eleanor's help with debts refers to a conversation with the queen and the chancellor "in the window" (S.C. 6/30/97 [s.d.]).

45. "Sexu quidem foemina, sed animo atque virtute plus viro" (*Opus chronicorum*, 49); "generosa et religiosa virago" (*Flores historiarum*, ed. Henry Richards Luard, 3 vols., RS 95 [London, 1890], 2:500), and "tam viriliter, tamquam virago potentissima" (ibid., 3:72); James Orchard Halliwell, ed., *The Chronicle of William Rishanger, of the Barons' Wars: The Miracles of Simon de Montfort*, Camden Society, 15 (London, 1840), 36. Cf. Stafford, *Queens, Concubines and Dowagers*, 30; Betty Bandel, "The English Chronicler's Attitude toward Women," *Journal of the History of Ideas* 16 (1955), 113–18; and Margaret L. King, *Women of the Renaissance* (Chicago, 1991), 192–93.

46. Legg, *English Coronation Records*, 37, 100, 108. These were twelfth-century borrowings from the *Ordo romanus* (John Joseph Brückmann, "English Coronations, 1216–1308: The Edition of the Coronation Ordines" [Ph.D. dissertation, Univ. of Toronto, 1964]), which must be seen in relation to contemporary developments in English queenship (see above, 149). This interpretation is closely related to material in Sherry B. Ortner and Harriet Whitehead, eds., *Sexual Meanings: The Cultural Construction of Gender and Sexuality* (Cambridge, 1981), whose theme is the male anxieties aroused by female involvement in, and possible disturbance of, activities associated with male prestige; see especially the essays by M. Strathearn ("Self-Interest and the Social Good: Some Implications of Hagen Gender Imagery" [166–91]) and M. Llewelyn-Davies ("Women, Warriors, and Patriarchs" [330–58]) on identification of the female with particular-

istic self-interest and the male with the welfare of the larger society. In contrast to the virginal implications of unbound hair, an overtly sexual, reproductive connotation is given the loosened hair by Claire Richter Sherman, "The Queen in Charles V's 'Coronation Book': Jeanne de Bourbon and the 'Ordo ad Reginam Benedicendam,'" *Viator* 8 (1977), 271–72; and Brigitte Bedos-Rezak, "Women, Seals and Power in Medieval France, 1150–1350," in Mary Erler and Maryanne Kowaleski, eds., *Women and Power in the Middle Ages* (Athens, Ga., 1988), 75, emphasizing the liminal spaces queens occupied. As with her seat to the king's left, the English queen's flowing hair was not rubricated until the 1380s, but French queens were so crowned long before the custom was first prescribed (Sherman, "Queen in Charles V's 'Coronation Book,'" 271–72); likewise unrubricated until the 1380s, English queens' scepters were bestowed at their coronations by 1236 (Parsons, "Ritual and Symbol," 62–63).

47. As Mullett implies (see n. 23 above), popular sentiment was more candid (Ives, *Anne Boleyn*, 283; cf. n. 38 above). Marian imagery at royal births evolved a coronation theme echoed in civic pageantry (Parsons, "Ritual and Symbol," 67; Mary Dormer Harris, ed., *The Coventry Leet Book*, 4 parts in 2 vols., EETS o.s. 134–35, 138, 146 [London, 1907–13], 1–2:287–88; Anglo, *Spectacle, Pageantry and Early Tudor Policy*, 253–54; Ives, *Anne Boleyn*, 277–78); Heslop relates Mary's regalia to prophecies of Christ's birth and hence to her divine motherhood, by extension perhaps linking queenly regalia to dynastic motherhood ("Virgin Mary's Regalia," 62). Only from the fifteenth century did queens' statues depict them with the Virgin's impressive beauty—but did this further or follow Marianization of the queens' image (Duby, *Temps des cathédrales*, 376–77, and "La vulgarisation des modèles culturels dans la société féodale," in *Hommes et structures du Moyen Age: Recueil d'articles* [Paris, 1973], 299–308)? Cf. Eleanor of Castile's tomb effigy at Westminster (1291), and the wall paintings of the Virgin and St. Margaret in South Newington church c. 1330–40 (E. W. Tristram, *English Wall Painting of the Fourteenth Century* [London, 1955], 70–73 and plates 16a–b). Even later, Marian qualities were attributed to Elizabeth Tudor and Victoria (Elkin Calhoun Wilson, *England's Eliza* [Cambridge, Mass., 1939], 200–29; Robin Headlam Wells, *Spenser's Faerie Queene and the Cult of Elizabeth* [Totowa N.J., 1983], 14–21; and John Wolffe, "The End of Victorian Values? Women, Religion, and the Death of Queen Victoria," in Sheils and Wood, *Women in the Church*, 485–88).

48. Turner, *Image and Pilgrimage*, 154; Miles, *Image as Insight*, 75–89; Gold, *Lady and Virgin*, 70–75. The growing influence of male-female bipolarities in medieval thought (Stuard, "Dominion of Gender," 165–70) must also be taken into account here.

49. Turner, *Image and Pilgrimage*, 154. On the multivalence of domi-

nant ritual symbols, Victor Turner, especially *The Forest of Symbols: Aspects of Ndembu Ritual* (Ithaca, N.Y., 1967). For a royal woman's use of such liminal imagery see Elizabeth Kristofovich Zelensky, "'Sophia the Wisdom of God': The Function of Religious Imagery during the Regency of Sofiia Alekseevna of Muscovy," in Fradenburg, *Women and Sovereignty,* 192–211.

50. Cf. Strohm, "Queens as Intercessors," 103–4.

51. Victor Turner, *Dramas, Fields and Metaphors: Symbolic Action in Human Society* (Ithaca N.Y., 1974), 196. On equality among those approaching the queen, cf. Bernard on the operation of the Virgin's mercy, above, 155.

52. Turner, *Image and Pilgrimage,* 253–54; cf. the model of appeal to a saint in Peter Brown, *The Cult of the Saints: Its Rise and Function in Latin Christianity* (Chicago, 1981), 118–19. Lucy de Grey of Codnor saw Eleanor of Castile in her bedchamber at Macclesfield (Parsons, "Ritual and Symbol," 67). Agnes de Sparkeford, a Somerset landholder, went to Eleanor at Clarendon for help in recovering land, and received a money fee after conveying the land to her (Sayles, *Select Cases,* 1:65–66, 2:20–23, 3:xcix n. 4; JUST 1/542 m. 8r); cf. the Haustede family above. The rector of Hanmer (Flintshire) and poor tenants from Overton went to Eleanor at Macclesfield in 1290 (JUST 1/1149 mm. 10r, 6r; cf. Natalie Fryde, ed., *List of Welsh Entries in the Memoranda Rolls, 1282–1343* [Cardiff, 1974], no. 144, 17). One R. Cissor of London, implicated in a fraud that cost a poor widow her tenement, went to the queen in Wales to confess and asked her to help the widow (S.C. 1/10/51 [Aberconway, 17 Mar. s.a., c. 1283]). There is little thirteenth-century evidence for procedures, but cf. Edward IV's mother, who saw petitioners in her audience chamber one hour a day (C. A. J. Armstrong, "The Piety of Cicely, Duchess of York: A Study in Late Mediaeval Culture," in Armstrong, *England, France, and Burgundy in the Fifteenth Century* [London, 1983], 142).

53. Turner, *Dramas, Fields and Metaphors,* 255, and *From Ritual to Theatre: The Human Seriousness of Play* (New York, 1982), 47. Strohm suggests queenly intercession as a critique of male behavior ("Queens as Intercessors," 103–4); cf. Joan Ferrante, "Public Postures and Private Maneuvers: Roles Medieval Women Play," in Erler and Kowaleski, *Women and Power in the Middle Ages,* 213–29, and see below.

54. L. Réau, *Iconographie de l'art chrétien,* 3 vols. in 6 (Paris, 1955–59), 2, pt. 2: 117.

55. Koziol develops the act of supplication as one of subjection to a superior, though accepting that it entailed prostration as represented in literature and art (cf. remarks on the image of the kneeling queen, n. 44 above) (*Begging Pardon and Favor,* 78–79, 95, 100). See also Kertzer, *Ritual, Politics and Power,* 50–56 (note that Kertzer feels such rituals of ruler-

ship are likely to be most highly developed where the gap between ruler and ruled is widest [see above, n. 24]); Victor Turner, *The Ritual Process: Structure and Anti-Structure* (Ithaca, N.Y., 1969), 166–203, esp. 176–77; and Maeke de Jong, "Power and Humility in Carolingian Society: The Public Penance of Louis the Pious," *Early Medieval Europe* 1 (1992), 29–52, esp. 49–50. See also Enright, "Lady with a Mead-Cup," 189–90.

56. Koziol, *Begging Pardon and Favor,* 101–2; Turner, *Ritual Process,* 129; Enright, "Lady with a Mead-Cup," 182–83, 202; Fradenburg, "Rethinking Queenship," in Fradenburg, *Women and Sovereignty,* 2, 8–9 (remarking on Parsons, "Ritual and Symbol"). These observations would be especially true if queens interceded at the banquet (see above); in this light, coronation intercessions might solve problems noted by Jacques le Goff in taking the banquet as a rite of aggregation in Van Gennep's sense ("A Coronation Program for the Age of St Louis: The Ordo of 1250," in János M. Bak, ed., *Coronations: Medieval and Early Modern Monarchic Ritual* [Berkeley, 1990], 55 n. 16). It is typical of what Fradenburg (5) calls the interstitiality of queens' power, and of queenly liminality, that intercession can also be seen as a critique of the domination it is here shown to help forge (cf. Strohm, "Queens as Intercessors," 103–4, and above). The above discussion echoes a critical point of Caroline Bynum's in that it embodies a male viewpoint of queens and queenly liminality: women were fully liminal only to men, not to other women ("Women's Stories, Women's Symbols," 49). This would imply that women understood the intercessory role differently from men; but the records dealt with here—created by men—rarely allow women's attitudes to be distinguished from men's in this respect.

57. Marc. 9:34: "Si quis vult primus esse, erit omnium novissimus, et omnium minister"; 1 Cor. 1:27: "infirma mundi elegit Deus, ut confundat fortia." On the latter as justification for medieval women's power to rebuke or correct male authority, see Barbara Newman, *Sister of Wisdom: St. Hildegard's Theology of the Feminine* (Berkeley, 1987), 1–4.

58. On intercession as ritual, Parsons, "Ritual and Symbol," 65–66; on queens' indispensability in royal ritual, A. M. Hocart, *Kings and Councillors: An Essay in the Comparative Anatomy of Human Society* (Cairo, 1936; reprint, Chicago, 1970), 79–80, 98, 136–37, 260–61. On the court and divine order, Koziol, *Begging Pardon and Favor,* 77–103; Clifford Geertz, *Negara: The Theatre State in Nineteenth-Century Bali* (Princeton, 1980), and "Politics Past, Politics Present: Some Notes on the Uses of Anthropology in Understanding the New States," in *The Interpretation of Cultures: Selected Essays by Clifford Geertz* (New York, 1973), 331–33 (cf. Kertzer, *Ritual, Politics and Power,* 108–9). See also Strohm, "Queens as Intercessors," 103–4; and Caroline Walker Bynum, *Jesus as Mother: Studies in the Spirituality of the High Middle Ages* (Berkeley, 1982), 154–59. On gender and

sovereignty, Fradenburg, "Rethinking Queenship," 2–3. There are echoes for Justinian's wife Theodora of the symbolic hermaphroditism of Byzantine sovereignty (cf. Miller, "Byzantine Sovereignty and Feminine Potencies," 259; Charles Barber, "The Imperial Panels at San Vitale: A Reconsideration," *Byzantine and Modern Greek Studies* 14 [1990], 40; and Baker, "Politics, Precedence and Intention," 211). An arresting instance of gender inversion is noted in pageantry for Margaret of Anjou at Coventry in 1456: a depiction of the dragon-killing St. Margaret—the only female to appear in the pageantry—implicitly juxtaposed the queen with the male dragon-slayer St. George (Harris, *Coventry Leet Book*, i, 291–92; J. N. King, "The Godly Woman in Elizabethan Iconography," *Renaissance Quarterly* 38 [1985], 52).

59. On the operation of symbols to maintain the separateness of contradictory values while highlighting their proximity to each other, with specific reference to virginity and fecundity, see Paul Hershman, "Virgin and Mother," in Ioan Lewis, ed., *Symbols and Sentiments: Cross-Cultural Studies in Symbolism* (London, 1977), 269–92, esp. 289–91; and Joyce E. Salisbury, "Single in Fruitfulness," *JMH* 8 (1982), 97–106.

Ceremonies and Privileges of Office: Queenship in Late Medieval France

Elizabeth McCartney

N MONDAY, 18 NOVEMBER 1504, Anne of Brittany was solemnly crowned queen of France in the abbey church at Saint Denis. Among the observers was her secretary, André de la Vigne, who watched the ceremony with interest, although not impartially. A privileged member of the royal court, he well understood the timely significance of the rituals performed in Anne's honor. In his account of this ceremony Vigne noted that from the moment Anne was invested with the regalia of her office—scepter, rod, crown, and, most significantly, her wedding ring—she "took possession, seizen, and full use of the kingdom of France, with the provision of having and receiving after the king, alone and without hindrance, the wealth, triumphs, glories, honors, preeminence, prerogatives, support, favors, and generally all other things which by rule of law came to her with the title of the most high and excellent queen of France".[1]

Vigne's assertion regarding the constitutional significance of the coronation ritual merits scrutiny and is the subject of this essay. That royal and distaff authorities were not joined was a fundamental tenet of French public law that recognized only a queen's lack of juridical capacity.[2] For various reasons, the proscriptive basis of queenship in late medieval France was of paramount concern to members of the royal court who, in 1504, began to examine the significance, both symbolic and juristic, of Anne's privileges of office. In turn, this interest in queenship encouraged new study of medieval texts and glosses of Roman, canon, and feudal law as a means of establishing this claim. Although such scholarship was an important component of French constitutional thought, modern scholars have had little interest in examining how the legal arguments developed in medieval France influenced sixteenth-century perceptions of queenship. This essay suggests why both the ceremonies and privileges of office that French queens in late medieval and early sixteenth-century France enjoyed should be studied in conjunction with the history of French public law.

The ceremonies performed in Anne's honor in 1504 were elaborate, carefully planned, and lengthy; combined, the various festivities took one month to complete.[3] The coronation ceremony began quietly on Saturday, 16 November, when the queen left the royal residence in Vincennes and was escorted to the abbey church of Saint Denis.[4] Here, she was received "with great reverence" on the church steps by the ecclesiastical dignitaries who would serve as the officiants at the coronation ritual. The most distinguished member of this group was the cardinal and papal legate Georges d'Amboise, a prominent figure at the royal court. Also in attendance were other archbishops and bishops of the realm, some of whom were to share responsibilities for officiating at the coronation ceremony.[5] Anne then entered the church and completed her devotions. Later, she was escorted to her residence, where she and the ranking members of her household resided until the performance of the coronation ceremony two days later.

Around eleven A.M., on Monday, 18 November, Anne was again escorted to the church steps. This ceremonial procession, also an integral part of the coronation ritual, was especially noteworthy because it included the most privileged members of the royal family, the princes of the blood, the queen's ladies-in-waiting, and other exalted members of the royal court. Before a large, international audience of dignitaries, Anne was crowned and honored as queen.[6] After the ritual of coronation was performed and the regalia of scepter, rod, crown, and ring were bestowed upon the queen, Mass was celebrated.[7] Following the service, Anne returned to her residence amid full fanfare, where festivities continued for the royal court with dinner and dancing. Early the following morning (Tuesday, 19 November), Anne again attended Mass and received reverences from her subjects who lined the streets in attendance.[8] Later in the morning she enjoyed a second ceremonial privilege of office: a postcoronation entry ceremony into the city of Paris.[9]

By the early sixteenth century, an elaborate protocol was a requisite component of such royal or "state" ceremonials and the same was true for the public festivities honoring a French queen.[10] That neither processional order nor emblems of dress were incidental components of rulership had been addressed recently by Charles VIII, who issued a royal edict that established a parity between the ceremonies performed in his honor and those for Anne of Brittany.[11] As for the king, those who participated in the queen's ceremony were members of the realm's most noble families, each of whom ensured that their vestimentary splendor reflected the dynastic greatness of the monarchy.[12] The privilege of serving royalty also belonged to ranking members of the royal court and the civic bureaucracies. Among the civic officials greeting Anne in 1504 were members of the city's government (the foremost of which were the *prévôt* and *échevins* and *conseillers*), as well as representatives from the University of Paris and other important officeholders in the financial and judicial branches of royal administration; each participant was identified by both dress and the appropriate emblems of office. The most privileged positions in the procession were accorded to the members of the Parlement of Paris (particularly the judicature's presidents, its ranking members, and the chancellor of France), who were the last in the procession to greet the queen.[13]

Predictably, those who were charged with delivering speeches on the occasion took care to laud Anne's preeminence as well as to voice their hopes for a glorious reign (which included trust that the dynastic fortune unique to the French monarchy would continue with the birth of a royal heir). As Anne toured the city, viewing the various monuments and tableaux painted for the occasion, various dramas and other entertainments were also performed in her honor.[14] Before the day's festivities concluded, the queen was honored by her Parisian subjects with a gift, specially commissioned for the occasion: a golden ship, the city's emblem.[15] The gift was one of three accessional privileges that Anne enjoyed in conjunction with her coronation ceremony: she also created a master in each guild and exercised the right of clemency (*droit de grâce*) by granting pardon to criminals detained in royal jails throughout the realm.[16] The ceremonies performed in Anne's honor (and the accessional privileges that she enjoyed) were part of a cult of rulership that was a celebrated component of the French Renaissance monarchy. That the occasion was significant was understood by all who attended, including the queen's secretary. In the course of the year, Vigne completed an account of the ceremony and presented the manuscript to the queen.[17] A second copy of the manuscript also exists, which has slight textual discrepancies.[18] What André de la Vigne could not have fully comprehended is how these accounts reflect developments in French public law which influenced the history of royal and distaff ceremonial.

Vigne's description of the coronation ceremony of 1504 is significant, in part, because few such accounts exist. With one notable exception—the coronation book written for the mid-fourteenth-century Valois king, Charles V, and the queen, Jeanne of Bourbon—the queen's coronation ritual had attracted scant attention.[19] The oldest documents are copies of the various coronation *ordines,* sometimes (albeit irregularly) augmented by the brief commentaries found in chronicles, usually those praising the august ancestry of successive Merovingian, Carolingian, Capetian, and Valois kings.[20] There are also a limited number of expense accounts which provide evidence that, like the rite for a king, the queen's coronation was a resplendent and costly ceremony. In addition to the manuscript on the ceremony of 1364, there is Jean Nicolaï's late fifteenth-century account of the ritual performed in Anne of Brittany's honor in 1492.[21] The third extant account of the queen's ritual is the one that Vigne produced in the course of 1504 in honor of Anne's second coronation.

Even a cursory comparison of the manuscripts describing the ceremonies of 1364, 1492, and 1504 provides evidence that the liturgical rite was of little interest to commentators in late medieval France. Unlike the coronation book of 1364, the later descriptions offer a synoptic account of the rite. Only one part of the service—the Mass performed after the queen's anointment, coronation, and enthronement—was recorded in detail.[22] Finally, there is a notable uncertainty regarding the correct order for bestowing upon the queen the regalia of her office. While such confusion was unthinkable for the royal rite, the difficulty that contemporaries encountered in understanding the symbolic importance of the queen's ritual was largely due to the histories of the respective ceremonies.

The ritual of coronation was one of the oldest and most solemn of royal rituals, although it was not one that remained unchanged in the face of the political and dynastic developments that occurred in medieval France.[23] Initially the ceremony was deemed to be a constitutive ritual, emphasizing each king's unique hereditary right to ascend to the crown. The symbolism of the king's regalia recalled the exalted nature of his sovereign authority, while the ritual of unction celebrated the quasimiraculous powers that only French kings enjoyed.[24] Over the centuries changes in the liturgical rite were introduced, as well as other ceremonial innovations, so that the constitutional importance of the royal ritual of coronation was derived from state ceremonial and French public law, which increasingly celebrated the dynastic basis of rulership.[25] The most spectacular development was the celebration of the postcoronation entry ceremony as one of the rituals marking royal advent.[26] Another practice—the granting of accessional privileges—also became an integral element of royal advent and was described by later writers as the "the right of joyous advent" ("droit de joyeux avènement à la couronne").[27]

The distaff component of royal ceremonial—the queen's rituals of unction and coronation—also reflected the changing basis of French public law. While the ceremony was almost as old as the ritual performed in the king's honor, it did not signify any claim to share the king's sovereign powers. Instead, both the liturgical rite, as well as the queen's regalia, emphasized her inability to ascend to the crown and assume temporal authority in her own right.[28] Even at its fullest development (the *ordo* used for the 1364 coronation of Charles V and Jeanne of Bourbon), the ceremony was far shorter than its royal counterpart. Moreover, since the queen's coronation ritual was not a "state" ceremonial, its history was more variable than the royal one. The customary practice in Capetian France was to hold a joint coronation for the king and queen. In instances where a king had ascended to the crown before his marriage (or remarriage), the queen's coronation ceremony was performed whenever political or dynastic considerations encouraged such celebration. The last joint coronation ritual occurred in 1364, when Charles V and Jeanne of Bourbon were crowned at the cathedral church of Reims. For later ceremonies, the practice of royal coronation continued at Reims, whereas the queen's ritual was performed at the abbey church of Saint Denis.[29] Despite its venerable tradition, the queen's ritual of coronation was not essential to the function of queenship. At least one queen in thirteenth-century Capetian France (Isabel of Aragon) was not crowned and, in the fifteenth century, the political consequences of Charles VI's attempts to disinherit his son caused an abeyance in the ceremonial practice that affected the fifteenth-century queens, Marie of Anjou and Charlotte of Savoy.[30] When, after a hiatus of slightly more than a century, the tradition of crowning resumed, interest in the liturgical rite was slight. Even the more solemn aspects of the ceremony—such as the moment of coronation—required study of medieval chronicles to be understood.

Regardless of the limitations evident in the coronation ritual, the ceremony was significant, reflecting both immediate dynastic and political concerns. Perhaps the most critical moment of the rite occurred when the queen was anointed—although not with the holy balm used in the royal ceremony—as a gesture to ensure that divine providence did not desert the royal house.[31] For the observers who watched Anne's coronation ceremony of 1492, hopes that the dynastic greatness of France would continue were voiced without the concern that surfaced in conjunction with the later coronation ceremony of 1504.[32] Unfortunately, Anne's earlier marriage to Louis XII (8 January 1499) had only encouraged mounting dynastic concern. At his accession in 1498, Louis XII was thirty-six years old, childless, and subject to repeated bouts of ill-health, as well as hunting accidents. A second concern was no less pressing. As heiress to the duchy of Brittany, Anne enjoyed considerable authority, which she had initially intended to augment by marrying Maximilian, king of the Romans.[33] Should this marriage have occurred, the duchy of Brittany could have become an imperial possession, thereby jeopardizing the security of the French realm. Charles VIII's unexpected death in 1498 required his successor, Louis XII, to act quickly and divorce his wife, Jeanne of France, in order to marry Anne of Brittany so that the French realm could still claim the duchy.[34] Thus, six years after the royal coronation ceremony was performed, Anne of Brittany became the first queen in French history to be honored with a second coronation.[35]

Given Anne's illustrious heritage as duchess of Brittany and her exalted status as queen, it is not surprising that her secretary wished to draw attention to the singular nature of her authority.[36] The account of the ceremony he presented to Anne was a carefully considered interpretation of the ritual and included a depiction of her coronation (see fig. 1) as well as one of the entry ceremony into the city of Paris (see fig. 2). Since relatively few depictions of a French queen's coronation exist for modern scholars to study, these images are particularly noteworthy. The most celebrated depictions of a queen's coronation are found in the full cycle of miniatures included in the manuscript produced for Charles V and Jeanne of Bourbon. As Claire Richter Sherman has noted, this work is unique, offering a full account of both the royal and distaff rites as well as a copy of the *ordines* used for the service.[37] Of particular interest is how visual devices were employed to honor Jeanne's importance as queen (particularly her expected role in assuring dynastic ambitions) without imparting any claim to temporal prerogatives of rulership. This feat was largely accomplished by deleting certain moments of the ritual that were performed publicly (such as the queen's procession to the church) and by using themes derived from Marian iconography so that Jeanne, like the Virgin Mary, was honored for her exalted status.[38]

The use of Marian iconography was especially clear in the miniatures depicting her regalia of office, particularly the queen's crown and her scepter, which is illustrated as a flowering rose (see fig. 3). Regardless of inconsistencies in depicting the queen's regalia, the miniatures found in the coronation book are exceptional and influenced later accounts of the ritual. Charles V's beautifully illuminated copy of the quasi-official history of France, the *Grandes chroniques de France,* contains a depiction of Jeanne of Bourbon ceremonially enthroned that was copied from the coronation book.[39] In turn, these sources encouraged a later commentator on Valois rulership, the chronicler Jean Froissart, to include a depiction of the postcoronation entry ceremony performed in Isabeau of Bavaria's honor in 1389 in his *Chroniques* (see fig. 4).[40] The composition of the depiction is a "condensed" account of the full cycles of the king's and queen's rituals.[41] These concerns are also evident in the two miniatures included in Vigne's manuscript of the coronation of 1504.

A comparison of the images of Anne of Brittany's coronation (see fig. 1) with the one found in the coronation book of Charles V and Jeanne of Bourbon (see fig. 5) suggests that the fourteenth-century account may well have been consulted as a model for the later illustration.[42] The similarities in composition are consistent with Vigne's assertion that he had studied medieval chronicles in order to understand better the practices involved in crowning a French queen. Unlike the illustrator of Jeanne of Bourbon's coronation, the artist of the sixteenth-century manuscript chose to depict the "official" crown—which Vigne described as the "crown of Saint Louis" ("couronne de Saint Louis")—and to emphasize the solemnity of the moment of coronation.[43] To do so required altering the positions of the queen's attendants as well as the officiants of the ceremony so that Anne and Amboise are the central figures of the composition. Care has also been taken to balance two concerns: the spectacle of the occasion (evident in the dress of the numerous observers who either attend the queen or watch from the gallery) with the solemnity of the liturgical rite, so that Anne's elevation as queen was as exalted as the king's. The same themes are found in the depiction of her postcoronation entry ceremony (see fig. 2). Once again, the crowned Anne is the focus of the composition; she is seated in a carriage and surrounded by her various attendants and officials, such as Cardinal d'Amboise, who is in the forefront. Here, the composition succeeds in emphasizing Anne's assumption of office, a prerogative now publicly celebrated in the presence of her Parisian subjects.

Although it is impossible to tell how fully—if at all—Vigne and the artist collaborated, the text and illuminations are consistent.[44] As had Jean Nicolaï, in his account of the ceremony of 1492, the queen's secretary took a special interest in recording the magnificence of the clothing worn by Anne's entourage in 1504. With an eye for detail, he described the richness of the cloth while also noting the noble birth and titles of the participants. His comment extended to the legal rights of widows, the most privileged of whom were the royal daughter and sometime regent, Anne de Beaujeu, duchess of Bourbon, and Marguerite de Lorraine, duchess d'Alençon.[45] Their prominence in the coronation miniature is unmistakable and provides a valuable clue regarding the constitutional significance of the coronation ceremony of 1504.[46]

What particularly interested Vigne was the claim that widows were entitled to enjoy fully their husbands' privileges and honors, even the ones associated with public office. That this right applied to a queen was not, however, acknowledged by one member of the royal court, Pierre de Rohan, seigneur de Gié. A fellow Breton and powerful royal minister, Gié had long kept a watchful eye over Anne of Brittany's affairs. A staunch supporter of royal authority, he was also especially keen to ensure that the duchy of Brittany remain a French possession.[47] Moreover, he was as distrustful of Anne as she was of him. The strands of mutual antipathy had been elevated to matters of state because of Gié's attempt to prevent Anne from leaving the court with the royal daughter, Claude of France, during one of Louis XII's bouts of ill health. Concerned that Anne would attempt to arrange an imperial marriage for Claude (and perhaps succeed in freeing the duchy of Brittany from French possession), he took steps to champion a royal marriage for Claude and Francis of Angoulême, heir apparent to the crown should

Louis and Anne fail to produce a son.[48] Initially, neither the king nor the royal council had much interest in Anne's allegation that Gié's actions amounted to more than an episode of misadventure. However a number of concerns eventually encouraged a closer scrutiny of the charges brought against Gié and, after careful consideration (and lengthy testimony on behalf of all involved parties), the royal council decided that Gié should stand trial for the crime of lèse-majesté.[49]

Whereas the council's decision owed much to personal antagonisms and ambitions, the case set constitutional precedent. Despite the gravity of the charge, the crime of lèse-majesté had not yet been fully defined in regard to the king's authority and it had yet to be applied in defense of a queen's sovereign rights. Nor was there much understanding of the juristic basis of queenship, particularly whether the impressive number of ceremonial and accessional privileges, as well as the legal, fiscal, and diplomatic immunities a queen enjoyed, were attributes of an office or automatic privileges because of a queen's legal status as royal consort (*uxor regis*).[50] In constitutional terms, this claim was significant because it recognized a distinction between the queen's person and office—a corollary to the doctrine of "twin bodied majesty"—that had yet to be recognized in French public law.[51]

In his defense, Gié argued that his actions were warranted because as a royal minister (as well as Francis of Angoulême's guardian), he enjoyed an authority superior to Anne's. Moreover, he alleged that Anne of Brittany no longer enjoyed the privileges and immunities of office because she had yet to be crowned as queen consort of Louis XII. Hence, her authority as a royal wife could not be held to be superior to that of a royal minister.[52] Gié's argument touched on one component of queenship that had been honored in the royal courts of medieval France: the privileged status of either a queen consort or a dowager queen. However, the practice was one that had received scant attention regarding legal issues and it had never been challenged so forthrightly before. To best assure a successful defense, the royal council decided to change the venue of the case so that it was heard in the jurisdiction of the Parlement of Toulouse, and not the Parlement of Paris. The decision was unusual, but necessary since Roman law provided abstract legal concepts associated with the immortal *dignitas* of public office (including notions of treason and transgression against legitimate authority). Arnaud Faure (Procureur général du roi à Toulouse) and Pierre Bonnin (Procureur général au grand conseil) were appointed to the case and considerable care was taken to assure that only the most prominent and learned jurists (both French and Italian) were appointed to represent the crown.[53] Anne herself was interested in monitoring these appointments as well as the later progress that was made toward prosecuting Gié. And, less than a month after he made his initial appearance before the royal council, Anne of Brittany was ceremonially crowned queen and feted publicly. With the trial still pending, her secretary, André de la Vigne, produced his account of the ceremony and presented it to the queen.

Certainly, the ceremonies of 1504 and Vigne's account of these events were intended to legitimize Anne's claim that she was entitled to share fully the king's sovereign prerogatives regardless of whether she had been honored with a second coronation. Vigne's assertion regarding the importance of the ring ritual leaves little question about his opinion of the juristic basis of queenship: as the king's wife, Anne did not need to have ceremonial confirmation of her authority. He had little interest in the liturgical rite which, in turn, had been modified so that no interregnum existed between Anne's marriage to Louis XII and the ceremony six years later. Most significantly, the coronation rite of 1504 supported the assertion that queenship was an office that could not be disinvested because of a king's death. As public law regulating succession to the crown prevented a king from being deprived of his authority, the same principles supported Anne's elevation from duchess to queen. As an incumbent of an office, she should not be prevented from enjoying prerogatives of rulership. This concern encouraged Vigne to study medieval chronicles so that he more fully understood the symbolism inherent in the ritual of coronation. The only piece of the queen's regalia that he described was the "official" crown, and he emphasized its weight. Such comment recalled how the ritual of coronation, symbolizing assumption of office, marked a transformation in Anne's authority so that she was entitled to enjoy the immortal (and inalienable) *dignitas* imparted to French rulers.[54]

The depiction of the coronation ritual included in Vigne's manuscript reflects all these concerns. The composition has been arranged so that the ritual of crowning the queen is a singular act, and one that involves only Anne of Brittany and the ranking officiant, Cardinal d'Amboise (whose influence at the royal court was now unrivaled because of Gié's disgrace).[55] Of the queen's attendants, two are particularly prominent: the two widows, most likely Anne of Beaujeu and

Marguerite de Lorraine, who were, as Vigne asserted, entitled to enjoy their husbands' privileges and honors freely because French law recognized no distinction between the marital rights a wife enjoyed during her husband's lifetime and those which she enjoyed after his death. Thus, the depiction of Anne's coronation in 1504 visually encouraged a legal analogy to be drawn between the two spheres of law, public and private, so that her authority as queen was unquestionable. The decision to depict the act of coronation—instead of her enthronement— may also have been inspired by the legal argument Arnaud Faure developed in Anne's defense.[56]

The opening statement of the defense drawn up by Pierre Bonnin and Arnaud Faure recalled the singular nature of royal and distaff authority, stressing that it was divinely ordained.[57] As *ministri Dei,* kings of France recognized no equal in temporal authority and, as Faure argued, the same was true for the realm's queens.[58] Drawing on precepts culled in feudal law codes (particularly the writings of Antonius Corsettus and Martinus Laudensis), Scripture, the glosses of the canonists such as Bartolus of Sassoferrato and Accursius, as well as on Roman law, he outlined the justification as to why Gié's action warranted the charge of lèse-majesté. First, Faure argued that as queen, Anne of Brittany was invested with public authority. Citing the Roman law maxim, *Bene a Zenone,* he argued that queens shared the privileges of office enjoyed by the realm's rulers, including the obligation of extirpating heresy.[59] Combining precepts from feudal law regulating succession to fiefs with Roman law addressing issues of marital rights, Faure adduced that a queen's privileges of office should be held to be as inviolable as the king's. To do so, he addressed the corporate nature of French society, drawing analogies between the marital practices of common law marriages and their royal counterpart. Thus, a queen had the same right to share fully the king's honors and privileges as did other married women, both non-noble and aristocratic. Since the argument central to the case was the question of Anne's right to continue to claim privileges of office independently of a second coronation, Faure examined the privileges of widowhood. Again, he followed arguments found in Roman law, particularly the gloss of the jurist Ulpian and the writings of Bartolus, each of whom had argued that a wife continued to enjoy privileges due from matrimony after her husband's death. Moreover, this practice was consistent with natural and divine law which recognized that marriage enhanced a woman's natural goodness.

Although the gloss written by Faure and Bonnin was short (consisting largely of compilations of legal precepts, *auctoritates*), it was thought through. There were few legal precedents and little political theory to support the allegation that Gié's actions constituted trespass against Anne's sovereign authority.[60] In the end, Gié was not found guilty of the crime of lèse-majesté, although he was deprived of his offices and exiled from the royal court. Neither Anne's dismay over the verdict nor her later attempts to deprive Gié's heirs of their patrimony discouraged further interest in examining the issues associated with the juristic basis of queenship.[61] A number of writers at the royal court defended Anne's preeminence, in part, by offering praise of her authority as both queen and duchess. Perhaps the most significant of such works was Alain Bouchart's history, *Les grandes croniques de Bretaigne*. Published in 1514, the text was a thorough recounting of political history intermixed with dynastic legend.[62] Since Bouchart was also a jurist, it is not improbable that he intended the history to be a commentary supporting Anne's unique and sovereign authority. A less well known work, a contemporary translation of Jacques de Cessoles's *Le jeu des eschez moralisé*, is also noteworthy since it developed a second argument touching on the juristic basis of queenship that was later incorporated into arguments defending a queen's right to enjoy sovereign prerogatives of rulership.

Le jeu des eschez moralisé is a vernacular translation of a popular thirteenth-century literary work, *De moribus hominum et officiis nobilium super ludo scacchorum*. While the sixteenth-century translator may well have started this project before the momentous events of 1504, he was nevertheless interested in Anne's legal rights; in turn, this interest produced a twist in the edition of Cessoles's treatise, which was not intended to defend the public authority of women.[63] The translator of the edition of 1504 appended to the text an introductory chapter which addressed the question of whether the privileges due to a queen constituted an office with powers that she alone was entitled to enjoy.[64] He too drew attention to the splendor inherent in the recently performed coronation, commenting on how the ceremony reflected the exalted nature of Anne's authority, while also noting that it was not a constitutive rite. To assert that these prerogatives included sovereign power, the translator adopted a notion found in feudal and customary law which supported primogenitural rights of inheritance by recognizing that the privilege of being seated to the right was a mark of honor and authority. No historical precedent was offered for this allegation, although such honor had been enjoyed by various queens in Capetian and Valois France.[65] Moreover, in regard to queenship, this ceremonial privilege was significant, in part, because it reversed the traditional seating accorded to a French queen during the ritual of coronation, which placed her to the king's left as a sign of her juridical incapacity.[66]

Whereas the translator hedged on his assessment of whether women were by nature more virtuous than men, he addressed forthrightly the issue regarding Anne's right to enjoy aspects of the king's sovereign authority. And he was adamant about one concern: a queen's preeminence should be deemed inviolable because it constituted an office which she alone was entitled to enjoy. Whereas the ceremonial splendor of the coronation ritual reflected the exalted nature of her authority, the prerogatives were not bestowed in the performance of the ritual. Drawing attention to French public law, he defended the juristic basis of queenship by noting that Anne's authority did not conflict with the laws governing royal succession. Instead, the two prerogatives—royal and distaff—were complementary because Salic law applied only to the question of whether women were entitled to claim hereditary right to the crown. After tracing the historic origins of the French practice, he defended the juristic basis of queenship by arguing that the title "Queen" was more than an honorary award. Like the other attributes of Anne's title ("very excellent and powerful"), such courtesies reflected public power so that "the title queen is that of ruler."[67]

This assertion was later supported by the Breton jurist François Marc, who wrote a gloss on the accessional privilege of pardoning criminals.[68] What interested Marc was not how freely Anne of Brittany enjoyed this privilege, but that it was a symbolic gesture that both reflected the exalted nature of the king's sovereign authority and represented an inalienable right derived from marriage. Marc's argument was brief and grounded in two principles of Roman law. The first, from Ulpian, defined the nature of majesty; the second supported the claim that marriage empowered a woman to enjoy her husband's privileges and honors. As did the sixteenth-century translator of Cessoles's treatise, Marc argued that a queen's lack of juridical capacity did not prevent her from enjoying attributes of sovereign power symbolizing the king's legislative authority. Whereas only a king, because of his unique hereditary right to the crown, was entitled to exercise power (*princeps soluto legibus est*), a queen enjoyed such privileges because of her status as a royal wife (*uxor regis*).

Marc's gloss has a special significance for the history of late medieval queenship because it addressed the question of why French queens were entitled to enjoy the accessional privilege of pardoning criminals, a gesture that was inextricably linked to the king's sovereign authority. This point had been tested in the late fifteenth century, when the Parlement of Paris denied the royal daughter and regent, Anne of Beaujeu, the right to enjoy freely the privilege of pardoning criminals. However, for Marc, the honor was one that reflected the exalted nature of the French monarchy—not just royal sovereign power—and counted as one of the attributes of the queen's office as well.[69]

The idea that Anne of Brittany was an incumbent of an office as exalted as the king's was also developed in ritual and monumental sculpture. With her death in 1514, Anne received the most elaborate funeral ceremony ever performed to date to honor a French queen. Its protocol was meticulously observed and attracted considerable interest among contemporaries. At least thirty manuscript accounts of the ceremony survive, many of which include depictions of the queen's effigy and regalia of her office—attributes of authority that left little doubt that French queens were entitled to share in the crown's immortal *dignitas* (see fig. 6).[70] The magnificent tomb later erected portrays Anne and Louis kneeling side by side in prayer. As Erwin Panofsky has noted, it is a spectacular enactment of the constitutional doctrine of "twin bodied majesty," which distinguished between the two components of authority—the incumbent and the immortal and inalienable rights of office.[71]

How fully royal and distaff authorities were enjoined was also of interest to two sixteenth-century jurists, Barthélemy de Chasseneuz (1480–1541) and Charles de Grassaille (1495–1582). By the time Chasseneuz published his treatise, *Catalogus Gloriae Mundi,* in 1529, he had demonstrated an impressive mastery of jurisprudence. Few challenges discouraged him from examining meticulously the maxims of Roman, canon, or feudal law. He was as undaunted by the improbable (his alleged defense of the woodworm of the town of Mamirolle in 1520) as he was intrigued with abstract notions pertaining to the corporate nature of French society.[72] Although an *avocat* in Autun and later president of a judicial court (the Parlement of Toulouse), he was exceptionally well informed on the inherent symbolism of "state" ceremonial. Combined, these interests encouraged him to examine the nature of the French monarchy. Ultimately, Chasseneuz asserted what the French had known for centuries: French kings were among the most exalted rulers on earth; he had no doubt that the same was true for the realm's queens.

In much the same spirit as his predecessors, he drew comparisons between a French king's and queen's preeminence and that accorded to either their biblical or celestial counterparts. That both royal and distaff powers were divinely bestowed was, he argued, evident in the respective regalia of office that each received during the rituals of coronation. After much discussion of the symbolism inherent in a French king's and queen's crown, Chasseneuz addressed questions concerning the constitutional significance of French ceremonial.[73] The royal rite reflected the majesty of the king's office, as well as the unique hereditary basis of the monarchy. Mindful of Salic law, Chasseneuz proceeded to discuss the distaff component of royal ceremonial. The history of the queen's coronation and postcoronation entry ceremonies did not particularly interest him, although it is clear from his discussion that he knew that neither ceremony was a constitutive one. He avoided mentioning the ceremonial abeyance that had occurred in the fifteenth century (as well as the politics of 1504) by comparing French practices of honoring married women with those that the ancient Romans followed.[74] The key claim in this gloss is that the privileges of matrimony were automatically assumed because a wife was entitled to share fully her husband's honors and prerogatives. Chasseneuz was also concerned to demonstrate that French public law mirrored the civil laws of the realm. In his study on the laws of the duchy of Burgundy, he again noted that French queens were entitled to share the king's privileges of office.[75] Moreover, the practice of honoring women was consistent with natural law; to affirm this claim, Chasseneuz offered a number of examples culled from mythical works, classical histories, and Scripture (Arthemisia, Minerva, Diana, Semiramis, Cleopatra, Judith, and Deborah).[76]

Chasseneuz defended the argument that a queen's prerogatives of office were derived from the king's sovereign authority in his discussions of marital rights and obligations. A woman was entitled to assume her husband's highest honors, in part, because of her natural goodness, which was not diminished by her husband's death; as did other women, a queen retained privileges of office during her widowhood.[77] For Chasseneuz, the most symbolic honor pertaining to the queen's authority was a ceremonial one: her privilege of being seated to the king's right, whereas both non-noble and aristocratic women were placed at their husbands' left.[78]

Chasseneuz's interest in Roman history and law was not incidental to this discussion. As had canonists and feudists centuries before him, he borrowed terminology and legal maxims (particularly *Bene a Zenone*) to assert the claim that a queen enjoyed a type of *dominium* over the realm. One distinction was essential, however.[79] Whereas a king enjoyed full sovereign authority (*princeps legibus soluto est*), the queen enjoyed a symbolic form of that power.[80] According to the glosses of various medieval writers, this meant that the prince was not bound by the laws, although a French queen—like a Roman empress—was not similarly freed. Whereas a queen was unable to assume full sovereign authority in her own right, she still enjoyed privileges of rulership which included, as Charles de Grassaille would later note, the right to pardon criminals.[81]

By the time Grassaille published his treatise, *Regalium Franciae Libri Duo*, in 1538, he had studied law under the guidance of Chasseneuz and was practising it in Carcassonne. Whereas much of his argument reflects the opinions of his mentor, he developed the juristic basis of queenship more thoroughly in two regards. Grassaille was especially interested in the most hallowed component of French public law, Salic law, which excluded female claimants to the French crown. Using chronicles as well as medieval legal texts, he reconstructed the historic origins of the practice and noted that this one component of French public law was unique to the realm.[82] He understood fully the essential difference between the French monarchy and all others: unlike royal women in England or Spain, a French queen could not exercise authority in her own right.[83] He also recognized a distinction between the dynastic and juristic basis of French public law, noting that Salic law was essential to assure the unique dynastic greatness of the French monarchy; on the other hand, it did not exclude the realm's queens from enjoying the same privileges and honors that were part of the king's prerogatives of office. In this regard, he provided the lines of argument that recognized dynastic notions of blood ties and lineage favoring a queen's authority as a royal mother.[84]

Grassaille's exposition of the juristic basis of queenship was clearly inspired by the gloss written to defend Anne of Brittany's sovereign authority as well as his mentor's work. He was particularly interested in questions pertaining to the symbolic importance of the king's and queen's regalia as well as the respective ceremonies of office. He also examined the question of whether either the royal ritual of coronation or the one performed in the queen's honor was essential to their authorities. Following in the footsteps of a number of medieval canonists and feudists, as well as the more recent arguments advanced by Bonnin and Faure in 1504 and Chasseneuz in 1529, he recognized that the splendor of the ceremony affirmed the exalted prerogatives of rulership that only a French king and queen were entitled to enjoy, although neither rite was a constitutive one.[85] And, while a French queen could not exercise temporal authority in her own right, such juridical incapacity was a reflection of the abstract nature of public law and did not apply to her legal rights as royal consort. Grassaille, too, developed arguments regarding the queen's authority as *uxor regis,* and noted that whatever honors a queen received during the king's lifetime continued after his death.[86] Tenets of the constitutional doctrine of "twin bodied majesty" are apparent throughout his discussion on royal and distaff prerogative. Significantly, in one regard, Grassaille pointed to a theoretical difficulty in applying the doctrine to the study of French queenship. Whereas the royal office included principles of immortal *dignitas* within the context of hereditary right to the crown, a queen's right to enjoy privileges of office could never be grounded in the dynastic basis of rulership since whatever honors she enjoyed were derived exclusively from her marital and maternal status and therefore could not be transmitted.[87] If, in constitutional terms, a French queen had only one body to the king's two, her status as *uxor regis* was still superior to that of all French subjects and other royal consorts.[88]

One of the most innovative aspects of Grassaille's gloss on queenship was the way he blended an interest in early medieval history with his study of law. Although he was not as diligent in recording the chronicles he had consulted as he was about compiling legal statutes, Grassaille nonetheless incorporated strands of the French humanist study of history (*mos gallicus*) into his interpretation of French public law. Thus, he balanced his assessment of the history of Salic law (and issues touching on a queen's lack of juridical capacity) with recognition of the many notable deeds of charity and guidance that various queens had performed.[89] If his interest in the politics of piety is suggestive of an unease regarding any woman's right to assume public responsibilities of office, Grassaille, like Chasseneuz, offered a thorough rebuttal to the arguments lamenting a woman's moral and biological inferiority, so that his assessment of the juristic basis of queenship ultimately supported a queen's right to assume full direction of the realm during a regency government.[90]

Figure 1. Andre Delavigne, Description of the Coronation of Anne of
Brittany, her Entry into Paris and Coronation Banquet, Paris, c. 1505, James
A. de Rothschild Collection, MS. 22, p. 2 [frontispiece]. Courtesy of the
National Trust Waddesdon Manor, Aylesbury, Bucks., Great Britain.

Figure 2. Andre Delavigne, Description of the Coronation of Anne of Brittany, her Entry into Paris and Coronation Banquet, Paris, c. 1505, James A. de Rothschild Collection, MS. 22, p. 76. Courtesy of the National Trust Waddesdon Manor, Aylesbury, Bucks, Great Britain.

Figure 3. British Library, Cotton Tiberius B VIII, Coronation Book of Charles V of France and Jeanne of Bourbon, fol. 70. Reproduced by permission of the British Library.

Figure 4. Bibliothèque Nationale, Paris, MS. fr. 2646; *Chronicle* of Jean Froissart, fol. vi. Reproduced by permission.

Figure 5. British Library, Cotton Tiberius B VIII, Coronation Book of Charles V of France and Jeanne of Bourbon, fol. 69v. Reproduced by permission of the British Library.

Figure 6. Bibliothèque Nationale, Paris, Collection Clairambault 483, fol. 26. Reproduced by permission.

Figure 7. The Newberry Library, Chicago, Ill., André du Chesne's *Les antiquitez et recherches de la grandeur et maiesté des roys de France* (Paris, 1609), frontispiece. Reproduced by permission.

Although the dynastic basis of the right to act as regent is not of interest in this essay, it was a paramount concern of generations of successive jurists who used the arguments of Marc, Chasseneuz, and Grassaille to refute allegations that a king's untimely death would render France a gynecocracy.[91] In turn, the troubled history of late sixteenth- and seventeenth-century France merged with a second interest, the unique dynastic glory of the French monarchy. The impressive corpus of studies of the history of French ceremonial and of the constitutional basis of the monarchy has not yet been fully tapped by scholars interested in understanding how contemporaries perceived the juristic basis of queenship. Perhaps the most succinct evidence attesting to how the arguments developed in early sixteenth-century France influenced later writers can be adduced from the frontispiece of André du Chesne's study of the history of royal ceremonial and the privileges of office (see fig. 7). His treatise, *Les antiquitez et recherches de la grandeur et maiesté des roys de France,* was published in 1609, one year before Henry IV's assassination, which in turn necessitated the proclamation of a regency government headed by the queen, Marie de Médicis. The frontispiece is a rare depiction of the king and queen, both of whom are crowned and enthroned under canopies. The composition reflects principles of French public law, emphasizing Henry IV's preeminence as king, his hereditary title to the crown, as well as Marie's right to share in his privileges of office, which, until 1610, she did fully and independently of the ritual of coronation.[92]

Notes

This article is derived from my forthcoming dissertation, "French Queens in the Cult of the Renaissance Monarchy" (Department of History, University of Iowa), directed by Ralph E. Giesey. Research was funded through grants and fellowships from the Department of History (University of Iowa), the Ada Louisa Ballard Dissertation Fellowship in the Humanities (Graduate College, University of Iowa), an American Association of University Women dissertation fellowship, and the Iowa Renaissance Studies Group, which supported study at the Newberry Library. I wish to thank publicly Ralph E. Giesey, Richard A. Jackson, John Carmi Parsons, and Constance H. Berman. I am also indebted to Hervé Pinoteau, William C. Jordan, Joseph Bergin, the anonymous readers of the earlier drafts of this paper, and two friends, the late Robert M. Fitch and Orene C. Fitch. And

I particularly wish to thank Sally-Beth MacLean and Jennifer Carpenter for unlimited patience in seeing this article through the press.

1. "... Ledict aneau sponsal signiffiant et denotant quelle espousoit et prenoit possession, saisine et joyssance du Royalume de France, a la charge den avoir et recevoir apres le Roy seulle et sans moyen les biens, tryumphs, gloires, honneurs, preemynences, prerogatives, pors, faveurs et generalle-ment toutes autres choses qui par Reigle de droict a tiltre de tres haulte et tres excellente Royne de France comme elle appartienient sans riens ex-cepter" (Vigne, *Commant la Royne a Sainct Denys sacree fut dignement en grant solempnyte, Pareillement comme estoit acoustree Quant a Paris elle fit son entree. Jay tout escript en ce petit traicte* [Waddesdon Manor (Aylesbury, Bucks.), James A. de Rothschild Collection, MS. 22, Andre Delavigne, Description of the Coronation of Anne of Brittany, her Entry into Paris and Coronation Banquet, Paris, c. 1505, 34–35]). See also Henri Stein, ed., "Le sacre d'Anne de Bretagne et son entrée à Paris en 1504," *Mémoires de la société de l'histoire de Paris et de l'île de France* 29 (1902), 268–305, esp. 268–69, 278. I thank Professor John Nothnagle for the translation of the text. Among scholars who have studied contemporary politics, symbolism, and constitutional concerns connected with the ritual of bestowing a ring are Ernst H. Kantorowicz, *The King's Two Bodies: A Study of Mediaeval Political Theory* (Princeton, 1957); Robert W. Scheller, "Ensigns of Author-ity: French Royal Symbolism in the Age of Louis XII," trans. Michael Hoyle, *Simiolus* 13 (1983), 75–141, esp. 137–39; Laurence M. Bryant, *The King and the City in the Parisian Royal Entry Ceremony,* Travaux d'human-isme et renaissance 216 (Geneva, 1986), esp. 93; Richard A. Jackson, *Vive le Roi!* (Chapel Hill, N.C., 1984), 85–90; and Robert Descimon, "Les fonc-tions de la métaphore du mariage politique du roi et de la république France, XVe–XVIIIe siècles," *Annales: Économies, sociétés, civilisations* 47 (1992), 1127–47.

2. For discussions of the development of public law in medieval France, see: Ralph E. Giesey, *The Juristic Basis of Dynastic Right to the French Throne,* Transactions of the American Philosophical Society n.s. 51, pt. 5 (Philadelphia, 1961), 17–22; Paul Viollet, "Comment les femmes ont été exclues, en France, de la succession à la couronne," *Mémoires de l'institut national de France,* Académie des inscriptions et belles-lettres 34, pt. 2 (1895), 125–78; Colette Beaune, *The Birth of an Ideology: Myths and Sym-bols of Nation in Late-Medieval France,* trans. Susan Ross Huston, ed. Fre-deric L. Cheyette (Berkeley, 1991), 245–65; Jacques Krynen, "Genèse de l'état et histoire des idées politiques en France à la fin du Moyen Age," in *Culture et idéologie dans la genèse de l'état moderne* (Rome, 1985), 395–412; Jean Barbey, *La fonction royale: essence et légitimité* (Paris, 1983), 324ff.; J. H.

Burns, *Lordship, Kingship, and Empire: The Idea of Monarchy, 1400–1525* (Oxford, 1992), 40–58; and Richard A. Jackson, ed., "The *Traité du sacre* of Jean Golein," *Proceedings of the American Philosophical Society* 113 (1969), 305–24.

3. Stein gives some of the expenses for the ceremonies of 1504 ("Sacre de Anne de Bretagne," 301–4); see also Bryant, *King and City,* 34–35; and Charles Oulmont, "Pierre Gringore et l'entrée de la reine Anne en 1504," in *Mélanges offerts à M. Émile Picot,* 2 vols. (Paris, 1913; Geneva, 1969), 2:385–92.

4. Stein, "Sacre de Anne de Bretagne," 270ff.; Théodore Godefroy notes that Louis XII notified the civic authorities in Paris (30 Oct.) and one week later (7 Nov.), the formal deliberations commenced regarding the proposed festivities; preparations were finally completed on 16 Nov., the day when coronation festivities began (*Le cérémonial françois,* 2 vols. [Paris, 1649], 1:690–92).

5. Stein identifies the following as the officiants who aided Cardinal Georges d'Amboise: P. de Luxembourg, cardinal of Le Mans, and "plusieurs archevesques, évesques, abbez," an ensemble which in 1504 included Tristan de Salazar, archbishop of Sens; René de Prie, bishop of Bayeux; Estienne Ponchier, bishop of Paris; and others ("Sacre de Anne de Bretagne," 270, 276 nn. 1 and 2, 277 and n. 1).

6. Stein lists the exalted members of Anne's entourage as well as the international dignitaries who attended the ceremony ("Sacre de Anne de Bretagne," 271–72, 275–76). For a brief discussion of the attendants see Jean-Pierre Leguay and Hervé Martin, *Fastes et malheurs de la Bretagne ducale, 1213–1532* (Rennes, 1982), 383–84. Anne of Brittany enjoyed an exceptionally large household, a privilege of queenship that was not as fully enjoyed by her daughter, Claude of France.

7. Stein, "Sacre de Anne de Bretagne," 277–78. The rite was short (most likely completed in less than an hour) and did not include the ritual of anointing nor many of the prayers; I thank H. Pinoteau for this information. See Michael Jones, *The Creation of Brittany: A Late Medieval State* (London, 1988), 389; Claire Richter Sherman, "The Queen in Charles V's 'Coronation Book': Jeanne de Bourbon and the 'Ordo ad Reginam Benedicendam,'" *Viator* 8 (1977), 255–98, esp. 269–70 and n. 48, giving examples of other French ceremonies as well as literature discussing the practice of deleting the ritual of consecration.

8. Stein, "Sacre de Anne de Bretagne," 281. Vigne states that Tuesday (19 Nov.) was the date, while Godefroy gives the date as 20 November 1504 (*Cérémonial,* 1:692); although Godefroy did not consult Vigne's manuscript, he did use the records of the Hôtel de Ville. A later, eighteenth-century copy of this entry found in B.N., MS. fr. 6509 ("Cérémonial pour

les prévôts des marchands et échevins"), fols. 3r–11v, is consistent with Godefroy's account.

9. Stein, "Sacre de Anne de Bretagne," 280–96, and Godefroy, *Cérémonial,* 1:690–95, are printed accounts of the postcoronation entry ceremony. Bryant has a brief summary of this ceremonial honor accorded to French queens (*King and City,* 93–97). For a general history of the development of the postcoronation entry ceremony, see also Lawrence M. Bryant, "The Medieval Entry Ceremony at Paris," in Janos M. Bak, ed., *Coronations: Medieval and Early Modern Monarchic Ritual* (Berkeley, 1990), 88–118; and Bernard Guenée and Françoise Lehoux, *Les entrées royales françaises de 1328 à 1515* (Paris, 1968).

10. The protocol observed in royal entry ceremonies reflected related developments in "state" ceremonial, as noted by Ralph E. Giesey, "Modèles de pouvoir dans les rites royaux en France," *Annales: Économies, sociétés, civilisations* 41 (1986), 579–99; and Giesey, "The King Imagined," in K. M. Baker, ed., *The French Revolution and the Creation of Modern Political Culture,* 3 vols. (Oxford, 1987), 1:41–59; also P. S. Lewis, "The Estates of Tours," in *Essays in Later Medieval French History* (London, 1985), 139–49.

11. Nicholas Ménin noted that the processional parity was a result of an *arrêt* issued during Charles VIII's reign (*Traicté historique et chronologique du sacre et couronnement des rois et des reines de France* [Paris, 1723], 236–37). Guyot's account was based on the research of a mid-sixteenth-century jurist, Jean Papon, *Recueil d'arrests notables des courts souveraines de France* (Paris, 1565), book 4, titles 3 and 6, art. 17. Stein notes that processional regularity was strictly followed in both the coronation and entry pageantries ("Sacre de Anne de Bretagne," 280); Bryant cites earlier evidence in "Medieval Entry Ceremony" (104–6) and in his *King and the City* notes that Louis XII, following Charles VIII's edict, had ordered that Anne receive the same ceremonial honors (93). The ceremonial parity interested many sixteenth- and seventeenth-century writers, such as the *greffier* Jean du Tillet, whose comments on this matter are included in several of his works: *Les mémoires et recherches* (Rouen, 1578); *Recueil des rois de france, leurs couronne et maison* (Paris, 1618); and *Mélanges historiques: Questions de préséance; mémoires sur les parlements et mémoires diplomatique* (B.N., MS. fr., 16, 634, esp. fol. 49v).

12. Stein, "Sacre de Anne de Bretagne," 272–75. Throughout his account of the coronation and postcoronation entry ceremonies, Vigne notes how the emblems of dress and office reflect status, rank, and power. Further study regarding the significance of dress and emblems of office is found in many of the essays in *City and Spectacle in Medieval Europe,* ed. Barbara A. Hanawalt and Kathryn L. Reyerson, Medieval Studies at Minnesota 6 (Minneapolis, 1994).

13. Stein, "Sacre de Anne de Bretagne," 287–88, for judicial personnel who attended and participated in the postcoronation entry festivities. Godefroy records the concern voiced by contemporaries regarding appropriate dress, noting as well the cost for the gowns worn by the *prévôt des marchands* and *échevins* (*Cérémonial,* 1:691). Françoise Autrand analyses contemporary institutional growth of royal power, government, office holding, and the symbolism of state ceremonial (*Naissance d'un grand corp de l'état* [Paris, 1981], 53–157, 203–57), as do Guenée and Lehoux (*Entrées royales,* 24–25). The presence of *Parlementaires* also touched on the practices of venality and the immortal notions associated with royal offices, which have been thoroughly studied. For a general discussion of the symbolism of emblems, see Alain Boureau, "État moderne et attribution symbolique: Emblèmes et devices dans l'Europe des xvie et xviie siècles," in *Culture et idéologie,* 155–78; and Michael Sherman, "Pomp and Circumstance: Pageantry, Politics, and Propaganda in France during the Reign of Louis XII, 1498–1515," *Sixteenth Century Journal* 9, no. 4 (1978), 13–32.

14. Oulmont, "Pierre Gringore et l'entrée de la reine Anne en 1504," 385–92.

15. Godefroy notes the gift's cost (*Cérémonial,* 1:691); Bryant discusses the practice within a wider ceremonial context (*King and City,* 31–34). Since the presentation of a gift reflected two concerns—the exalted nature of ceremonial displays of majesty as well as the realm's prosperity—considerable care was taken to ensure that it symbolized the splendor of the occasion without requiring the levy of additional taxes. N. Rondot discusses the concern of defraying excessive costs (*Bernard Salomon, peintre et tailleur d'histoires* [Lyon, 1987], 48–63).

16. There is limited evidence that the privileges of receiving gifts, pardoning criminals, and creating masters of guilds developed in the late thirteenth and fourteenth centuries. Henri Martin notes that prisoners were released in conjunction with the coronation of Louis VIII and Blanche of Castile (6 Aug. 1223) (*Histoire de France depuis les temps les plus reculés jusqu'en 1789,* 4th ed., 17 vols. [Paris, 1855], 4:116); Louis Douët-d'Arcq notes that the fourteenth-century queen Jeanne of Boulogne granted pardons in conjunction with entry ceremonies on at least two occasions (24 Feb. 1351 and 1 Apr. 1356) ("Inventaire des meubles de la reine Jeanne de Boulogne [1360]," in *Bibliothèque école des Chartres* [Paris, 1879], 548). For a list of the gifts presented to the queen, see Ernest Petit, *Histoire des ducs de Bourgogne,* 9 vols. (Dijon, 1905; reprint, Millwood, N.Y., 1976), 9:80. Paris, A.N., Châtelet, Y 6-1, fol. 77v has a copy of the royal legislation issued to authorize Anne of Brittany to pardon criminals in conjunction with the postcoronation entry ceremony of 1492. English queens also enjoyed this privilege; see John Carmi Parsons, "Ritual and Symbol in

English Medieval Queenship to 1500," in Louise Olga Fradenburg, ed., *Women and Sovereignty* (Edinburgh, 1992), 64–65. Discussions of political theory underlying the practice of creating masters of guilds include J. P. Canning, "Law, Sovereignty and Corporation Theory, 1300–1450," in J. H. Burns, ed., *The Cambridge History of Medieval Political Thought, c.350–c. 1450* (Cambridge, 1988), 454–76, esp. 473–75; and Antony Black, *Guilds and Civil Society in European Political Thought from the Twelfth Century to the Present* (London, 1984), 124–42.

17. The Waddesdon Manor manuscript is discussed by both Scheller, "Ensigns of Authority," 135, and Jones, *Creation of Brittany,* 371–409, esp. 387–88.

18. Paris, Bibliothèque Sainte Geneviève, MS. 3036, which is the copy Stein edited; see Jones, *Creation of Brittany,* 388 and n. 78.

19. Edward S. Dewick, ed., *The Coronation Book of Charles V of France,* Henry Bradshaw Society 16 (London, 1899); C. R. Sherman, "Queen in Charles V's 'Coronation Book,'" 255–98, and "Taking a Second Look: Observations on the Iconography of a French Queen, Jeanne de Bourbon (1338–1378)," in Norma Broude and Mary D. Garraud, eds., *Feminism and Art History: Questioning the Litany* (New York, 1982), 101–17.

20. Among the earliest printed accounts of coronation *ordines* are Godefroy, *Cérémonial,* vol. 1, and John Selden, *Titles of Honor,* 2d ed. (London, 1631). Commentary on the royal rite includes Percy Ernst Schramm, "Ordines-Studien 2: Die Krönung bei den Westfranken und den Franzosen," *Archiv für Urkundenforschung* 15 (1938), 42–47; Schramm, *Der König von Frankreich: Das Wesen der Monarchie vom 9. zum 16. Jahrhundert,* 2d ed., 2 vols. (Weimar, 1960), 2:237–41; Richard A. Jackson, "Manuscripts, Texts and Enigmas of Medieval French Coronation Ordines," *Viator* 23 (1992), 35–71; Jackson, "Les manuscripts des *ordines* de couronnement de la bibliothèque de Charles V, roi de France," *Moyen Age* 82 (1976), 67–88; Jackson, *Vive le Roi;* and the essays in *Le sacre des rois* (Paris, 1985).

21. J. de Gaulle, "Sensieult le couronnement et entrée de la royne de France en la ville de Paris, fait ou mois de fevrier an de grasce mil quatre cens quatre vingtz et onze en ceste maniere," *Bulletin de la société de l'histoire de France* (1845–46), 111–21; Godefroy gives only a brief account of this ceremony, noting that Anne was "grandement accompagne . . . tous les estats" (*Cérémonial,* 1:469–70).

22. Stein, "Sacre de Anne de Bretagne," 277–80. For the symbolism of the ceremonies of Mass and offerings see Jackson, *Vive le Roi,* 21–22, 49–53; and Sherman, "Queen in Charles V's 'Coronation Book,'" 285–86. Vigne also expressed interest in the portion of the rite which included the blessing and bestowal of Anne's wedding ring and the ceremony of crowning the queen, which required the participation of the ranking blood princes in the queen's entourage.

23. For interpretations of the development of ritual and constitutional thought see Ernst H. Kantorowicz, "Mysteries of State: An Absolutist Concept and Its Late Mediaeval Origins," *Harvard Theological Review* 48 (1955), 65–91, esp. 72ff.; Fritz Kern, *Kingship and Law in the Middle Ages,* trans. S. B. Chrimes (Oxford, 1939), 27ff.; Ralph E. Giesey, "Inaugural Aspects of French Royal Ceremonies," in *Coronations,* 35–45, esp. 36–38; Jacques Le Goff, "A Coronation Program for the Age of Saint Louis: The Ordo of 1250," *Coronations,* 46–57; Hervé Pinoteau, *Vingt-cinq ans d'études dynastiques* (Paris, 1982); M. David, *La souveraineté et les limites juridiques du pouvoir monarchique du IXe au XVe siècle* (Paris, 1965); Elizabeth A. R. Brown, *Franks, Burgundians, and Aquitanians and the Royal Coronation Ceremony in France,* Transactions of the American Philosophical Society n.s. 82, pt. 7 (Philadelphia, 1992), esp. 3–12, 23–80.

24. The symbolism of the royal ritual of coronation and the king's regalia is one of Hervé Pinoteau's interests; see his various essays in *Vingt-cinq ans d'études dynastiques,* especially "Quelques réflexions sur l'oeuvre de Jean Du Tillet et la symbolique royale française," 100–140.

25. Regarding the connection between the dynastic basis of royal succession and the history of royal coronation, see Giesey, *Juristic Basis,* 12–17; Jackson, *Vive le Roi,* 203–10; Anne D. Hedeman, *The Royal Image: Illustrations of the Grandes Chroniques de France, 1274–1422* (Berkeley, 1991), 30–73; Bryant, "Medieval Entry Ceremony," 88–118; and Robert W. Scheller, "Imperial Themes in Art and Literature of the Early French Renaissance: The Period of Charles VIII," trans. Michael Hoyle, *Simiolus* 12 (1981–82), 5–69, esp. 10ff.

26. Scheller, "Ensigns of Authority," 101 n. 117, for literature on the subject.

27. Bryant, *King and City,* 21–50.

28. The following authors have considered how the *ordines* of coronation rituals reflect temporal limitations on a queen's authority: Janet L. Nelson, *Politics and Ritual in Early Modern Europe* (London, 1986); Pauline Stafford, *Queens, Concubines and Dowagers: The King's Wife in the Early Middle Ages* (Athens, Ga., 1983); Françoise Barry, *La reine de France* (Paris, 1964), 79–99; Parsons, "Ritual and Symbol," 60–77; Marion F. Facinger, "A Study of Medieval Queenship: Capetian France, 987–1237," *Studies in Medieval and Renaissance History* 5 (1968), 1–48; Dewick, *Coronation Book;* Sherman, "Queen in Charles V's 'Coronation Book'"; Anne D. Hedeman, "The Commemoration of Jeanne d'Evreux's Coronation in the *Ordo ad consecrandum* at the University of Illinois," *Essays in Medieval Studies: Proceedings of the Illinois Medieval Association* 7 (1990), 13–28; Brown, *Franks, Burgundians, and Aquitanians,* 96–98, 133–35; and McCartney, "French Queens."

29. Sherman, "Queen in Charles V's 'Coronation Book,'" 268–69; Gabrielle M. Spiegel discusses the political ideology that late Capetian and Valois kings associated with the abbey church at Saint Denis ("The Cult of Saint Denis and Capetian Kingship," *Journal of Medieval History* 1 [1975], 43–69, esp. 62). Bodleian, MS. Douce 92, a manuscript written during Louis XII's reign and presented to him, contains an account of the "history" of the abbey church and its inextricable association with French kings since Charlemagne's reign. See also B.N., MS. fr. 5706 ("De la dévotion des rois de France à Saint Denis").

30. Louis Carolus-Barré, "Le testament d'Isabelle d'Aragon, reine de France, épouse de Philippe III le hardi," *Annuaire-bulletin de la société de l'histoire de France*, 1983–84 (1986), 131–37; I thank H. Pinoteau for calling my attention to the ceremonial abeyance in the fifteenth century. Both the thirteenth- and fifteenth-century practices were due to contemporary political concerns. Regardless of the ceremonial abeyance, fifteenth-century queens did enjoy numerous privileges, including ceremonial entries into other cities in the realm: B.N., MS. fr. 10,426, fols. 62 and 63, lists two examples from 1442, when Marie of Anjou was feted in the cities of Toulouse and Carcassone; and Godefroy gives another example (1 Sept. 1447), when Marguerite of Scotland was honored with a ceremonial entrance into the city of Paris (*Cérémonial,* 1:671–72). In the fifteenth century, accessional honors and privileges were often granted in conjunction with various dynastic celebrations, including births of royal daughters, as noted by E. Sermet, *Le droit de grâce* ([Toulouse, 1901], 82), when Louis XI extended the *droit de grâce* to the poet, François Villon. The dynastic connections between the pardoning of criminals and celebrations of royal births were also noted by the anonymous fifteenth-century commentator on Salic law cited by John Milton Potter, "The Development and Significance of the Salic Law of the French," *English Historical Review* 52 (1937), 249 n. 1.

31. Differences between the royal rite of unction and the one performed for French queens have received careful study by a number of scholars, including Jackson, *Vive le Roi,* 13, 31–32, 42–43, 176–78, 203–5, 218; and Sherman, "Queen in Charles V's 'Coronation Book,'" 270; see also Marc Bloch, *Les rois thaumaturges: Étude sur le caractère surnaturel attribué à la puissance royale particulièrement en France et en Angleterre* (Strasbourg, 1924), for an assessment of the ritual within the cult of the monarchy.

32. The birth of the dauphin, Charles-Orland, was greatly celebrated and numerous accounts attest to the realm's joy, including Antoine-Jean-Victor Le Roux de Lincy, *Vie de la reine Anne de Bretagne,* 2 vols. (Paris, 1860), 1:114–15; B.N., MS. fr. 2834, fols. 174r–74v; B.N., Latin 9849, fols. 188r–188v; L-G. Pélissier, "Documents sur la première année du règne de

Louis XII, tirés des archives de Milan" (*Bulletin historique et philologique de comité des travaux historiques* [1890], 47–124), records the international fetes.

33. Jones notes that dating from Anne's marriage by procuration to Maximilian, king of the Romans (19 Dec. 1490), she was honored as queen on various documents dated 1490–91 (*Creation of Brittany*, 117). The politics of this marriage were often studied by seventeenth-century *érudits* such as Théodore Godefroy, who in his *Histoire de Charles VIII* (Paris, 1617) used contemporary accounts including the writings of André de la Vigne. See also Anne-Marie-Joseph Trébuchet, *Anne de Bretagne, reine de France* (Paris, 1822), and Le Roux de Lincy, *Vie de la reine Anne de Bretagne*. See also Alexandre Lenoir, *Description d'une tapisserie, rare et curieux faite à Bruges* (Paris, 1819), on a tapestry made to commemorate the occasion.

34. Chroniclers customarily emphasized that Anne's marriage to Louis XII was both hastily arranged and brief. See Jean-François Drèze, *Raison d'état, raison de dieu: Politique et mystique chez Jeanne de France* (Paris, 1991), 71–72, 84–87, 96; and M. de Maulde, *Procédures politiques du règne de Louis XII*, Collections des chroniques nationales françaises 44 (Paris, 1885), xxxviiff. Archives Communales (Rouen), A9, contains copies of letters (23 and 24 Jan. 1498 [n.s.]), informing the local citizenry of Louis XII's intention to marry Anne of Brittany, affirming that his marriage to Jeanne of France had been annulled, and attesting to the king's desire for a royal son. See Hyacinthe Morice, *Mémoires pour servir de preuves à l'histoire ecclesiastique et civile de Bretagne* (Paris, 1746), vol. 3, cols. 794–800, 813–15, regarding the marriage contract and provisions; and Antoine Dupuy, *Histoire de la réunion de la Bretagne à la France* (Paris, 1882), 2:100ff.

35. Jones notes that in 1501 Louis XII was anxious to hold the coronation and postcoronation entry festivities, although they were postponed until 1504 (*Creation of Brittany*, 389); Louis XII's coronation was performed on 27 May 1498. Among the archival evidence attesting to the preeminence Anne enjoyed as queen prior to 1504 is an account of the ceremonies honoring an imperial visit to the French royal court in 1501. B.N., MS. Dupuy 542 has a copy of a contemporary description of the reception for the Archduke Philip of Austria and Jeanne of Castille (fols. 29r ff.) As in the later ceremony for coronation, this account emphasizes both Anne's preeminence as well as that enjoyed by other distinguished women who served the queen at the royal court.

36. Vigne's interest in praising Anne's exalted status as duchess was a common theme in late fifteenth-century literature discussing Breton concerns. Jones analyzes such literature within the context of political issues, including the ways in which the dukes of Brittany attempted to turn their duchy into an independent state (*Creation of Brittany*, 10ff. and 309–28*)*;

Scheller, "Ensigns of Authority," gives examples of ceremonies and devices used to honor Anne's status as duchess and queen prior to 1504 (83ff.).

37. Sherman, "Queen in Charles V's 'Coronation Book.'"

38. Marian iconography was particularly apt for the coronation of 1364. Sherman notes that the ceremony was performed on Trinity Sunday, 19 May, at the abbey church in Reims where the iconography of the portal encouraged a visual analogy to be drawn between the heavenly and earthly queens ("Queen in Charles V's 'Coronation Book,'" 256–57); Christian de Mérindol (*Le roi René et la seconde maison d'Anjou* [Paris, 1987], 50–51, 196–98) and Drèze (*Raison d'état*, 16, 27–28, 32, 37–45, 52–57) give examples of Marian iconography within the cult of the monarchy in fourteenth-century France and its application regarding Marie of Anjou's queenship and that of the monarchy. Scheller ("Ensigns of Authority," 139) and Pinoteau ("Quelques réflexions sur l'oeuvre de Jean Du Tillet," 137) discuss usage in the sixteenth century. Dynastic associations inherent in the Marian trope limiting a queen's temporal authority are found in the political writings of Jean Golein; see Jackson, "*Traité du sacre*," and Jean Juvénal des Ursins in P. S. Lewis, ed., *Écrits politiques de Jean Juvénal des Ursins*, 2 vols. (Paris, 1978). See also Parsons ("Ritual and Symbol," 66–69) and Sherman ("Queen in Charles V's 'Coronation Book,'" 279–80) regarding the iconography of the queen's scepter and rod; and Brigitte Bedos Rezak, "Women, Seals, and Power in Medieval France, 1150–1350," in Mary Erler and Maryanne Kowaleski, eds., *Women and Power in the Middle Ages* (Athens, Ga., 1988), 61–82, for other examples of Marian iconography found in contemporary seals.

39. Hedeman, *Royal Image*, esp. pls. 4 and 6; and her "Copies in Context: The Coronation of Charles V in His *Grandes Chroniques de France*," in *Coronations*, 72–87, esp. 73–75, 79–81, and 87 n. 25.

40. B.N., MS. fr. 2646, fol. vi. Godefroy gives an account of the postcoronation entry ceremony, which was taken from two contemporary chroniclers, Jean Froissart and Jean Juvénal des Ursins (*Cérémonial*, 1:637–49); see Jean Froissart, *Chroniques de France*, ed. Kervyn de Lettenhove, *Oeuvres de Froissart* (Bruxelles, 1872), 14: 5–25. For a full published account of the entry ceremony see Marius Barroux, *Les fêtes royales de Saint-Denis en mai, 1389* (Paris, 1936), and Gordon Kipling's forthcoming study.

41. Hedeman, "Copies in Context," uses Robert Scheller's work to discuss the strategies of compositional arrangement found in such depictions (72–73).

42. For a description of the ceremony of 1364, see Sherman, "Queen in Charles V's 'Coronation Book,'" 280–81 and pl. 13. Marian iconography would have been of special interest to late fifteenth-century writers at the royal court. Jones notes that Anne's collection of manuscripts in-

cluded several poems attesting to the glory of the Blessed Virgin Mary (*Creation of Brittany*, 382); Marian tropes are also found in her Book of Hours.

43. See Sherman, "Queen in Charles V's 'Coronation Book,'" 281–83, for practices of coronation, which required two sets of crowns. Pinoteau has identified the royal crown as the *couronne de Charlemagne*, which he notes was first used in 1180, and the queen's crown, *couronne de la reine*, which was also first used in the same service ("L'ancienne couronne française dite 'de Charlemagne,' 1180?–1794," in *Vingt-cinq ans d'études dynastiques*, 375–430); Blaise de Montesquiou-Fezensac and Danielle Gaborit-Chopin further describe this regalia and its history (*Le trésor de Saint-Denis: Inventaire de 1634* [Paris, 1973]).

44. Scheller, "Ensigns of Authority," 135–37; Jones, *Creation of Brittany*, 367–88 and n. 1.

45. Stein, "Sacre de Anne de Bretagne," 273–74; five widows were part of Anne's entourage: Anne de France, duchesse de Bourbon; Charlotte d'Albret, duchesse de Valentinois; Marie de Luxembourg, contesse de Vendosme; Matheline de Périer, dame de La Guierche; Gillette de Coëtivy, wife of Jacques d'Estouteville, prévôt of Paris. Sherman shows that the same visual depictions of widowhood were incorporated into the four-teenth-century account ("Queen in Charles V's 'Coronation Book,'" 273ff.).

46. Stein, "Sacre de Anne de Bretagne," 280. Vigne notes cursorily that the performance of the coronation ceremony attested to the "augmenta-tion du bien de la chose publique et entretenement de la paix et union de royaume de France."

47. The following studies address questions of Gié's influence at the royal court and his personal ambitions for power: J. A. Guy, "The French King's Council, 1483–1526," in *Kings and Nobles in the Later Middle Ages*, ed. Ralph A. Griffiths and James Sherborne, (Gloucester, 1986), esp. 279, 283, 289–90; Maulde notes that Gié's motives were at least partly inspired by his own hopes to secure hereditary rights to properties in the duchy of Brittany (*Procédures*, vi–vii, xiii–xiv, xxxv). See Richard Bonney, *The European Dynastic States 1494–1660* ([Oxford, 1991], 83) for a synopsis of the political concern regarding the accession of the duchy of Brittany during Charles VIII's reign; P. S. Lewis, "Of Breton Alliances and Other Matters," in *Essays in Later Medieval French History*, 69–90, for the fourteenth cen-tury; and Leguay and Martin, *Fastes et malheurs*, 390–433.

48. See Yvonne Labande-Mailfert, *Charles VIII et son milieu (1470–1498)* ([Paris, 1975], 475ff.), regarding Anne's actions after Charles VIII's death; and Maulde, *Procédures*, lviiiff. Gié's defense of his actions was of interest to a number of sixteenth- and seventeenth-century scholars, including

Bertrand d'Argentré (*conseillier du roy* and *président* of the Parlement in Rennes), *L'histoire de Bretagne* (Paris, 1588), 804ff.

49. Maulde, *Procédures,* 23–32 (for Pontbriant's allegations), 32–39, 107–8 (for Louise of Savoy's charges), 57–59 (for the *arrêt* of the *grand conseil*), and 241ff. (for the decision to try Gié on the charge of lèse-majesté).

50. Maulde, *Procédures,* i–v; Jones discusses this issue within the context of recent scholarship on the question of treason in late medieval France (*Creation of Brittany,* 329–50). For the later history of the doctrine, see Ralph E. Giesey, Lanny Haldy, and James Millhorn, "Cardin Le Bret and Lese Majesty," *Law and History Review* 4 (1986), 23–54. Both Facinger ("Study of Medieval Queenship," 1–48) and William C. Jordan ("Isabelle d'Angoulême, by the Grace of God, Queen," *Revue belge de philologie et d'histoire* 69 [1991], 821–52, esp. 839ff.) study the public, political authority of queens in Capetian France and note the special powers they often enjoyed as royal mothers and widows.

51. Successive generations of writers did examine the prerogatives enjoyed by French queens by studying archival sources, chronicles, and medieval legal texts (see my dissertation, "French Queens"). One of the first (as well as one of the most influential) writers was the sixteenth-century *greffier,* Jean du Tillet. His treatise, *Recueil,* includes discussion of the ranking legal and administrative officers (for example, the positions of chancellor and *procureur général*) who served French queens since medieval France as well as the extraordinary rights regarding legal representation that queens shared with their royal husbands (257–58); see Barry, *Reine de France,* 104ff.; and Brown, *Franks, Burgundians, and Aquitanians,* 56.

52. Maulde, *Procédures,* lxxxvii, 144–72.

53. Maulde lists those who were appointed to the case (ibid., v, cviff.).

54. Discussion of the ritual of coronation includes Stein, "Sacre de Anne de Bretagne," 277–78; Jackson, *Vive le Roi,* 20–21; Sherman, "Queen in Charles V's 'Coronation Book'"; and Jean-Claude Bonne, "The Manuscript of the Ordo of 1250 and Its Illuminations," in *Coronations,* 58–71. A singular emphasis on Anne's preeminence as newly crowned queen is especially evident in the third miniature in the Waddesdon Manor manuscript. MS. 22, fol. 106, depicts the festivities of the postcoronation banquet. The significance of Anne's office is underscored by depicting the richness of her dress, crown, and the tapestries and canopy placed on her chair. These details separate her authority from that of the other participants in the feast, such as her attendants, the widowed ladies-in-waiting, who are seated by her side.

55. Maulde, *Procédures,* lxxix–lxxxvi, for Georges d'Amboise's involvement.

56. Ernst H. Kantorowicz's essay, "The Sovereignty of the Artist: A Note on Legal Maxims and Renaissance Theories of Art" (in *Essays in Honor of*

Erwin Panofsky, ed. Millard Meiss [New York, 1961], 1:267–79), and Ian Maclean's *Interpretation and Meaning in the Renaissance: The Case of Law* ([Cambridge, 1992], 37–50) discuss analogies between legal texts and artistic and literary works developed in Renaissance culture. Anthony Grafton ("Humanism and Political Theory," in *The Cambridge History of Political Thought, 1450–1700,* ed. J. H. Burns and Mark Goldie [Cambridge, 1991], 9–29) and Grafton and Lisa Jardine (*From Humanism to the Humanities: Education and the Liberal Arts in Fifteenth- and Sixteenth-Century Europe* [London, 1986]) discuss the humanist practice of adapting legal texts to support contemporary political and social concerns. For a discussion of French legal humanism, see Donald R. Kelley, "Law," in *Cambridge History of Political Thought, 1450–1700,* 66–93.

57. For a printed copy of the legal defense see Maulde, *Procédures,* 242–43. The symbolism inherent in the divinely bestowed ritual of coronation was also a theme of the entry ceremony of 1504, a point which the later eighteenth-century *érudit,* Henri Sauvel (*avocat* in the Parlement of Paris) noted in his *Histoire et recherches de la ville de Paris* (Paris, 1724), 643–44.

58. Kantorowicz, "Mysteries of State," discusses the use of theological metaphors and "political theology" developed to defend royal prerogative (67ff.); in *The King's Two Bodies,* he lists the major works on this subject (92 n. 16); Scheller, "Ensigns of Authority," discusses the early sixteenth-century context (81), while Barbey provides insights regarding how such legal notions were applied in contemporary political theory in fifteenth-century France (*Fonction royale,* 157–66).

59. This portion of the legal argument recalled the symbolism inherent in the liturgical rite for the queen's coronation, as noted by Dewick (*Coronation Book,* fol. 68v, col. 47) and Sherman ("Queen in Charles V's 'Coronation Book,'" 269–70, 282–84), as well as the constitutional arguments of medieval writers such as Guillaume Durandus and Robert Grosseteste, who were interested in the symbolism inherent in the ritual of coronation. Natalie Zemon Davis has also considered the symbolism of ritual; see Davis, "Women in Politics," in *A History of Women in the West,* ed. Natalie Zemon Davis and Arlette Farge, 3 vols. (Cambridge, 1993), 3:171.

60. Traditionally such arguments recognized only the limitations on a queen's authority, a subject studied by Ernst H. Kantorowicz in his essay "Kingship under the Impact of Scientific Jurisprudence," in Marshall Clagett, Gaines Post, and Robert Reynolds, eds., *Twelfth-Century Europe and the Foundations of Modern Society* (Madison, Wis., 1961); J. R. Strayer, "The Laicization of French and English Society in the Thirteenth Century," in Sylvia L. Thrupp, ed., *Change in Medieval Society: Europe North of the Alps,*

1050–1500 (New York, 1964), 103–5; and Susan Miller Okin, *Women in Western Political Thought* (Princeton, 1979), 28–96. Parsons notes how contemporaries viewed rituals of office in late medieval England as a means of "enacting limitations" on a queen's power ("Ritual and Symbol," 61); René Metz discusses legal statutes in canon and private law which limited a woman's authority (*La femme et l'enfant dans le droit canonique médiéval* [London, 1985], iv, 86–108).

61. Maulde, *Procédures,* v, cxix–cxxviii; the decision was pronounced 9 Feb. 1506.

62. Elizabeth Armstrong notes that the work was undertaken with Anne's encouragement (which presumably included financial incentive), although it was published after her death (*Before Copyright: The French Book-Privilege System 1498–1526* [Cambridge, 1990], 87). Leguay and Martin record that Bouchart had been an *avocat* in the Parlement of Brittany as well as secretary to François II, duke of Brittany (*Fastes et malheurs,* 385). Jones considers the question of legal studies pursued by Bretons during the late fifteenth century (*Creation of Brittany,* 317ff.).

63. Beaune, *Birth of an Ideology,* 249–50 and n. 14, 392. Beaune's discussion of this text is based on B.N., MS. fr. 1728; my discussion follows the printed text, B.N., Rés. R 251 (Paris, 1504); the explicit is dated 6 Sept. 1504.

64. B.N., Rés. R. 251, *Le jeu des eschez moralisé,* prologue (a ii), includes the translator's remarks that this book was intended to be a gift to the queen. For the introductory chapter ("De la forme de la Royne de ces meurs [*sic*] et de son estat"), see fols. 7v–13r.

65. B.N., Rés. R. 251, fol. 7v (and my dissertation, "French Queens").

66. See Parsons, "Ritual and Symbol," 63–64.

67. Cessoles, *Le jeu des eschez moralisé,* fol. 10v: "Et doit honnorer lestat de sa dignite: et non pas l'estat d'elle. Et elle qui est dicte Royne doit regarder quelle nait pas le nom sans cause. Car elle doit avoir le nom et le fait. Et ce nom Royne est dit gouverneur." This assertion is supported by the frontispiece engraving (fol. a1v), depicting Louis XII and Anne, both crowned, playing chess in the presence of various members of the royal court and Three Estates.

68. François Marc, *Nove decisiones supreme curie Parlamenti delphina,* 2 parts in 1 vol. (Grenoble, 1532), pt. 1, decision 1, viii, and pt. 2, fol. 88. Marc's short exposition suggests his understanding of the glosses written by Bartolus of Sassoferrato and Baldus of Ubaldis; for a brief synopsis of Baldus's opinions see Canning, "Law, Sovereignty, and Corporation Theory," 467–69.

69. That the privilege did symbolize aspects of sovereign authority, associated with notions of lèse-majesté which French queens enjoyed, was

noted by a number of later writers, including the seventeenth-century jurist René Choppin, who gives the example of 1502 and cites Marc's gloss (Choppin, *Commentaire sur les coutumes de la prevosté et vicomté de Paris* [Paris, 1614], book 3, sect. 25, 824–25). Marc's interest in the example of 1502 is significant, in part, because it supplies further evidence that contemporaries viewed the festivities of that year as legitimizing Anne's sovereign authority as queen; for accounts of the festivities see Robert Gaguin, *Les grandes croniques: escellens faitz et vertueux gestes* (Paris, 1514), ccvl verso (B.N., Rés. L 35. 15); see also Archives départementales (Rhône; Lyon), CC 557 (deliberations held regarding the 1502 entry into the city of Lyon), which contains three cahiers attesting to the exceptional importance that this entry had for contemporary observers; Archives départementales (Dijon), Série B (Reg. 169), contains accounts of the preparations for Anne's ceremonial entry into this city as well; d'Argentré, *Histoire de Bretagne,* 804ff.; and Scheller, "Ensigns of Authority." Combined, such inchoate sources suggest how fully such celebrations honored Anne's sovereign authority, although her coronation ceremony and postcoronation entry ceremony into the city of Paris were postponed until 1504.

70.   See Jones, *Creation of Brittany,* 372, 407–9; manuscript and archival accounts containing a full description of the ceremony also include B.N., MS. fr. 18,534 (fols. 88–128), and A.N., K 79 (Pièces 16, accounts pertaining to the Parlement of Paris's involvement in the preparations for the ceremonies). There is also the published account of the funeral, Pierre Choque, *Récit des funérailles d'Anne de Bretagne,* ed. L. Merlet and M. de Gombert (1858; reprint, Geneva, 1970); this account is based on B.N., MS. fr. 5094.   For the symbolism of the funeral ceremony see Ralph E. Giesey, *The Royal Funeral Ceremony in Renaissance France* (Geneva, 1960), 33–34, 65, 75–76, 166, and figs. 11 and 12; Giesey, *Le roi ne meurt jamais,* trans. D. Ebnötter (Paris, 1987), 67 n. 41, 82 n. 27, 109, 123, 246, 253–54; and Giesey, *Cérémonial et puissance souveraine: France, XVe–XVIIIe siècles* (Paris, 1987), 21–32. As Giesey notes, a number of disputes arose regarding individual and corporate rights and there was also the same uncertainty that had surfaced in descriptions of the coronation regalia regarding the correct order for bestowing the attributes of office, particularly whether the scepter should be placed in the right or left hand. Bernard de Montfaucon, *Les monumens de la monarchie françoise qui comprennent l'histoire de France* (Paris, 1729–33), refers to this uncertainty, listing the members of the queen's entourage and noting that Anne de Bourbon retained the privileged position in this ceremony that she had enjoyed earlier in 1504 (3:128–35, esp. 130–31). Regarding fourteenth-century funeral ceremony honoring French queens see Hedeman, *Royal Image,* for a depiction of the fourteenth-century queen Jeanne of Bourbon's effigy and funeral ceremo-

ny held in 1379. There are descriptions of the ceremony in B.N., MS. fr. 18, 534 ("Cérémonies observées aux obseques des roys [*sic*], roynes [*sic*]"), fols. 7v–9r; and A.N., KK 310–12; B.N., MS. fr. 10,426, fol. 37, has a brief account of the simpler ceremony held in honor of Isabeau of Bavaria, which notes that the queen's effigy was displayed with the scepter to her right. Armstrong gives other works published to commemorate Anne of Brittany (*Before Copyright*, 123, 179).

71. Horst W. Janson, ed., *Tomb Sculpture* (New York, 1961), 79–80; A.N., K 153–56, liasse III, no. 8, and A.N., K 79, pièces 6, have copies of the descriptions of the monument dated 1794. See Kantorowicz, *King's Two Bodies*, regarding the doctrine of *dignitas* (383–437); and, for medieval France, Georgia S. Wright, "A Royal Tomb Program in the Reign of Saint Louis," *Art Bulletin* 56 (1971), 223–43; Elizabeth A. R. Brown, "Burying and Unburying the Kings of France," reprinted in *The Monarchy of Capetian France and Royal Ceremonial* (Aldershot, 1991), 241–66; and Alain Boureau, *Le simple corps du roi* (Paris, 1988), 16–42.

72. Besançon, Archives Municipales (CG 377a) contains the documents relevant to this alleged trial. This particular case is not as well known as Chasseneuz's alleged defense of rats in the town of Autun, a trial which Edward P. Evans discusses, also noting the legal literature of the later sixteenth century which includes references to this trial (*The Criminal Prosecution and Capital Punishment of Animals* [London, 1906; reprint, London, 1987], 18–21ff.). For an interpretation of such cases see Esther Cohen, *The Crossroads of Justice: Law and Culture in Late Medieval France* ([Leiden, 1993], 121ff.), although N. Humphrey has expressed caution in accepting views such as Cohen's (*Criminal Prosecution*, xiiff.). I thank William C. Jordan for sharing both his interest and knowledge of this aspect of legal history with me. Ian Maclean has a brief assessment of Chasseneuz's importance to the development of sixteenth-century jurisprudence (*Interpretation and Meaning in the Renaissance*, 24–25).

73. Chasseneuz, *Catalogus*, fols. 1v–8v, 123ff., 142r–43r. Chasseneuz develops fully the Christological comparisons (fols. 95ff., 115–19) which writers such as Guillaume Durandus had used; his treatise, *Rationale divinorum officiorum*, was a popular work in the sixteenth century. In *The Political Thought of Baldus de Ubaldis* (Cambridge, 1987), Joseph Canning notes how the humanist jurisprudence of the sixteenth century (including that of Chasseneuz) reflected the opinions of medieval jurists such as Bartolus (228–29). Kantorowicz, *King's Two Bodies*, discusses Baldus's views regarding the sempiternity of the invisible crown and the medieval perceptions of abstract notions of majesty that are the basis of Chasseneuz's argument (336–83, esp. 336–39). Also, connections between political theory and ceremonial addressed in institutional assemblies are discussed by

Bryant in *King and City,* where he notes that for the delegates of the Estates General assembly of 1484, the bestowal of accessional privileges reflected the confirmation of the perpetual and irrevocable alliance that existed between the crown and the French people (46–48). See also Kelley, "Law," in *Cambridge History of Political Thought,* regarding how writings of Chasseneuz and other jurists reflected abstract notions of royal prerogative and attributes of sovereignty (78ff.).

74. Chasseneuz, *Catalogus,* fols. 62r–64r, 69r, 147r–147v; a more complete discussion of the legal maxims and arguments of "equiparation" is in my dissertation, "French Queens." Kantorowicz, "Sovereignty of the Artist," 275–76; Guy, "French King's Council," 278; C. Valone, "Piety and Patronage: Women and the Early Jesuits," in *Creative Women in Early Modern Italy* (Philadelphia, forthcoming)—all discuss the use of classical examples in Renaissance society.

75. Chasseneuz, *Catalogus,* fol. 68r; B. Chasseneuz, *Repertorium in Commentaria Edredii* (Lyon, 1535), fols. 124v–126v. Armstrong notes that the privilege to Chasseneuz's treatise on the Burgundian law codes is dated 1515 (*Before Copyright,* 30, 173).

76. Chasseneuz, *Catalogus,* fols. 50v–51r. Chasseneuz's references to Semiramis suggest that he knew Boccaccio's works as well as the arguments developed by various Italian humanists of the quattrocento, who debated questions pertaining to a woman's ability to enjoy public authority and power. See Grafton and Jardine, *From Humanism to the Humanities,* 29–57. Constance Jordan discusses arguments posited to limit the public authority of women (*Renaissance Feminism: Literary Texts and Political Models* [Ithaca, N.Y., 1990]).

77. Chasseneuz, *Catalogus,* fols. 50r, 68v–69r.

78. Ibid., fols. 147r–147v, using the gloss of Lucas de Penna. For discussion of English and French coronation practices see Parsons, "Ritual and Symbol," 63–64. Regarding ceremonial seating to the right and abstract notions of justice, see Kantorowicz, *King's Two Bodies,* 342, 416; and Giesey, *Juristic Basis,* 25 and n. 19, 26–28. This concept was frequently used by sixteenth- and seventeenth-century writers (most of whom followed in Chasseneuz's footsteps) when they studied questions pertaining to queenship. For a discussion of this literature, see "French Queens" and my essay, "The King's Mother and Royal Prerogative in Early Sixteenth Century France," in John Carmi Parsons, ed., *Medieval Queenship* (New York, 1993), 117–41.

79. The legal maxim, *Bene a Zenone,* was a well-known and often cited gloss for medieval jurists. Kenneth Pennington discusses this maxim in regard to general development of political theory (*The Prince and the Law* [Berkeley, 1993], 18–22, 78–98).

80. Chasseneuz, *Catalogus,* fol. 147v. Pennington (*Prince and Law,* 76–118) and Dieter Wyduckel (*Princeps Legibus Solutus: Eine Untersuchung zur frühmodernen Rechts- und Staatslehre* [Berlin, 1979], 48–51, 151) discuss this legal maxim as it was applied to support the development of royal prerogative and, ultimately, notions pertaining to "absolute" royal authority. Chasseneuz's analogy was consistent with the long-standing practices of medieval jurists to apply natural law to notions of "office," especially questions pertaining to legislative prerogative; on this issue see Kantorowicz, "Sovereignty of the Artist," 275–76. For a discussion of how mid-sixteenth-century royal politics incorporated arguments of "equiparation," see Michael H. Merriman, "Mary, Queen of France," in *Mary Stewart: Queen in Three Kingdoms,* ed. Michael Lynch (Oxford, 1988), 30–52.

81. Charles de Grassaille, *Regalium Franciae Libri Duo* (Lyon, 1538), fols. 60r–61r. Grassaille was one of the first writers in the sixteenth century to be interested in the symbolism associated with this practice, and discussed the practice within the context of lèse-majesté. Although both he and Chasseneuz had a keen interest in Roman imperial history, neither one appears to have known that the practice of pardoning criminals was one that the Romans invoked in conjunction with dynastic celebrations, a subject of study for the nineteenth-century historian Théodor Mommsen (*Le droit public romain,* trans. P. F. Girard [Paris, 1889–96], 88ff.). Michel Antoine researched thoroughly how frequently this practice was used by French kings since the fourteenth century ("Notes sur les lettres de rémission transcrites dans les registres du trésor des Chartes," *Bibliothèque de l'école des Chartes* 103 [1942], 317–24). Jackson discusses the late medieval practice, noting arguments touching on issues of abstract royal authority (*Vive le Roi,* 94–114); in *King and City* Bryant discusses how the practice developed in conjunction with entry ceremonies (22–50). In my dissertation, "French Queens," I discuss use of the privilege by successive French queens and the views of sixteenth- and seventeenth-century writers regarding the symbolic and dynastic associations of this usage.

82. Grassaille, *Regalium,* fols. 234r–245r, 250r–256r.

83. Ibid., fols. 235r–236rff. For developments regarding constitutional thought in late medieval Spain, see Ralph E. Giesey, *If Not, Not: The Oath of the Aragonese and the Legendary Laws of Sobrarbe* (Princeton, 1968); and Angus Mackay, "Ritual and Propaganda in Fifteenth-Century Castile," *Past and Present* 107 (May, 1985), 3–43. For a discussion of legal arguments regarding the authority of Spanish kings and queens, see Antonio Perez Martin, "El renacimiento del poder legislativo y la genesis del estado moderno en la corona de Castilla," in André Gouron and Albert Rigaudiere, eds., *Renaissance du pouvoir legislatif et genèse de l'état* (Montpellier, 1988), 189–202, esp. 189 and n. 1.

84. Grassaille, *Regalium,* fols. 24r, 201r, 237r, 250r–251r; and McCartney, "King's Mother" and "French Queens."

85. Grassaille, *Regalium,* fols. 20r–24r, 29r, 262r–263r. Scheller, "Ensigns of Authority," also notes textual similarities between Grassaille's text and that of 1504 (101 and n. 115).

86. Grassaille, *Regalium,* fols. 258r–267r; and McCartney, "French Queens."

87. Grassaille, *Regalium,* fol. 261r; McCartney, "King's Mother" and "French Queens." For a recent discussion of the dynastic notions inherent in Kantorowicz's theory of the "King's Two Bodies" and medieval legal thought, see Boureau, *Simple corps du roi,* 16–24. See also Giesey, *Juristic Basis,* for discussion of notions of "seminally impressed kingship." Marie Axton, *The Queen's Two Bodies* (London, 1977) discusses this notion regarding English queens, as does Diana E. Henderson, "Elizabeth's Watchful Eye and George Peele's Gaze: Examining Female Power beyond the Individual," in *Women and Sovereignty,* 150–69, esp. 158.

88. Grassaille, *Regalium,* fol. 268r. Two examples of later writers who followed the lines of Grassaille's argument are Pierre-Jean-Jacques-Guillaume Guyot, *Traité des droits, fonctions, franchises, exemptions, prérogatives et privilèges annexés en France à chaque dignité* (Paris, 1786–88), 241–42; and Ménin, *Traicté historique,* 241.

89. Grassaille, *Regalium,* fols. 264r–267r. The lines of Grassaille's argument regarding piety and charity were also practised by women in the Italian Renaissance (see Valone, "Piety and Patronage"). See also Donald R. Kelley, *Foundations of Modern Historical Scholarship* (New York, 1970) and more recently, his chapter entitled "Law," in *Cambridge History of Political Thought,* 78ff. Other discussions of the tenets of medieval constitutionalism in sixteenth-century France include Kantorowicz, "Mysteries of State," 75ff.; Ralph E. Giesey, "Medieval Jurisprudence in Bodin's Concept of Sovereignty," in *Jean Bodin: Berhandlungen der Internationalen Bodin-tagung in München,* ed. H. Denzer, Münchener Studien zur Politik 16 (Munich, 1973), 167–86.

90. I consider this question more fully in my dissertation, "French Queens." One example of a later writer who followed such views is Petri Fabri (Peter Faber or Pierre Faure), president of the Parlement of Toulouse and a descendant of Arnaud Faure, who developed the legal defense of 1504. See Fabri's work, *ad Tit. Antiqui, ex libro Pandectarum Imperatoris Iustiniani quinquagesimo* (Paris, 1585), esp. fols. 8–23.

91. The dynastic basis of queenship is of special interest to me, particularly the question as to how it was developed through legal texts and royal ceremonial as a means to affirm a queen's right to act as regent. Both H. Lightman, "Sons and Mothers: Queens and Minor Kings in French Con-

stitutional Law" (Ph.D. dissertation, 1981, Bryn Mawr College), and A. Poulet, "La régence et la majorité des rois au Moyen Age" (Thèse, Université des Sciences Humaines de Strasbourg, Faculté des Sciences Historiques, Strasbourg, 1989), discuss the political developments and juridical arguments that developed in late medieval France regarding the question of regency right and French public law.

92. Regarding the ceremonial and accessional privileges that Marie de Médicis enjoyed, see McCartney, "French Queens." Giesey, *Cérémonial et puissance souveraine,* discusses André du Chesne's interest in "state" ceremonial, as well as the developments in theory since the late fifteenth century which influenced du Chesne's treatise (33–47). See also Brown, who notes du Chesne's use of Jean du Tillet's treatise (*Franks, Burgundians, and Aquitanians,* 7); and Bonney, *European Dynastic States,* 486.

Contributors

JENNIFER CARPENTER is a lecturer in history at the University of Otago, Dunedin, New Zealand. She is completing her doctorate at the Centre for Medieval Studies of the University of Toronto, and her thesis will be a study of the *vitae* of the thirteenth-century *mulieres religiosae* of the southern Low Countries.

LIBBY GARSHOWITZ is a member of the Department of Near Eastern Studies at the University of Toronto and director of the Jewish Studies Programme there. She teaches medieval and modern Hebrew language, literature, and intellectual history. Her main research and publishing interests include the life and thought of Jews of medieval Spain and Jewish-Christian relations and extend to contemporary Israeli literature. The present essay is the result of ongoing research on women whose lives are/were disrupted by war, persecution, and displacement.

LOIS L. HUNEYCUTT completed her doctoral studies in 1992 at the University of California, Santa Barbara, under the direction of C. Warren Hollister and Jeffrey B. Russell. Currently assistant professor of history at California State University, Hayward, she is completing a biographical study of Queen Mathilda II of England (1100–18).

SALLY-BETH MACLEAN is executive editor of the Records of Early English Drama series and author of *Chester Art: A Subject List of Extant and Lost Art including Items Relevant to Early Drama,* EDAM Reference Series 3 (Kalamazoo, Mich., 1982), as well as various articles on traveling medieval players, patronage, and parish drama. She is presently collaborating on a book on the Queen's Men with Scott McMillin.

ELIZABETH MCCARTNEY, doctoral candidate in the Department of History at the University of Iowa, is completing her dissertation, "French Queens and the Cult of the Renaissance Monarchy," under the supervision of Ralph E. Giesey, and presently holds a fellowship in the "Women and Power in Medieval Central Europe" program at the Central European University, Budapest. She has previously published "The King's Mother and Royal Prerogative in Early Sixteenth-Century France," in John Carmi Parsons, ed., *Medieval Queenship* (New York, 1993).

JACQUELINE MURRAY is associate professor of history at the University of Windsor. She has translated Agnolo Firenzuola's *On the Beauty of Women* (Philadelphia, 1992) with Konrad Eisenbichler, and with Michael M. Sheehan has published *Domestic Society in Medieval Europe* (Toronto, 1991). She is currently completing a study on women in confessors' manuals and a comprehensive *Bibliography of Marriage and the Family in the Middle Ages*.

JOHN CARMI PARSONS is currently senior fellow of the Centre for Renaissance and Reformation Studies at Victoria University in the University of Toronto and has been assistant professor in the Department of History at the University of Toronto. He has published *The Court and Household of Eleanor of Castile in 1290* (Toronto, 1977); *Eleanor of Castile: Queen and Society in Thirteenth-Century England* (New York, 1994); *Medieval Queenship* (New York, 1993), an anthology; and articles on medieval English queenship.

JOCELYN WOGAN-BROWNE lectures in English at the University of Liverpool, UK. She publishes editions and translations of early Middle English and Anglo-Norman texts and recently, with two of her postgraduate students, a *Concordance to Ancrene Wisse: MS Corpus Christi College, Cambridge 402* (Cambridge, 1993). She also publishes studies on women, early insular literature, and other subjects. She is currently completing the first translation of Clemence of Barking's twelfth-century *Life of St. Catherine* for Dent and a study, *Authorized Virgins: The Literature of Female Celibacy c. 1150–1350*, for Oxford University Press.

Index

Page numbers in italics refer to illustrations.

DATE DUE

MAR 1 3 2004			
			Printed in USA